The Pragmatics of Intercultural Communicative Competence

LANGUAGES FOR INTERCULTURAL COMMUNICATION AND EDUCATION

Series Editors: **Michael Byram**, *University of Durham, UK* and **Anthony J. Liddicoat**, *University of Warwick, UK*

The overall aim of this series is to publish books which will ultimately inform learning and teaching, but whose primary focus is on the analysis of intercultural relationships, whether in textual form or in people's experience. There will also be books which deal directly with pedagogy, with the relationships between language learning and cultural learning, between processes inside the classroom and beyond. They will all have in common a concern with the relationship between language and culture, and the development of intercultural communicative competence.

All books in this series are externally peer-reviewed.

Full details of all the books in this series and of all our other publications can be found on http://www.multilingual-matters.com, or by writing to Multilingual Matters, St Nicholas House, 31–34 High Street, Bristol, BS1 2AW, UK.

LANGUAGES FOR INTERCULTURAL COMMUNICATION AND
EDUCATION: 43

The Pragmatics of Intercultural Communicative Competence

Language Use and Intercultural Understanding in Foreign Language and Study Abroad Contexts

J. César Félix-Brasdefer

MULTILINGUAL MATTERS
Bristol • Jackson

DOI https://doi.org/10.21832/FELIX4365
Library of Congress Cataloging in Publication Data
A catalog record for this book is available from the Library of Congress.
Names: Félix-Brasdefer, J. César, author.
Title: The Pragmatics of Intercultural Communicative Competence: Language Use and Intercultural Understanding in Foreign Language and Study Abroad Contexts/J. César Félix-Brasdefer.
Description: Bristol; Jackson: Multilingual Matters, 2025. | Series: Languages for Intercultural Communication and Education: 43 | Includes bibliographical references and index. | Summary: "This book presents a pragmatic perspective on the development of intercultural communicative competence by language learners in the foreign language classroom and in study abroad contexts. The book concludes with a reflection on what it means to be an intercultural speaker and the benefits for the learner of developing intercultural competence"—Provided by publisher.
Identifiers: LCCN 2025000249 (print) | LCCN 2025000250 (ebook) | ISBN 9781800414358 (paperback) | ISBN 9781800414365 (hardback) | ISBN 9781800414389 (epub) | ISBN 9781800414372 (pdf)
Subjects: LCSH: Language and languages—Study and teaching. | Communicative competence—Study and teaching. | Intercultural communication—Study and teaching. | Pragmatics. Classification: LCC P53.255 .F45 2025 (print) | LCC P53.255 (ebook) | DDC 418.0071—dc23/eng/20250211
LC record available at https://lccn.loc.gov/2025000249
LC ebook record available at https://lccn.loc.gov/2025000250

British Library Cataloguing in Publication Data
A catalogue entry for this book is available from the British Library.

ISBN-13: 978-1-80041-436-5 (hbk)
ISBN-13: 978-1-80041-435-8 (pbk)

Multilingual Matters
UK: St Nicholas House, 31–34 High Street, Bristol, BS1 2AW, UK.
USA: Ingram, Jackson, TN, USA.
Authorised Representative: Easy Access System Europe - Mustamäe tee 50, 10621 Tallinn, Estonia, gpsr.requests@easproject.com.

Website: https://www.multilingual-matters.com
X: Multi_Ling_Mat
Bluesky: @multi-ling-mat.bsky.social
Facebook: https://www.facebook.com/multilingualmatters
Blog: https://www.channelviewpublications.wordpress.com

Copyright © 2025 J. César Félix-Brasdefer.

All rights reserved. No part of this work may be reproduced in any form or by any means without permission in writing from the publisher.

The policy of Multilingual Matters/Channel View Publications is to use papers that are natural, renewable and recyclable products, made from wood grown in sustainable forests. In the manufacturing process of our books, and to further support our policy, preference is given to printers that have FSC and PEFC Chain of Custody certification. The FSC and/or PEFC logos will appear on those books where full certification has been granted to the printer concerned.

Typeset by SAN Publishing Services.

Contents

Figures and Tables ... ix
Acknowledgements ... xi
Transcription Conventions ... xiii

Introduction ... 1
   Intercultural Understanding and the Intercultural Speaker in a Global World ... 2
   Pragmatic Competence and Intercultural Communicative Competence ... 3
   Language Use as Emergent through Intercultural Interaction ... 4
   Social Action and Joint Activity ... 5
   Metapragmatic Awareness of Language Use in Context ... 6
   Outline of the Book ... 8

1 Intercultural Communicative Competence as Language Use: A Pragmatic Perspective ... 11
   Introduction ... 11
   Situating Pragmatics from a Social and Interactional Perspective ... 12
   Defining Intercultural Competence ... 15
   Models of Intercultural (Communicative) Competence ... 19
   Dimensions of Communicative Competence ... 25
   Intercultural Communicative Competence: A Pragmatics Perspective ... 32
   Conclusion ... 37

2 Pragmatic Competence and Metapragmatic Awareness in Intercultural Understanding ... 38
   Introduction ... 38
   Defining the Construct of Pragmatic Competence ... 39
   Perspectives of Pragmatic Competence ... 43
   Pragmatic Competence from an Intercultural Pragmatics Perspective ... 51
   Conclusion ... 54

3	Pragmatic-Discursive Perspective on Language Use and Intercultural Understanding	56
	Introduction	56
	Pragmatic-Discursive Approach to Intercultural Interaction	57
	Intercultural Interaction through Joint Action	58
	Intention and Attention	60
	Pragmatic Contexts	63
	Emergent Common Ground	65
	Data Analysis	66
	Metapragmatic Awareness	67
	Variability	69
	Conclusion	72
4	Pragmatic Learning and Intercultural Understanding in the Foreign Language Classroom	74
	Introduction	74
	Developing Pragmatic Competence in the Foreign Language Classroom	75
	Teaching Pragmatic and Intercultural Competence	78
	Intercultural Perspective on Teaching and Learning	79
	Classroom-Based Study of Learning Spanish as a Foreign Language	84
	Requesting in the Foreign Language Classroom	91
	Apologizing in the Foreign Language Classroom	98
	Refusing in the Foreign Language Classroom	106
	Metapragmatic Awareness and Reflection	111
	Metapragmatic Reflection of Speech Acts in Interaction	118
	Conclusion	123
5	Negotiating Refusals: Sociopragmatic Awareness and Insights from Study Abroad Learners	125
	Introduction	125
	Refusals	126
	Sociopragmatic Knowledge, Metapragmatic Awareness and Reflection	129
	Study Abroad as a Site for Social Interaction and Reflection	131
	Negotiation of Refusal Practices and Metapragmatic Awareness	134
	Refusing in Informal and Formal Intercultural Interactions	138
	Insights on Refusal Practices and Sociopragmatic Knowledge	150
	Verbalizations as Insights for Raising Metapragmatic Awareness	155
	Conclusion	157

6 Intercultural Impoliteness, Reflexive Awareness,
   and Agency in Study Abroad Contexts   159
     Introduction   159
     Considerations of (Im)politeness in Intercultural
     Pragmatics   160
     Identity, Mediation and Agency in Study Abroad
     Contexts   163
     Evaluations of Impoliteness and Rapport Management   165
     Research on Evaluations of Intercultural Impoliteness   167
     Perception of Offense Abroad through Impoliteness Events 168
     Perceived Offense in Intercultural Impoliteness Abroad 173
     Reflexive Metapragmatic Awareness   180
     Conclusion   183

Conclusion   186
References   192
Index   208

Figures and Tables

Figures

Figure 1.1	Byram's (2021) model of intercultural competence and intercultural communicative competence	22
Figure 1.2	Integrated model of intercultural communicative competence	33
Figure 3.1	Pragmatic-discursive approach to intercultural interaction	58
Figure 5.1	Refusal responses, stage 1: Invitation-response (-D, -P)	139
Figure 5.2	Refusal responses, stage 2: Insistence-response (-D, -P)	139
Figure 5.3	Refusal responses, stage 1: Suggestion-response (+D, +P)	139
Figure 5.4	Refusal responses, stage 2: Insistence-response (+D, +P)	139
Figure 5.5	Prosodic analysis of the first refusal to invitation	146
Figure 5.6	Prosodic analysis of the second refusal to insistence	146
Figure 5.7	Prosodic analysis of the third refusal to insistence	146
Figure 5.8	Prosodic analysis of the fourth refusal to insistence	146
Figure 5.9	Prosodic analysis of rejection to a professor's suggestion to take class	150
Figure 6.1	Primary types of perceived offense	173

Tables

Table 1.1	Defining intercultural (communicative) competence	18
Table 2.1	Defining pragmatic competence	40
Table 4.1	Learner characteristics with and without previous study abroad experience	85
Table 4.2	Roleplay situations: Requests, apologies, refusal to an offer	86
Table 4.3	Instructional treatment, pretest and posttest	88
Table 4.4	Frequency of request type by learning context	92
Table 4.5	Request perspective by learning context	92
Table 4.6	Frequency of mitigators by learning context	93
Table 4.7	Frequency of apology type by learning context	99
Table 4.8	Frequency of intensifiers in apology by learning context	99
Table 4.9	Refusing an offer of food from host mother: Stage 1 and stage 2	107
Table 5.1	Learner characteristics in study abroad contexts	135
Table 5.2	Roleplay situations according to politeness systems	136
Table 5.3	Sequential distribution of refusal responses by situation	141
Table 5.4	Verbal probes during the retrospective verbal interview	151
Table 6.1	Setting of intercultural encounters of impoliteness events abroad	169
Table 6.2	Perception of offense in intercultural impoliteness events	171
Table 6.3	Perceived offense of hearer's intention	181
Table 6.4	Reflexive awareness of non-verbal cues in intercultural impoliteness	182

Acknowledgements

I would like to express my gratitude to the many people who were involved during the conceptualization and development of this book. First, I would like to thank my undergraduate and graduate students who inspired me to write a book on intercultural pragmatics with a focus on diversity, global citizenship, and intercultural understanding. My undergraduate students participated in various pilot studies, which helped refine the instruments used in this book. In particular, I would like to thank the following people who helped collect and analyze the data, and reviewed previous versions of these chapters: Elise Baker, Brianna Best, Christopher Brenes, Bruno Staszkiewicz García, Enrique Rodríguez, Christine Song, Erika Sosa and Audrey Waite. My appreciation goes to my graduate students (fall 2024) who read pre-final versions of this manuscript during our seminar on Intercultural Pragmatics, and whose feedback and insightful questions helped refine the final version.

This book would not have been possible without the financial support I received at Indiana University, in particular from the Department of Spanish and Portuguese and grants from the College Arts and Humanities Institute. My sincere thanks go to the students who agreed to participate in this project, the research assistants, and the faculty and staff at Indiana University, including the Office of Education Abroad for facilitating access to students studying abroad.

I would also like to thank several people at Multilingual Matters: Anna Roderick, Flo McClelland, Constance Collier-Qureshy, Mythili Devi and the reviewers who provided thoughtful comments. Thanks to Multilingual Matters for their permission to reprint Byram's (2021) figure on intercultural competence and communicative competence.

I would like to express my sincere gratitude to Professor Istvan Kecskes whose research on intercultural pragmatics inspired the present book. His seminal book on Intercultural Pragmatics (Oxford University Press, 2014) includes foundational concepts such as the socio-cognitive approach, pragmatic competence, context, common ground, salience, politeness and impoliteness, and common ground. It was a pleasure to have collaborated with him when he was President of the American Pragmatics Association. Thank you for your friendship and mentorship. You will be missed.

Finally, I would like to thank three important people in my life to whom I dedicate the pages of this book, Terri, Gabriel and Salaar. To my wife, for her patience, moral support, professional advice, and unconditional love. Terri, thanks for your careful reading and feedback on previous versions of the chapters. To my son Gabriel who witnessed the write up of the book from the beginning to the end, for asking about the progress of the chapters and the data collection process, and for his interest in intercultural communication between Mexico and the United States. And to Salaar, our exchange student from Pakistan, from whom I learned new insights on intercultural communication in the Pakistani culture and linguistic diversity. Collectively, they made this book a pleasant experience.

Transcription Conventions

(Adapted from Jefferson, 2004)

These are the transcription conventions that were used in the examples.

A. Contiguous utterances
- =   Equal signs indicate no break-up or gap. They are placed when there is no interval between adjacent utterances and the second utterance is linked immediately to the first.

B. Overlaps
- [A left bracket indicates the point of overlap onset.
-]   A right bracket indicates the point at which two overlapping utterances end, if they end simultaneously, or the point at which one of them ends during the course of the other. It is also used to parse out segments of overlapping utterances.

C. Intervals
- ( )   Parentheses indicate the time in seconds and when placed within an utterance, mark intervals or pauses in the stream of talk.
- -   A dash marks a short untimed pause within an utterance.

D. Characteristics of speech delivery
- ↑↓   The up and down arrows mark sharp rises or falls in pitch.
- :   A colon marks a lengthened syllable or an extension of a sound.
- :::   More colons prolong a sound or syllable.
- word   Underlining is used to indicate some form of stress or emphasis, either by increased loudness or higher pitch.
- .   A period marks a fall in tone.
- ,   A comma marks continuing intonation.
- ?   A question mark signals rising intonation.

E. Other markings
- (( ))   Double parentheses are used to mark the transcriber's descriptions of events

Introduction

Over 25 years ago, Byram (1997) proposed a model of Intercultural Communicative Competence (ICC) to teach and assess various dimensions of Intercultural Competence (IC) in the foreign language (FL) classroom. Byram's seminal work, including his revised edition (2021), has inspired researchers to expand his model, examining the relationship between intercultural competence and pragmatics (Schauer, 2024), and between performativity and agency (Beecroft, 2022). Based on his work, others have analyzed topics of second language (L2) pragmatics through the lens of intercultural understanding, agency, and reflexivity (Liddicoat & Scarino, 2013; McConachy, 2018; McConachy & Liddicoat, 2022; McConachy et al., 2022). In this book, I adopt a pragmatic perspective to examine language use and understanding among learners who engage in intercultural interaction, critical reflection, collaboration, and contextual analysis of speech acts, as well as understandings of polite and impolite behavior. I examine intercultural communication in two particular contexts, learners in the FL classroom and in study abroad settings. Further, along with others (Jackson, 2019; Schauer, 2024; Taguchi & Roever, 2017), I continue the discussion to examine the link between IC and pragmatics through the lens of *intercultural understanding*, which is defined as 'awareness of and respect for diverse (linguistic) behaviors, beliefs, and values in different linguistic and cultural communities, particularly awareness of how assumptions about social relationships, social categorizations, and power interface with speakers' judgments about language use in context' (McConachy & Liddicoat, 2022: 2).

In this book, the concepts of IC and ICC will be used interchangeably, with the understanding that the former often implies communicative competence, and thus encompasses the following components: linguistic, pragmatic, sociolinguistic, discourse, interactional and strategic (see Chapter 1, Figure 1.2).

Pragmatics is generally defined as language use in context with contributions from both the speaker and the hearer, and how individuals produce and understand explicit and implicit meaning such as pragmatic routines, direct and indirect speech acts, politeness and impoliteness, irony and humor. In Chapter 1, I adopt a broad view of pragmatics to examine meaning in interaction, language use, and context as dynamic and changeable. A definition of pragmatics for intercultural understanding includes the following elements: pragmatic contexts (cognitive, situational, interactional, emergent), the speaker's intention (*a priori*, emergent and co-constructed through interaction) and attention to the contextual features of the situation, the hearer's understanding of what is said, and the ways in which intercultural speakers negotiate and assess meaning in social contexts.

The chapters in this book emphasize the interdependence of language and culture. When learners communicate, they choose language to express their social identities, behaviors, ideologies and social norms. Culture is generally defined as 'a complex frame of reference that consists of patterns of traditions, beliefs, values, norms, symbols, and meanings that are shared to varying degrees by interacting members of a community' (Ting-Toomey, 1999: 10). From an intercultural pragmatics angle, culture is conceptualized as 'a socially constituted set of various kinds of knowledge structures … it has fuzzy boundaries … and changes both diachronically and synchronically' (Kecskes, 2014: 4). More importantly, during the act of communication, learners bring their own cultural frames, previous knowledge, assumptions, ideology, behaviors and ways of thinking that represent their own cultural expectations of a speech community. In relation to cultural understanding, learners do not always have to follow the pragmatic conventions and cultural norms of native speakers (NSs). In Chapters 4–6, I focus on the topic of pragmatic resistance (Ishihara, 2019; McConachy, 2023) to show that learners in FL and study abroad contexts may choose to deviate from pragmatic norms of NSs, often choosing social norms, identity and behaviors that align with their L1 culture(s) and language(s).

Intercultural Understanding and the Intercultural Speaker in a Global World

Unlike previous research in L2 pragmatics that contrasts the learner's production and receptive skills to that of the NS (Bardovi-Harlig, 2013; Kasper & Rose, 2002; Rose & Kasper, 2001), I challenge the notion of the NS, which is often viewed as the model for learners and teachers (see also Byram, 1997, 2021; Wilkinson, 2020). I focus on the intercultural speaker as a global citizen with multiple identities and an awareness of diversity: as a learner, agent, mediator and individual (Beecroft, 2022; Byram, 1997, 2021; Byram & Zarate, 1994; Liddicoat & Scarino, 2013; Wilkinson, 2020). Intercultural speakers, as global citizens, communicate with others who are culturally and linguistically different from themselves; they bring their own knowledge, skills, behaviors and attitudes to communicate effectively and appropriately. As agents and mediators, learners exert agency to choose to agree or disagree, remain silent or challenge the interlocutor's viewpoints. In Chapters 4–6, I examine interactions that showcase how learners in these two contexts co-construct social meaning and perceive understandings of impolite behavior and how learners exert agency and develop intersubjectivity to achieve emergent common ground in order to communicate effectively and appropriately in spoken settings. I adopt the socio-cognitive approach (Kecskes, 2014, 2020) as well as a discourse perspective on pragmatics (Félix-Brasdefer, 2019b; Kasper, 2006) to complement my analysis of ICC through agency, metapragmatic awareness, reflexivity, collaboration and analysis of language use. The chapters in this book address global issues, such as pragmatic resistance, agency, mediation, intercultural diversity, intercultural impoliteness and metapragmatic awareness. While these concepts have been introduced and analyzed in previous work, mainly from a teaching and learning perspective (Ishihara, 2019; McConachy & Liddicoat, 2022; McConachy et al., 2022; Schauer, 2024), I will expand on them from a pragmatic-discursive perspective and through a lens of intercultural understanding in FL and study abroad contexts.

Byram's model of ICC has recently been re-analyzed and extended to account for intercultural learning in language education (McConachy et al., 2022). Under this view, the intercultural speaker acts as a learner, agent, and mediator to achieve common ground in intercultural interaction. The development of ICC requires cultural awareness, reflexivity and collaborative interaction through reflective analysis of pragmatic routines and speech acts at the discourse level (Félix-Brasdefer, 2019b; Kasper, 2006; McConachy, 2018). Thus, I focus on the learner's ability to co-construct meaning in intercultural interaction and foster intercultural understandings of polite or impolite behavior in FL and study abroad contexts.

Pragmatic Competence and Intercultural Communicative Competence

This book examines the interdependence of two competencies that comprise communicative language ability, namely, pragmatic competence and intercultural competence. In her study of teachers' perceptions of intercultural understandings, Schauer (2024) examined the link between pragmatics and intercultural competence, and concluded, based on the teachers' views, that pragmatic competence represents a constituent of intercultural competence (see also Jackson, 2019, for a similar conclusion). Others have examined L2 pragmatics as a process of learning intercultural understanding, involving the negotiation of 'new ways of behaving and coming to operate within alternative frameworks for conceptualizing social reality and managing of social relationships' (McConachy & Liddicoat, 2022: 7). Adopting a discursive perspective on pragmatics, I examine the negotiation of meaning-making that is co-constructed between two or more interlocutors, such as speech acts (apologies, requests, refusals) or dimensions of polite and impolite behavior.

Pragmatic competence concerns the learner's ability to produce and comprehend language use in action, for example, in speech acts and in institutional and non-institutional contexts, such as the classroom, a host family dinner, a café, or in service encounters (cafés, supermarkets, call centers). Chapter 2 expands our understanding of pragmatic competence from different research traditions, including L2 pragmatics and intercultural pragmatics (see Barron, 2020; Félix-Brasdefer, 2021b; Taguchi, 2017).

With regard to intercultural communicative competence, a distinction is often made between intercultural competence and the communicative aspect of communicative competence (Byram, 1997, 2021; Kecskes, 2014). On the one hand, intercultural competence is exhibited when people communicate in their own language with individuals who have different cultural affiliations. It includes an understanding of knowledge, attitudes, skills to communicate and relate and awareness (e.g. a US American interacting in English with an Australian). On the other hand, ICC focuses on the communicative aspect of FL learners who communicate in a language and in a culture different from their own. It includes reflection on and understanding of the linguistic conventions, cultural norms and sociocultural expectations (e.g. a US speaker learning Spanish communicates in Spanish with people from Mexico or Argentina, or with other learners of Spanish). As shown in Chapter 2, ICC is generally defined as a complex set of interconnected abilities needed to perform effectively and appropriately according to the sociocultural expectations of the first and target culture(s). Some of the components include the speaker's own and others' knowledge, skills, attitudes, behaviors, and awareness during the negotiation and assessment of intercultural interaction.

A pragmatic perspective on intercultural understanding considers foundational concepts such as the speaker's intention and the hearer's attention, cognitive and social context, emergent situational context, co-constructed meaning, cultural awareness, reflexivity and variability. And, following the intercultural perspective on language use (McConachy, 2018), the chapters in this book direct the learner's attention to features of the social and interactional context and emphasize metapragmatic awareness to encourage learners to reflect on, analyze and talk about contextual features of the situational context. Overall, a pragmatic perspective on intercultural interaction and understanding takes into account three elements: language use as emergent through intercultural interaction, social action through joint activity and metapragmatic awareness of language use in context, which I explain below.[1]

Language Use as Emergent through Intercultural Interaction

We use language to accomplish action in social contexts. From an ethnographic perspective, Malinowski (1923, 1935) postulated two functions of language, namely, language as a mode of action and of phatic communion. He noted that '[...] the main function of language is not to express thought, not to duplicate mental processes, but rather to play an active pragmatic part in human behavior' (1935: 7). In his view, utterances are attached to their context and to action, or what people are doing through the exchange of words or the exchange of information. The second function – phatic communion, is used to fulfill a social function such as small talk, greetings or farewells. From a sociological perspective, Firth (1935, 1950) noted that the meaning of a language is functional and, as in Malinowski's work, its meaning is embedded in the culture. Firth proposed a semantic function (1935: 27) in which the meaning of a word or a sentence is determined by a particular context of a situation. Further, Bühler's (1990) tripartite model of language functions complemented Jakobson's (1960) typology of six language functions. The first three functions (referential, emotive and conative) are similar. The additional functions of language in Jakobson's model include: the poetic function (focus on the message), the phatic function (similar to Malinowski's phatic communion, which focuses on the social function of language), and the metalinguistic function, which focuses on the relation between the code and the situation, as in 'what do you mean by *conative*?' Each of the language functions in Jakobson's typology should be analyzed with a model of six 'constitutive factors in any speech event' (1960: 353), namely, the addresser (expressive), the addressee (conative), the message (poetic), the context (referential), contact (phatic), and the metalingual or the metalinguistic function (code). These functions will be reflected in an analysis of intercultural interaction, including the production and understanding of language use.

From an intercultural pragmatic perspective (Kecskes, 2014, 2020), intercultural speakers create meaning in situationally emergent contexts. When a learner communicates with another learner or with a NS of the target culture, they engage in the creation of an interculture, defined as 'situationally emergent and co-constructed phenomena that rely both on relatively definable cultural norms and models as well as situationally evolving features' (2014: 15). The interculture, such as in the negotiation of an invitation-refusal interaction, is emergent and co-constructed, and includes knowledge prior to the situation and knowledge that is co-constructed, collaborative, and emergent.

Social Action and Joint Activity

The concept of *action* has been approached from various interdisciplinary fields, including philosophy, anthropology, sociology, psychology and recent models of discourse analysis. In his *Philosophical Investigations*, Wittgenstein (1958) observed that the concept of meaning is related to the way in which language functions in communication. Words are not isolated entities, but rather actions used with different functions. He further observed that 'language-games' have multiple functions or actions, such as giving orders and obeying them, describing, reporting or speculating about an event, asking, thanking, cursing, greeting, praying, etc. According to Austin (1962: 117), the notion of *action* is reflected in the 'performance of an illocutionary act,' which includes the securing of an uptake (e.g. an invitation-response sequence). From a pragmatic perspective, Levinson (1992: 71) proposed the notion of *activity type* to refer to actions as 'verbal contributions' that occur in social interaction. Specifically, the underlying idea of action within the 'activity-type' framework is oriented towards a sociocultural context in social interactions where actions are accomplished (with specified participant roles and within the constraints of the situation). It is important to note that the notion of *action* under Levinson's framework is linked to activity types in the following ways: the social circumstances, the discourse structure of the interaction, the participants' roles and expectations and the inferences that must be drawn from the activity such as a question–answer format in classrooms, radio show interviews and court cases. From a discourse perspective, Clark (1996) used the term 'joint activity' to refer to language as social action with the participation of at least two interlocutors (e.g. in a sales transaction). Clark's notion of joint activity assumes that both interlocutors share *common ground* for the successful negotiation of the interaction. Finally, Habermas (1987) adopts a pragmatic and discursive approach to the analysis of meaning through communicative acts. He noted that communication is multi-functional in that it is accomplished through *reaching understanding, coordinating action*, and *socializing actors* (1987: 63).

In this book, I follow Clark's (1996) notion of joint actions and joint activity and Kecskes's (2014) discursive approach to intercultural interaction to examine the production and comprehension of meaning through language use. The concept of social action refers to joint actions that are coordinated in joint activity between learners or between a learner and NSs of different cultures. Language use always occurs in joint activity and in situated contexts that are negotiated and co-constructed.

Metapragmatic Awareness of Language Use in Context

To develop an intercultural understanding of language use in action, instructors and researchers need to find ways to provide students with a strong emphasis on reflection and analytical awareness of language use in context. Intercultural interaction takes place in a situated context, be it verbal (face-to-face, phone), in writing, or through technology-mediated communication. To maximize the ability to communicate effectively and comprehend social meaning in interaction, learners need to pay attention to the contextual features of the interactional context, 'reflecting on the construction of meaning from multiple (...) perspectives and developing insight into the influence of cultural assumptions and frames of understanding in communication' (McConachy, 2018: 7). Metapragmatic awareness concerns 'whatever goes on in people's minds when language serves expressive and communicative purposes' (2018: 117). Intercultural speakers not only pay attention to linguistic forms, but they also talk about language use, degrees of appropriate and inappropriate behavior, as well as social and linguistic variation. Metapragmatic awareness through dialogical verbalized reflection fosters collaborative dialogue through an engaged reflection on the learner's pragmalinguistic choices which mediate how language is used in appropriate settings, thus emphasizing awareness of sociocultural knowledge. As will be explained in Chapters 4–6, sociopragmatic awareness is a process that involves the learner's ability to talk about and reflect on their understanding of social norms, social power, social distance, degree of imposition, as well as levels of (in)directness and (im)politeness. When learners verbalize their thought processes, they engage in reflection and an analysis of social meaning in situated contexts.

The notion of context has been approached from other sociocultural and cognitive perspectives. For Austin (1962), the notion of context refers to the appropriate circumstances within a theory of social pragmatics. According to Searle (1969), the nature of context is cognitive because the felicity conditions must hold prior to the performance of a speech act. Context is viewed as predetermined, unchangeable, cognitive and as knowledge that may not be subject to the negotiation of face in social interaction. From a relevance theory perspective (Sperber & Wilson, 1986 [1995]; Wilson, 2017; Wilson & Sperber, 2004), context is cognitive and refers to the 'set of premises used in interpreting an utterance.' A context 'is a psychological construct, a subset of the hearer's assumptions about the world' (Sperber & Wilson, 1986: 15). For Levinson (1992), context falls under an activity type in which the situation is determined, such as a family dinner, for example; the roles of the participants are specified and their contributions are constrained by the sociocultural expectations of the situation. And, according to Goffman, context is determined by both the 'rules of the group and the definition of the situation' (1967: 6). Goffman's (1981) notion of context takes place in 'social situations' that frame and organize talk in situated settings.

Following the socio-cognitive approach to intercultural interaction, context is viewed as cognitive and emergent in interaction. The intercultural speaker brings information to the interaction, such as prior knowledge, assumptions, beliefs and behaviors. The goal for the intercultural speaker is to co-construct social meaning during the ongoing interaction in the 'emergent situational context,' in order to arrive at a mutual understanding and common ground (Kecskes, 2014 [Chapters 6 & 7]).

The concepts analyzed above have direct implications for the analysis of language use in context and intercultural understanding. Language is used to construct interpersonal talk, such as agreeing, disagreeing or challenging the other's viewpoints. Social actions are realized through collaborative talk among intercultural speakers who accomplish joint actions according to the sociocultural expectations of the members of a particular community of practice. My understanding of context (cognitive, social, interactive) is dynamic, co-constructed and emergent, according to the demands of the interactional context. And, through metapragmatic awareness learners engage in contrastive analysis, collaborative talk and reflection on the contextual features of the situation (McConachy, 2018; McConachy & Spencer-Oatey, 2020; Verschueren, 2021). A pragmatic perspective on language learning broadens our understanding of the construct of ICC, and ultimately intercultural citizenship, among learners in the FL classroom and in study abroad contexts (Kong & Spenader, 2024).

Outline of the Book

Chapters 1–3 set the theoretical and methodological foundation for intercultural understanding and negotiation of meaning, present a revised model of ICC for the analysis of language use in context and describe a model for the analysis of intercultural interaction from a pragmatic and discursive perspective. Chapter 1 adopts a pragmatic perspective to examine some of the key issues in order to extend our understanding of language use in intercultural interaction. I explain fundamental elements for an understanding of ICC, such as the role of culture in language learning, understanding and cultural awareness; thus, the interdependence of language and culture is emphasized. The chapter concludes with a revised model that combines both intercultural and communicative dimensions. Chapter 2 examines the construct of pragmatic competence from four different perspectives: interlanguage pragmatics, inference and communication, sociocultural pragmatics and intercultural pragmatics. Based on each of these perspectives, I examine how the notions of pragmatic awareness and metapragmatic awareness are conceptualized in different research traditions. I focus on metapragmatic awareness to engage learners in reflection, discussion, analysis and collaborative talk. I conclude with my understanding of pragmatic competence from an intercultural pragmatic perspective with intercultural speakers – as learners, mediators and agents – who use language to communicate effectively and appropriately. Chapter 3 describes a pragmatic-discursive approach for examining intercultural interaction through joint action. It includes the following components as shown in Figure 3.1: interlocutors (speaker/hearer), intercultural interaction, pragmatic contexts, intention/attention, emergent common ground, data analysis, metapragmatic awareness and variability.

Chapters 4–6 present an analysis of intercultural interactions and an understanding of language use in context, such as the production and comprehension of speech acts, and understandings of politeness and impoliteness. The data in these chapters is taken from learners in the FL classroom and in study abroad contexts. It includes the negotiation and assessment of speech acts (apologies, requests, refusals) through roleplay interactions, Likert scales, verbal reports, reflections of language use and contextual analysis, and politeness events, or critical incidents, which describe narrations of the learner's previous experiential activities.[2] Chapter 4 adopts an intercultural perspective to examine the learning of pragmatic knowledge and the effects of teaching pragmatics in the FL classroom. I present an analysis of a classroom-based study that looks at the development of pragmalinguistic and sociopragmatic awareness among FL learners of Spanish with and without previous experience abroad. The analysis includes pragmalinguistic and sociopragmatic awareness of cultural and interactional norms, awareness of regional variation and agency, and awareness of improvement and lack of pragmatic competence. It focuses on learners' ability to negotiate speech acts in interaction (requests, apologies, refusal of an offer), followed by their metapragmatic reflection on language use and the effects of pragmatic instruction at the end of 16 weeks. Chapter 5 begins with an overview of verbal and non-verbal strategies, including a prosodic analysis, used during the negotiation of refusal speech act sequences. After assessing research on L2 pragmatics in study abroad contexts, I offer an overview of sociopragmatic awareness and the role of attention and reflexivity in social interaction. Then, I present an analysis of two situations: declining a friend's invitation to a birthday party and rejecting a professor's advice, followed by an analysis of the learners' insights, cognitive processes and metapragmatic awareness based on the learners' verbalizations immediately after a roleplay task. I offer a prosodic analysis of refusal responses to examine pragmatic meanings based on prosodic features such as intonation, rhythm, duration and stress that contribute to the speaker's pragmatic meaning. Chapter 6 changes the focus to intercultural impoliteness through the analysis of impoliteness events. It begins with an overview of theoretical considerations of impoliteness, an assessment of agency and identity construction, and perceptions of offense in intercultural contexts. After the method is described, an analysis of understandings of impolite behavior is presented and discussed from an intercultural and sociopragmatic perspective with attention to the perception of offenses and face threats in study abroad settings.

The book ends with concluding remarks on intercultural interaction and cultural understanding from a pragmatic perspective, metapragmatic and intercultural awareness, the proposed model of ICC (Chapter 1), the pragmatic-discursive approach for examining intercultural interaction and understanding through the learning of L2 pragmatics (Chapter 3), pedagogical implications for teaching intercultural competence, and the role of the intercultural speaker's multiple identities as a learner, agent, mediator and an individual in a global world. I conclude with remarks on intercultural citizenship.

Notes

(1) Some of this information is taken from Félix-Brasdefer (2015: 6–13) and adapted to the context of intercultural competence.
(2) The Institutional Review Board at my institution granted permission to collect the data for this study.

1 Intercultural Communicative Competence as Language Use: A Pragmatic Perspective

Introduction

What does it mean to be interculturally and pragmatically competent in a second or in multiple languages? In the foreign language (FL) classroom and immersive study-abroad contexts, intercultural speakers – as language learners – communicate with others who are culturally and linguistically different from them; they bring their own knowledge, skills, behaviors and attitudes to communicate effectively and appropriately. Following the pioneering work of Byram's (1997, 2021) model of intercultural communicative competence (ICC), this chapter adopts a pragmatic view to examine some of the key issues in order to extend our understanding of language use in intercultural interaction. A pragmatic perspective accounts for notional features such as speaker intention and attention, hearer's understanding of what is said, cognitive and social contexts, emergent situational context, co-constructed meaning, interculturality and variability. Byram's pioneering framework of ICC has been re-analyzed and extended to examine different aspects of intercultural understanding through the learning and teaching of second language pragmatics (L2 pragmatics) (McConachy, 2018; McConachy & Liddicoat, 2022), performative competence through *savoir agir* (Beecroft, 2022), language education and learner agency and mediation (McConachy et al., 2022), and the link between intercultural competence and pragmatics (Schauer, 2024). As it will be shown in this chapter, the development of ICC requires cultural awareness and collaborative interaction through a reflective analysis of pragmatic routines and speech act sequences at the discourse level (Clark, 1996; Félix-Brasdefer, 2019b; Kasper, 2006; McConachy, 2018, 2023).

While most research in ICC centers on English, testing and assessment to measure outcomes, in this book, I focus on how learners of second or multiple languages negotiate, understand, learn and use language in context in the FL classroom and in study-abroad contexts.

In this chapter, I propose a model of ICC that helps the learner produce and understand language use in action through the negotiation of cognitive (*a priori*) and emergent contexts in intercultural interactions (Kecskes, 2014, 2020). I provide a definition of pragmatics that will be used in this book, followed by my understanding of pragmatic meaning in intercultural interaction. Following this, I offer an assessment of definitions of the construct of intercultural competence, followed by my definition of ICC. With regard to the communicative aspect of intercultural competence, I offer an appraisal of seven phases that are often included in research on communicative competence: linguistic, sociolinguistic, discourse, pragmatic, interactional, strategic and intercultural. I end this chapter with a proposed model of ICC from a pragmatic and discursive perspective. The chapter concludes with the notion that intercultural speakers (as learners, mediators and agents) need to be equipped with knowledge that combines both intercultural and communicative dimensions in order to communicate effectively and successfully in intercultural encounters.

Situating Pragmatics from a Social and Interactional Perspective

In this section, I describe the scope of pragmatics from an intercultural perspective to examine the dynamics of social action in intercultural situations with learners of second or more languages in FL and study-abroad contexts. At the end of this section, I provide the definition of pragmatics that I will use in this book to examine meaning in intercultural interaction.

Scope of pragmatics and pragmatic meaning

The term pragmatics was coined by the American philosopher Charles W. Morris (1938), who developed a theory of signs, known as semiotics, which comprises pragmatics, syntax and semantics. According to the author, pragmatics concerns the relationship between signs (e.g. an object, a word) and a person who interprets them in specific communicative situations. Pragmatics can be broadly studied from two perspectives, namely, the narrow view, or the Cognitive-Philosophical view (or Anglo-American pragmatics) and the broad view, or the Sociocultural-Interactional view (or European-Continental pragmatics) (see Culpeper [2021], who proposed using the narrow and broad views of pragmatics to avoid confusion).

Under the narrow view, pragmatics is defined as 'the systematic study of meaning by virtue of, or dependent on, language use' (Huang, 2014: 4). Within this perspective of the narrow view, pragmatics is considered to be one of the components of mental grammar (similar to phonology, morphology, semantics or syntax) and includes topics such as deixis, inferences and implicature, (in)definiteness, reference, presupposition and formal aspects of speech act theory. In contrast, under the broad view, pragmatics adds an empirical focus and adopts 'a functional perspective on all core components and "hyphenated" areas of linguistics and beyond' (Huang, 2014: 5) – such as sociolinguistics, psychology, sociology, educational linguistics and discourse analysis. Following this view, pragmatics represents a broad or functional view that encompasses 'a general cognitive, social, and cultural perspective' of language use in interaction (Verschueren, 1999: 7). The broad view of pragmatics focuses on social aspects of language, such as meaning in interaction, language use, context as dynamic and interpersonal aspects of communication. To avoid confusion, Culpeper (2021) rightly notes that the dichotomy of European-Continental versus Anglo-American is not helpful. In light of this continuum, Huang (2017a) observed a convergence between the two schools of thought. For example, previous research has been conducted on implicature, speech acts and presupposition from a Continental perspective; additionally, some key topics in the Anglo-American tradition such as syntax and anaphora are now considered 'hyphenated' domains of linguistics, such as computational linguistics and historical/clinical pragmatics (Huang, 2017a: 4). Hence, as noted by Huang, each tradition benefits from the other: analyzing theoretical topics of cognitive pragmatics and philosophy of language from a functional perspective, while emphasizing empirical research, including the intercultural component of pragmatics.

In addition, some researchers adopt an integrative view of pragmatics which integrates notions from both the narrow and the broad view to offer a comprehensive approach that focuses on interaction, discourse, and language use and variation (e.g. Barron *et al.*, 2017; Culpeper & Haugh, 2014; Koike & Félix-Brasdefer, 2021). In this book, I adopt a broad view or integrative approach to pragmatics, which will be described in more detail in Chapter 3.[1]

As a field of linguistics, pragmatics has been broadly defined as the study of language use in context and the ways in which the speaker and the hearer produce and understand meaning in social interaction. It has been approached from different angles, including cognitive, social, cultural, pedagogical and acquisitional perspectives. For example, Levinson (1983) adopts an inferential view of pragmatic meaning. For this author, pragmatics is concerned with 'detailed inferences about the nature of the assumptions participants are making, and the purposes for which utterances are being used. In order to participate in ordinary language use one must be able to make such calculations, both in production and in interpretation'

(Levinson, 1983: 53). From an interactional perspective, Yule's definition of pragmatics is concerned with 'meaning as communicated by a speaker (or writer) and interpreted by a listener (or reader)' (Yule, 1996: 3). Similarly, Crystal defines pragmatics as 'the study of language from the point of view of users, especially of the choices they make, the constraints they encounter in using language in social interaction and the effects their use of language has on other participants in the act of communication' (1997: 301). From a social perspective, pragmatics is approached from a 'general cognitive, social, and cultural perspective' (Verschueren, 1999: 7); pragmatics 'studies the use of language in human communication as determined by the conditions of society' (Mey, 2001: 6).

Overall, the aforementioned definitions include the following elements to account for a comprehensive understanding of pragmatics: inference, speaker intention, hearer's interpretation of speaker meaning, cognitive and social contexts, and the negotiation of meaning in emergent situational contexts. Since pragmatics examines meaning, it is important to identify what kind of meaning we negotiate in intercultural interaction.

Pragmatic meaning

An understanding of pragmatic meaning is crucial for successful intercultural interaction. When learners negotiate meaning in foreign-language or study-abroad contexts, they engage in social interaction at the utterance (e.g. requesting) or discourse level (e.g. speech act sequences such as request-response), and they produce and understand different types of meanings to communicate effectively and appropriately. Following Grice (1975), Levinson (1995) proposed three types of meaning: (1) sentence-type meaning; (2) utterance-type meaning; and, (3) utterance-token meaning. The first one is semantic meaning, while the other two are connected to pragmatic understanding of conventional and non-conventional explicit and implicit meaning during the co-construction of meaning through joint action (Chapter 3, Figure 3.1). *Sentence-type meaning* refers to propositional meaning that is encoded in the words, phrases and sentences. It is context-free and does not refer to the speaker's intention. Propositional meaning of a sentence consists of the individual meanings that make up the meaning of the sentence as a whole. *Utterance-type meaning* refers to 'a level of systematic pragmatic inference based *not* on direct computations about speaker-intentions, but rather on *general expectations about how language is normally used*', and this type of meaning includes 'speech acts, presuppositions, felicity conditions, conversational presequences, preference organization and [...] general conversational implicatures' (1995: 93). Finally, *utterance-token meaning* (or speaker-meaning) refers to Grice's notion of speaker's intentions that are recognized by the hearer in a particular situation in order to draw inferences about the speaker's intentional meaning. This meaning concerns non-conventional meaning or Grice's (1975) particularized implicature, that is, meaning that is inferred based on what the speaker meant or implicated, and the meaning is derived through conversational implicature, such as understanding the meaning of an ironic or sarcastic remark. This meaning is situation and context-specific and depends on the speaker's intentions and the hearer's recognition of those intentions. This type of meaning is irregular and does not account for the heterogeneity of the patterns of language use. As noted by Levinson (1995), this level of meaning 'underestimates the regularity, recurrence, and systematicity of many kinds of pragmatic inferences' (1995: 93).

The three types of meaning outlined above are needed for successful intercultural interaction. Of these, the last two are essential for communication to be effective and appropriate: utterance-type and utterance-token meaning. **Utterance-type meaning** is the intermediate level where we can observe regularity in everyday social interaction through the negotiation and understanding of speech acts, preference organization (e.g. acceptances or refusals), conversational sequences and conventional implicatures (Levinson, 1995: 93). It accounts for systematicity in social norms and conventions of language use, and 'orderly heterogeneity' (Weinreich *et al.*, 1968: 100). Following Terkourafi (2012), utterance-type meaning is the level where pragmatic variation takes place – that is, pragmatic meanings vary according to micro- (situation, power, social distance) and macro-social variables (e.g. gender, age, region, etc.).

Overall, my understanding of pragmatics comprises cognitive, social and cultural aspects during the construction of meaning in intercultural interaction. It considers contributions from the user (speaker, writer) and the effects that their intentions have on the feelings and emotions of the addressee (hearer, observer). Speaker meaning can be intentional or co-constructed during the course of the interaction (see Chapter 3, Figure 3.1). This definition also includes the evaluations that speakers make during course of interaction, such as perceptions of polite and impolite behavior, ironic remarks, or the comprehension of humor or figurative speech. I focus on utterance-type meaning to account for the negotiation and understanding of meaning that is regular, emergent, co-constructed and constantly evolving according to the demands of the interaction (Kecskes, 2014, 2020).

Defining Intercultural Competence

Culture

A fundamental concept of intercultural competence is culture, which is multifaceted and socially constituted. Culture is generally defined as 'a complex frame of reference that consists of patterns of traditions, beliefs, values, norms, symbols, and meanings that are shared to varying degrees by interacting members of a community' (Ting-Toomey, 1999: 10). Spencer-Oatey (2008b) defines culture as 'a fuzzy set of basic assumptions and values, orientations to life, beliefs, policies, procedures and behavioral conventions that are shared by a group of people, and that influence (but do not determine) each member's behavior and his/her interpretations of the "meaning" of other people's behavior' (2008b: 3). Cultural norms are understood as group expectations of what it means to be appropriate or inappropriate in particular situations. From an intercultural pragmatics perspective, in the actual situational context, intercultures are 'co-constructed, a process which may contain elements from the participants' existing cultural background and *ad hoc* created elements as well' (Kecskes, 2014: 5). For example, consider a conversation in English, taking place in the United States, between two international students (high school students), one from Mexico and one from Pakistan. They talk about cultural differences such as religion, high schools and their political systems. They agree and disagree, express repair, make clarification requests and eventually find common ground during the course of the interaction. Through the negotiation of their views, an interculture – the interaction – is created, blended and negotiated. Both participants are mindful of their sociocultural contexts. They bring their own prior cognitive and social knowledge and negotiate their intentions according to the demands of the interaction, sociocultural expectations, understandings and expectations of the participants (Kecskes, 2014, 2020).

A key component of IC is knowledge of culture through interaction and reflection. Specifically, negotiation and understanding of the conventions and regularities of social behavior, beliefs, norms, values and ideologies. Knowledge of culture changes according to the assumptions and expectations of the participants who create the interculture through social interaction and their awareness of the use of verbal and non-verbal cues (e.g. low or high intonation, eye gaze). Thus, our understanding of culture changes according to the demands of the emergent situational context.

Intercultural (communicative) competence

The concept of *intercultural competence* has been approached from different theoretical and methodological perspectives, including intercultural communication (e.g. Chen & Starosta, 2005; Gudykunst, 2004; Holliday, 2018; Klyukanov, 2021; Scollon & Scollon, 2001; Ting-Toomey, 1999) and international education (Deardorff, 2006, 2015; Deardorff & Arasaratnam-Smith, 2017). The communicative aspect of intercultural competence is present in selective models of communicative competence described in the next section, and it is currently analyzed as ICC (e.g. Byram, 1997, 2021; Fantini, 2019; Fantini & Tirmizi, 2006; Meier, 2015). The focus is on communication with the learner's ability to negotiate meaning in FL and study-abroad contexts, using interdependent competences (i.e. linguistic, discourse, sociolinguistic) in addition to knowledge, cultural awareness, attitudes, as well as cognitive and behavioral skills. Two concepts are crucial for our understanding of ICC: the intercultural speaker as agent and mediator (Byram & Golubeva, 2020; Byram & Zarate, 1994; Kramsch, 1998; Liddicoat, 2022; McConachy, 2018; Wilkinson, 2020). As an agent, the learner makes their own decision to act or to remain silent, and as a mediator, they facilitate and engage in collaborative interaction and cultural understanding.

The concept of intercultural competence has been defined from different interdisciplinary perspectives. The following labels have been used: intercultural competence, intercultural effectiveness, intercultural communication competence, global competence, transcultural communication competence, cross-cultural competence, interpersonal competence, intercultural interaction competence, intercultural competence development and intercultural communicative competence. Table 1.1 displays 12 definitions of intercultural competence as used in various sociocultural contexts and from different perspectives.

The definitions in Table 1.1 use different terminology to explain the multiple dimensions of intercultural competence when interacting with people from other cultures; namely, people who are also linguistically different. Of the 12 definitions listed, six labels are used: intercultural competence, intercultural communicative competence, intercultural communication competence, intercultural interaction competence, transcultural communication competence and intercultural effectiveness. These definitions highlight two key components of intercultural competence: the speaker's ability to communicate *effectively* (the speaker's ability to manage their goals in communication) and *appropriately* (the ability to achieve so as to be acceptable and assessed by the interlocutor) with others who are culturally different (Jackson, 2019: 480–81). These components emphasize the linguistic, cultural and psychological demands and outcomes as a result of verbal or non-verbal intercultural interactions. This includes cognitive, affective (concerning attitudes) and behavioral dimensions.

In sum, the construct of intercultural competence comprises three interrelated components: cognition, attitudes and behaviors. Most of the definitions focus on interculturality through the negotiation of meaning in intercultural interactions, where social meanings are created and negotiated in an emergent context (Kecskes, 2014, 2020). These definitions center on the speaker's abilities to perform effectively and with an increased cultural awareness (Byram, 1997, 2021; Hammer, 2012). Similarly, after her exhaustive review of the various dimensions of intercultural competence, Deardorff identified three interconnected dimensions of intercultural competence: 'awareness, valuing, and understanding of cultural differences; experiencing other cultures; and, self-awareness of one's own culture' (Deardorff, 2006: 247). Building on Byram's work,

Table 1.1 Defining intercultural (communicative) competence

Author & Year / label used	Definition
Bennett and Bennett (2004) Intercultural competence	'the ability to communicate effectively in cross-cultural situations and to relate appropriately in a variety of cultural contexts' (2004: 149).
Byram (1997, 2021) Intercultural communicative competence	Includes two components, communicative (linguistic, sociolinguistic and discourse knowledge) and intercultural competence. While the former refers to the communicative component, the latter encompasses '[k]nowledge of others; knowledge of self; skills to interpret and relate; skills to discover and/or to interact; valuing others' values, beliefs, and behaviors; and relativizing one's self' […] 'Critical cultural awareness, as an ability to evaluate, critically and on the basis of an explicit, systematic process of reasoning, values present in one's own and other cultures and countries' (2021: 66); 'effective exchange of information' (2021: 43).
Chen and Starosta (2005) Intercultural communication competence	'the ability to effectively and appropriately execute communication behaviors to elicit a desired response in a specific environment' (2005: 241).
Cui and Awa (1992) Intercultural effectiveness	Intercultural effectiveness of sojourners in a foreign language refers to 'effective intercultural communication' which comprises a composite of characteristics such as 'language and interpersonal skills, social interaction, cultural empathy, personality traits, and managerial ability' (1992: 312–15).
Deardorff (2004) Intercultural competence	'the ability to communicate effectively and appropriately in intercultural situations based on one's intercultural knowledge, skills, and attitudes' (2004: 194).
Fantini and Tirmizi (2006) Intercultural communicative competence	'a complex of abilities needed to perform effectively and appropriately when interacting with others who are linguistically and culturally different from oneself' (2006: 12).
Hammer (2012) Intercultural competence	'involves increasing cultural self-awareness; deepening understanding of the experiences, values, perceptions, and behaviors of people from diverse cultural communities; and expanding the capability to shift cultural perspective and adapt behavior to bridge across cultural differences' (2012: 116).
Klyukanov (2021) Intercultural communication competence	A system of knowledge and skills enabling us to communicate successfully with people from other cultures. 'The ICC system is made up of three interconnected components: Cognitive, Affective, Behavioral' (2021: 4).
Meier (2015) Intercultural communicative competence	'focuses on abilities especially pertinent to effective communication between those of different cultural backgrounds…' (2015: 26).
Spitzberg and Changnon (2009) Intercultural competence	'the appropriate and effective management of interaction between people who, to some degree or another, represent different or divergent cognitive, affective, and behavioral orientations to the world' (2009: 7).
Spencer-Oatey and Franklin (2009) Intercultural interaction competence	'competence not only to communicate (verbally and non-verbally) and behave effectively and appropriately with people from other cultural groups, but also to handle the psychological demands and dynamic outcomes that result from such interchanges' (2009: 51).
Ting-Toomey (1999) Transcultural communication competence	To be a competent transcultural communicator, 'we need to transform our knowledge of intercultural theories into appropriate and effective performance' (1999: 261).

Guilherme (2022) revised Byram's notion of cultural awareness into critical intercultural awareness. According to the author, this term is preferred because it provides the 'readers with illustrations of a decolonial "intercultural translation" across and within languages(s) and culture(s) rather than simply on the (post)colonial meeting of languages and cultures' (2022: 112).

The intercultural speaker needs intercultural communicative competence, including intercultural competence and other competences that will be described in the last section of this chapter: linguistic, sociolinguistic, pragmatic, interactional, sociocultural, discourse and strategic. Based on the aforementioned research on intercultural competence, I will use the following definition of ICC that includes intercultural speakers as learners, mediators and agents, in both FL and study-abroad contexts.

I define intercultural communicative competence as a complex set of interconnected abilities needed to perform effectively and appropriately according to the sociocultural expectations of the first and target culture(s). Some of these abilities include the speaker's and others' knowledge, skills, attitudes, behaviors and awareness during the negotiation and assessment of intercultural interaction. Intercultural speakers need to engage in intercultural understanding, reflexivity, metapragmatic awareness and agency to make their own informed decisions. Intercultural speakers pay attention to the sociocultural features of the interaction through the emergent situational context. They are agents who adjust and calibrate their intentions according to the dynamic demands of the linguistic and non-verbal exchanges when interacting with others who are both culturally and linguistically different from one's self.

Models of Intercultural (Communicative) Competence

In the following section, I review five models that have advanced our understanding of intercultural competence (Bennett, 1993, 2004; Bennett & Bennett, 2004; Deardorff, 2006; Hammer, 2012) and ICC (Byram, 1997, 2021; Fantini, 2006, 2019, 2020). The focus of ICC is on communication from a FL and study abroad perspective, and also from an educational perspective, where the emphasis is on instruction and assessment. For additional details on these and other models, see Arasaratnam-Smith (2017) and Jackson (2019).

Intercultural sensitivity development

This section describes the main tenets of two models that examine how people move from ethnocentric or monocultural mindsets to ethnorelative or intercultural mindsets: Bennet's developmental model of intercultural sensitivity, and Hammer's Intercultural Development Continuum. Based on observations made during intercultural workshops, classes and exchanges with students, Bennett (1993, 2004; also Bennett & Bennett, 2004) proposed a framework that explains how intercultural speakers construe experience over time, known as 'The Developmental Model of Intercultural Sensitivity' (DMIS). The model consists of six stages, organized into two worldviews of intercultural sensitivity: ethnocentric (denial, defense, minimization) and ethnorelative (acceptance, adaptation, integration). **Denial** states that 'one's own culture is experienced as the only real one' (Bennett & Bennett, 2004: 152), and foreign cultures are ignored. **Defense** shows that one's own culture is experienced as the only good one; cultural differences are denigrated as they perceive their culture as superior; this subsequently manifests in the stereotyping of other groups. **Minimization**, the final stage of ethnocentrism, contrives elements of a singular culture to be a universal experience, while differences are still acknowledged. In **acceptance**, the first stage of ethnorelativism, other cultures (including their values, beliefs and behaviors) are accepted as equally complex, respecting other cultural contexts. **Adaptation** includes the ability to shift perspective to a different worldview – that is, people begin to experience the world from the perspective of other cultures, leading to the appropriateness of mutual recognition, and enabling intercultural communication. Finally, in **integration**, the last state on the ethnorelative continuum, one's experience is expanded to include movement in and out of different worldviews; people at this stage have already internalized bicultural and multicultural worldviews and are 'truly multicultural and global' (Bennet & Bennett, 2004: 158). Overall, the DMIS describes how people in intercultural contexts move from ethnocentric to ethnorelative worldviews. Bennett's model seems suitable mainly to intercultural speakers in immersion contexts.

A revised version of Bennett's model is Hammer's (2012) model of the Intercultural Development Continuum (IDC). The IDC model emphasizes that building intercultural competence 'involves increasing cultural self-awareness; deepening understanding of the experiences, values, perceptions and behaviors of people from diverse cultural communities' (2012: 116). Hammer's model, based on Bennett's model of DMIS, is reduced to five stages and two cultural mindsets, ranging from a monocultural mindset (denial and polarization [or Bennett's defense]) through the transitional orientation of minimization, to the intercultural or global mindsets (acceptance and adaptation). Hammer's polarization stage can take the form of defense, with cultural practices perceived as divisive (e.g. my cultural practices are superior to other practices) or reversal, which values other cultural practices and denigrates those of one's own culture (e.g. other cultures are better than mine). For Hammer, minimization represents the transitional stage between the monocultural and the intercultural mindset. For the DMIS, the integration state concerns the 'construction of an intercultural identity rather than the development of intercultural competence' (Hammer, 2012: 119). Hammer's IDC is the result of the intercultural development inventory (IDI) which consists of a survey assessing the development of intercultural competence mainly for speakers in intercultural contexts, such as employees interacting with people from other cultures or students studying abroad. The goal of Hammer's model is to assess how speakers develop an awareness of intercultural sensitivity over time.

Both Bennett's and Hammer's models of intercultural development focus on how people develop intercultural sensitivity in diverse intercultural contexts, emphasizing changes in intercultural sensitivity and cultural self-awareness over time. Moreover, Hammer's revised model, with minimization considered a transitional stage, represents a suitable alternative to assess intercultural development over time if the goal is to examine sensitivity, diversity and cultural awareness in intercultural contexts. These models focus on developing intercultural competence in diverse environments with people from various cultural, educational and ethnic backgrounds.

Deardorff's process model of intercultural competence

Using a Delphi technique, Deardorff (2006) asked 23 international scholars on intercultural competence to select and assess characteristics of intercultural competence. Based on the findings and her previous work (2004, 2006), Deardorff proposed the Process Model of Intercultural Competence which consists of four developmental states, beginning from a personal state to an interpersonal level: (1) attitudes (respect, openness, curiosity and discovery); (2) knowledge/comprehension and skills; (3) internal outcomes (e.g. adaptability, flexibility, empathy); and (4) external outcomes (i.e. effective and appropriate communication and behavior in intercultural situations). According to this model, intercultural competence should be seen as an ongoing process of intercultural development, with intercultural speakers constantly learning about personal and intercultural dimensions of the target culture. The importance of this model is that it emphasizes attitudinal development to enable the development of knowledge and skills. While internal outcomes focus on the intercultural component, external outcomes center on the delivery of the exchange of information, including effective and appropriate communication.

Byram's model of intercultural communicative competence

In his seminal work, Byram (1997) presented a model of ICC, which includes both linguistic competences (largely based on van Ek's [1986] language-based model) and the components of intercultural competence. The model remains intact in his 2021 revised edition, with a few minor revisions and extensions (2021: 60–66; see also the exquisite appraisal of Byram's model in their introduction, Golubeva et al., 2022).[2] Byram's model (1997, 2021: 62) is shown in Figure 1.1.

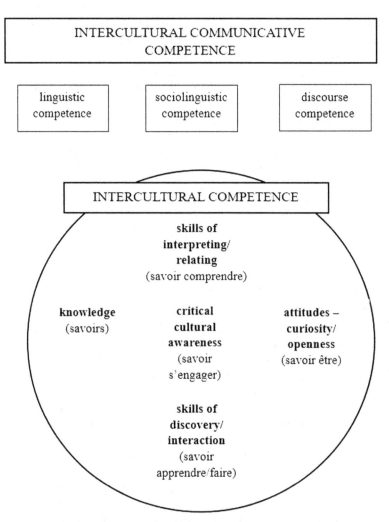

Figure 1.1 Byram's (2021) model of intercultural competence and intercultural communicative competence

The three linguistic components are generally defined as follows: linguistic competence, the ability to apply knowledge of the rules of the language to produce and interpret spoken and written language; sociolinguistic competence, 'the ability to give meaning to the language produced by an interlocutor [NS or other] in order to negotiate with other interlocutors' (Byram, 2021: 60); and discourse competence, the ability to use, discover and negotiate strategies for the production and interpretation of monologic or dialogic intercultural texts. The second dimension of ICC, intercultural competence, includes five components: knowledge (general knowledge of individual interaction and of social groups and their products and practices in one's own and in one's interlocutor's country or cultures); attitudes (curiosity and openness, willingness to discover and take risks, readiness to engage with conventions and rites of verbal and non-verbal communication and interaction); skills of interpreting and relating (ability to interpret a document or event from another culture); skills of discovery and interaction (ability to acquire new knowledge about cultural practices and communication and interaction skills); and critical cultural awareness (ability to evaluate critically, interact and mediate in intercultural exchanges).

While Byram's model has been adopted by many researchers in the design of pedagogical activities (e.g. Garcia & Di Maggio, 2021; Guo & Rodríguez, 2021; McHugh & Uribe, 2021; Tiffany, 2021; Wagner *et al.*, 2018), the focus remains on FL teaching and assessment. For example, Diaz (2013) stated that the connection between language and culture is not clear, with some discrepancies about applications of the model in intercultural teaching and assessment. Additionally, two of the linguistic competences require some precision: the sociolinguistic component focuses on speaker's meaning, which is concerned with pragmatics, instead of awareness of language and dialectal variation, style shifting, social factors (e.g. age, gender), etc. Sociolinguistics considers how language use is conditioned by linguistic and social factors, such as gender, age, region and education, among others. For example, the intercultural speaker should be aware that there is regional variation in how people use language in the United States, the United Kingdom, Canada, Australia and other regions where English is the official language or is used as *a lingua franca*. The discourse component seems broad, as it makes reference to interactional competence, as described by other researchers (e.g. Young, 2019). It concerns how people organize discourse through their ability to open and end an interaction, engage in an agreement or disagreement, and knowing when it is appropriate to initiate a turn or overlap. In the last section of this chapter, 'Intercultural Communicative Competence: A Pragmatics Perspective', I explain my understanding of these two components (see Figure 1.2). Although my proposed model generally aligns with Byram's in key aspects, mine differs in that I adopt a pragmatic perspective to examine language use with intercultural speakers who are seen as agents and mediators during the negotiation of meaning in intercultural interaction.

Fantini's intercultural communicative competencies dimensions' model

Fantini's model is the result of empirical and methodological studies which examined the socialization process or development of ICC through dimensions and attributes (2006, 2019, 2020; also, Fantini & Tirmizi, 2006). His model of ICC is rooted in the concept of communicative competence (see Hymes, 1972a, and reviews of communicative competence above). The author's definition of ICC encompasses 'a complex of abilities needed to perform *effectively* and *appropriately* when interacting with others who are linguistically and culturally different from oneself' (Fantini & Tirmizi, 2006: 12; original emphasis). Fantini's model includes five components: (1) characteristics/attributes (flexibility, humor, curiosity, tolerance for ambiguity, patience, openness); (2) three skills (ability to establish/maintain relationships, ability to communicate with minimal loss and ability to collaborate with others); (3) four dimensions (attitudes/affects, skills, knowledge and awareness); (4) target language proficiency; and (5) levels of attainment or development.

Fantini's model has some similarities to Byram's with regard to the emphasis on communicative competence (i.e. ability to communicate effectively and appropriately), attitude (flexibility, openness, curiosity), and the four dimensions – specifically awareness, which is placed at the center of the other dimensions in both. Further, his model considers the learner's proficiency level in the target culture; however, it is not clearly explained how that proficiency is measured. Finally, his model views intercultural competence as a gradual or developing ability over time and includes learners with different levels of proficiency and experiences of residence abroad. Awareness is fundamental for the development of intercultural competence because it promotes reflection and retrospection on sociocultural (setting, situation) and pragmatic concepts (e.g. social power and distance, perception of polite/impolite behavior, use and perception of address forms).

Taken together, Bennett's and Hammer's models offer ways to examine developmental stages of intercultural competence through increased cultural awareness of knowledge (first and target cultures), values, beliefs, attitudes, skills and behaviors, but do not consider the linguistic and pragmatic knowledge necessary to communicate effectively and appropriately in social interaction. Deardorff's model focuses on how intercultural competence is understood considering aspects of assessment in an educational setting (Deardorff, 2006). The final two models, proposed by Fantini and Byram, focus on ICC with some differences, but more attention is needed on the pragmatic component through increased cultural awareness. Overall, these models serve as foundational frameworks, advancing our understanding of various aspects of intercultural communication in foreign and study abroad contexts.

In the next section, I review selective models of communicative competence to understand the communication dimension of ICC. I will focus on the pragmatic dimension (production and assessment of social norms), as well as other components that need to be added to the construct of ICC in FL and study abroad contexts.

Dimensions of Communicative Competence

This section presents an appraisal of selected models that address different dimensions of the construct of communicative competence, beginning with initial proposals (Habermas, 1970; Hymes, 1962, 1972a; Savignon, 1972) and ending with our current understanding and a refinement of the pragmatic, sociolinguistic, interactional and intercultural components. Within the framework of generative grammar, Chomsky (1965) introduced the concepts of competence and performance in modern linguistic theory, with the native speaker-listener model in a homogeneous speech community. While competence refers to the speaker's tacit knowledge of the language or the unconscious knowledge of grammatical competence (e.g. phonology, morphology, syntax and semantics), performance refers to action, or the speaker's individual use of language. Habermas (1970: 367) was one of the early researchers who argued against Chomsky's monolingual notion of linguistic competence, and proposed the term *communicative competence,* which includes qualifications of speech and symbolic interaction and represents 'the mastery of an ideal speech situation'.

This view of communicative competence takes place in social interaction through social action at the discourse level in order to achieve 'intersubjectivity of mutual understanding' (1970: 372). However, Chomsky's view pays little attention to linguistic, social and pragmatic variation, focusing more on the 'ideal speech situation', which may be more appropriate for monolingual speakers, and less so for L2 or multilingual intercultural speakers. This view generally aligns with the grammatical or linguistic component of ICC (Byram, 1997, 2021) – the learner may use and comprehend language employing the lexico-grammatical resources available (phonology, morphology, syntax, semantics) – but lacks attention to linguistic variation across dialects of a language and languages themselves. After Habermas' initial insights regarding a social action theory, the construct of communicative competence took a different turn, beginning with Hymes' (1962, 1972a, 1972b) sociolinguistic perspective on communicative competence.

This section is organized according to phases representing the components gradually added to the construct of communicative competence in the field of foreign and second-language learning and testing: sociolinguistic, discourse, sociocultural, pragmatic, interactional and intercultural competence. At the end of this section, I present selected models of intercultural competence, followed by a proposed model that focuses on ICC in foreign and study-abroad contexts.

The sociolinguistic phase

In his seminal article 'on communicative competence', Hymes (1967, 1972a) argued against Chomsky's narrow focus of competence. Chomsky viewed the competence-performance distinction as context-free with an ideal native speaker-listener in a homogeneous speech community, leaving knowledge of culture and variation aside. He proposed a theory of competence 'to show the ways in which the systematically possible, the feasible, and the appropriate are linked to produce and interpret actually occurring cultural behavior' (1972a: 286). Hymes (1972a: 277–78) defined communicative competence as 'competence as to when to speak, when not, and as to what to talk about with whom, when, where, in what manner'. His understanding of this concept included two main components: linguistic and sociolinguistic competence. The anthropological linguist (1972a: 290) focused on a description of sociolinguistic competence with three interrelated concepts: heterogeneity in speech communities or communicative repertoire (i.e. different varieties of a language, codeswitching); linguistic routines and sequential organization (e.g. speech acts in interaction, appropriate circumstances); and the domains of language behavior by which one language (variant dialect or style) is habitually used rather than another. However, Hymes's understanding of communicative competence centered on the native speaker in homogeneous communities and was not intended to be used in interactions with intercultural speakers/language learners in contact with other languages and cultures. His understanding of communicative competence was limited to sociolinguistic competence, which implicitly included pragmatic competence, such as the ability to produce and interpret linguistic routines or speech acts in the appropriate circumstances (e.g. requesting, apologizing), as well as sociocultural competence.

The concept of communicative competence was later approached from an applied linguistics perspective with the refinement of sociolinguistic competence, as well as other components. In their discussion of communicative approaches to L2 language teaching, Canale and Swain (1980), inspired by Savignon's (1972) work on the L2 communicative classroom, considered communicative competence as the interaction of three types of knowledge: grammatical (linguistic) competence, sociolinguistic competence and strategic competence. Grammatical (linguistic) competence refers to grammatical accuracy both orally and in writing, including the rules of phonology, morphology, syntax and semantics. Sociolinguistic competence comprises two sets of rules: sociocultural rules and rules of discourse. While the former refers to 'the ways in which utterances are produced and understood *appropriately*' within a given sociocultural context such as a restaurant or classroom (1972: 30), emphasis in original, the latter includes rules of cohesion (i.e. grammatical links within and between sentences) and coherence (i.e. appropriate combination of communicative functions). Strategic competence includes verbal and non-verbal strategies to avoid communication breakdown, including the appropriate opening and closing of a conversation, knowing how to deal with false starts and hesitations, understanding conversation turn-taking and knowing how to address speakers of different statuses in authentic communicative situations. This theoretical framework focused on communicative language teaching and testing and set the pathway to examine how learners of second languages develop various abilities to communicate effectively and appropriately. According to this perspective, the conceptualization of sociolinguistic competence encompasses aspects of culture and discourse, with less emphasis on macro-social factors that condition variation such as gender, age, education and social status.

The discourse phase

Knowledge of the rules of discourse was later added to our understanding of communicative competence. Canale (1983) added a fourth component, discourse competence, to the three components included in Canale and Swain (1980). According to this author, discourse competence concerns how speakers 'combine grammatical forms and meanings to achieve a unified spoken or written text in different genres,' such as an argumentative essay, a scientific report, or a business letter (1983: 9). Specifically, discourse competence concerns how different meanings in a text are connected to convey attitudes and communicative functions, such as asking for information and responding, or opening and closing a conversation. Further, from a classroom model of communicative competence, Savignon (1983) kept the first three components proposed in Canale and Swain (1980, grammatical, sociolinguistic, strategic), and added a fourth, discourse competence. This was later added to Canale (1983), which focused on the interpretation of how sentences were connected at the discourse level. The component is also part of Celce-Murcia's revised model (2007), where discourse competence (i.e. selection, sequencing, and arrangement of words), appears at the center of her model. It should be noted, however, that the sociolinguistic and discourse components of Canale and Swain (1980) and Canale (1983) both refer to different dimensions of pragmatic meaning, such as the relevance of context, appropriateness and the speaker's intention to convey communicative functions or speech acts (Austin, 1962; Searle, 1969, 1975). It includes elements of pragmatics since, for some authors, discourse competence encompasses the learner's ability to infer meaning in discourse in particular contexts, alluding to speech acts and the *values, intentions,* and *purposes* of the reader/hearer, as well as those of the writer/speaker' (Savignon, 1983: 38).

The sociocultural phase

From a European foreign language learning perspective, van Ek (1986) proposed a five-pronged model adding two competences to existing models. His model included the following components: linguistic, sociolinguistic, discourse, strategic, sociocultural and social. The sociolinguistic component is aligned with Hymes's (1972a) concept of the features of the communicative situation, including the setting, the relationship between the participants, and the speaker's communicative intention. Sociocultural competence concerns 'awareness of the sociocultural context in which the language concerned is used by native speakers and of ways in which this context affects the choice and the communicative effect of particular language forms' (1972a: 59). According to the author, this competence includes an understanding of the turn-taking mechanisms of the target culture and an understanding of the communicative event in social practice. Social competence includes the speaker's 'will and skill to interact with others; engaging freely in a social activity, and the personality of the learners' (1972a: 65). This model advances our understanding of the importance of the sociocultural context and the speaker's social characteristics and skills for relating and interacting. Van Ek's model, however, focuses on the native speaker and bilingual speakers; little attention is given to the social and relational needs of the intercultural speaker who interacts with other learners or monolingual speakers of different languages. Later, Celce-Murcia *et al.* (1995), proposed a five-pronged model of communicative competence, the first four components were similar to those of previous models (linguistic, discourse, strategic, sociocultural), with the addition of actional competence (i.e. speech act competence), to be discussed in the pragmatic phase below. According to Celce-Murcia *et al.* (1995), the sociocultural component is a revised version of the sociolinguistic component (Canale & Swain, 1980), indirectly adding pragmatic knowledge (i.e. how to express messages appropriately) and knowledge of language variation in relation to sociocultural norms of the target language. Formulaic competence concerns the learner's ability to produce and comprehend fixed and prefabricated chunks that speakers use in everyday social interaction (e.g. routines like *How are you; I'm fine thanks* or idioms like *to kick the bucket* or *it's raining cats and dogs*).

Within the model of communicative language teaching, Savignon (2002) proposed an integration of four components of communicative competence (Canale, 1983; Canale & Swain, 1980; Savignon, 1983): grammatical, discourse, strategic and sociocultural. The sociocultural component represents a broader view of Canale and Swain's sociolinguistic competence. Sociocultural competence 'requires an understanding of the social context in which language is used: the roles of the participants, the information they share, and the function of the interaction' (Savignon, 2002: 9). Unlike the previous models that focus on the NS, Savignon emphasized the role of the learner in communicative language teaching and testing with regard to functional competence, such as the negotiation of meaning through communicative tasks such as asking for information or greeting a classmate or a teacher. Overall, Savignon's model focuses on how the various components of communicative competence develop gradually with practice, experience, and, I would add, constant interaction and awareness of the cultural norms, values, behaviors and beliefs of the learner's culture, as well as knowledge of one's own culture and that of others.

The pragmatic phase

The pragmatic component is reminiscent of Hymes's construct of communicative competence in his reference to using language appropriately in context, 'as to when to speak, when not, and as to what to talk about with whom, when, where, in what manner' (1972a: 277). In his model of communicative language ability from a language learning and testing perspective, Bachman (1990), and later revisions (Bachman & Palmer, 1994: 67–68), divided **language knowledge** into two broad categories, each one with various subcomponents:

- *Organizational knowledge* includes grammatical knowledge (similar to Canale & Swain's [1980] grammatical competence) and *textual knowledge* (again, similar to Canale's [1983] discourse competence in spoken or written texts i.e. cohesion, rhetorical or conversational organization).
- *Pragmatic knowledge* includes both functional knowledge or 'illocutionary competence' (Bachman, 1990) (i.e. communicative goals of the language user and the features of the language use settings, the speaker's intentions to perform speech acts) and *sociolinguistic knowledge*, comparable to Canale and Swain's sociolinguistic component (i.e. knowledge of dialect/varieties, knowledge of registers and knowledge of cultural references and figures of speech).

Bachman and Palmer's pragmatic component combines pragmatic and sociolinguistic knowledge for assessment and testing purposes, and little attention is given to the interactional aspect of negotiating the learner's communicative intentions with others. The focus is on the learner as an individual who possesses pragmatic knowledge. Likewise, Celce-Murcia et al.'s (1995) actional competence is similar to Bachman's (1990) illocutionary knowledge, the ability to perform direct and indirect speech acts, and speech act sets (Cohen & Olshtain, 1981). In her revised model, Celce-Murcia (2007) included pragmatic knowledge (how to express messages appropriately) as part of sociocultural competence. Finally, Usó-Juan and Martínez-Flor (2006) included pragmatic competence as part of their model of communicative competence integrating the four skills (speaking, listening, reading, writing). For these authors, pragmatic competence is similar to Bachman's (1990) illocutionary and sociolinguistic knowledge, and Celce-Murcia et al.'s (1995) actional competence.

Knowledge of pragmatics, in the aforementioned models of communicative competence, is often combined with sociolinguistic and sociocultural knowledge. The focus of pragmatic competence is limited to the learner's ability to perform and understand speech acts, such as requesting, apologizing or refusing. It should be noted that an understanding of this component is often limited to what the learner knows about the language, instead of what they can do with language in social interaction. Specifically, this narrow view of pragmatic competence is understood as illocutionary knowledge, that is, the ability to produce and understand speech acts, and recognize the speaker's intention, excluding speech acts in interaction and discursive dimensions of pragmatics. Overall, the negotiation of speech acts requires the ability to deploy interactional resources to co-construct meaning with two or more interlocutors, as described in the interactional competence.

The interactional phase

Hymes (1972a) made indirect reference to this component when he described communicative competence as using language in social action through socialization, as well as in his discussion of *performance*, following Goffman's work (1967), as 'interactional competence' (1972a: 284). Due to the co-constructed nature of this competence, the interactional component is rarely included as an explicit component of the framework of communicative competence from an applied and teaching perspective. One exception is Celce-Murcia (2007) who included this component in her model of communicative competence: linguistic, discourse, sociocultural, strategic, formulaic and **interactional**. For this author, interactional competence includes three subcomponents: actional competence (i.e. knowledge of speech acts), conversational (i.e. turn-taking, sequential organization) and non-verbal/paralinguistic (i.e. gesture, body movement, eye contact, use of space by interlocutors, silence). This broad view of interactional competence includes aspects of pragmatics, sociology and paralinguistics, such as non-verbal communication. Little attention, however, is given to the intercultural speaker's ability to co-construct meaning with others in specific discourse practices; and again, the focus is on the native speaker that learners intend to emulate.

From an interactive perspective, the concept of interactional competence has been examined in depth in the fields of second-language learning, teaching and assessment. It takes a different direction from the aforementioned models referred to as the componential or narrow view of pragmatics (Culpeper, 2021). Kramsch (1986: 367) introduced interactional competence to refer to the learner's ability to co-construct social meaning with others in light of previous and current cognitive and situational contexts:

> [s]uccessful interaction presupposes not only a shared knowledge of the world, the reference to a common external context of communication, but also the construction of a shared internal context or 'sphere on intersubjectivity' that is built through the collaborative efforts of the interactional partners.

From a conversation-analytic perspective, Kasper (2006: 86) defined interactional competence as the ability 'to understand and produce social actions in their sequential contexts', including analytical concepts such as turn-taking, sequence and action formation, repair, preference organization, and the ability to co-construct social and discursive identities through sequence organization. Researchers on interactional competence adopt **conversation analysis** (Sacks *et al.*, 1974; Schegloff, 2007) as the methodological framework for analyzing social action in interaction. Importantly, for Kramsch, interaction 'entails negotiating intended meanings, i.e. adjusting one's speech to the effect one intends to have on the listener' (Kramsch, 1986: 367).

From a teaching and assessment perspective, Young (2011, 2019; also He & Young, 1998) conceptualized interactional competence as the learner's ability to co-construct social meaning 'by all participants in a discursive practice' (2019: 93). Under this view and counter to the componential view of communicative competence (e.g. Canale, 1983; Canale & Swain, 1980; Celce-Murcia, 2007; Usó-Juan & Martínez-Flor, 2006), interactional competence is not implicit knowledge that the learner brings to the interaction; instead, it is an ability that evolves over the course of interaction in situated discourse practices. Young describes four characteristics of interactional competence (2019: 96):

- occurs in spoken interaction;
- includes the participants' understanding of the pragmatic meanings of communicative acts;
- is co-constructed by all participants in a discursive practice;
- refers to participants' participation in specific discursive practices (i.e. recurrent episodes of spoken interaction in context such as a vendor–customer sales transaction or student–advisor session).

Young (2019) mentions a set of resources that interlocutors deploy to create intersubjectivity in discursive practice. These include identities, participation framework, linguistic (i.e. register and mode of meaning to create experiential, interpersonal and textual meaning [Halliday & Matthiessen, 2004]) and various interactional resources (e.g. speech acts, turn-taking, repair, boundaries).

Based on the aforementioned discussion, interactional competence cannot be understood merely as one component of communicative competence, as it relies on other skills to co-construct social action with one or more participants in unique discourse practices. The aim is to achieve intersubjectivity and understanding by the participants' co-constructed intentions through social interaction. Additional work on interactional competence in applied linguistics has been conducted by researchers who examine how learners co-construct social action in foreign language and second-language contexts (e.g. Félix-Brasdefer, 2021b; Hall, 2018; Hall & Pekarek Doehler, 2011). This competence has also been applied to second-language teaching and testing, as evidenced by the welcome contributions in Salaberry and Kunitz's (2019) edited volume, as well as in study abroad contexts with learners who develop their ability to interact with members of the target culture (Dings, 2014; Kinginger & Carnine, 2019; Salaberry *et al.*, 2019; Shively, 2015).

The intercultural phase

In most of the aforementioned models of communicative competence, intercultural competence is rarely included as a separate component. One exception is found in the work of Usó-Juan and Martínez-Flor (2006: 16–17) who incorporated this component into their proposed model of communicative competence that integrates the four skills, that is, speaking, writing, listening and reading. For these authors, intercultural competence involves both sociocultural knowledge (similar to Celce-Murcia *et al.* [1995], including sociocultural awareness and sociolinguistic knowledge) and non-verbal signals such as body language, use of space, touching or silence. However, this component has predominantly been examined from a sociocultural and intercultural communication view. From an intercultural pragmatics perspective, Kecskes (2014) made reference to knowledge of pragmatics taking into account the cognitive, social and emergent situational context. Sociocultural knowledge is emergent in interaction and relies on cultural norms and participants' shared knowledge that is created and co-constructed during the course of the interaction (2014: 140).

Taken together, these phases offer a general understanding of the construct of communicative competence from different perspectives, mainly oriented to language teaching and assessment. However, some of these definitions do not seem clear, as they overlap with other competencies, such as sociolinguistic, interactional and discourse. In particular, the sociolinguistic dimension has been conceptualized differently, mainly from a discourse view. Finally, the pragmatic dimension is not clearly articulated or integrated into a model of communicative competence.

In the next section, I review the concept of ICC from a broad view, a pragmatic and discursive perspective through the lens of intercultural understanding.

Intercultural Communicative Competence: A Pragmatics Perspective

Drawing on previous work (Byram, 1997, 2021; Celce-Murcia, 2007; Fantini 2019, 2020; Schauer, 2024), Figure 1.2 shows my conceptualization of ICC in FL and study abroad contexts. ICC is multifaceted and is conceptualized as a composite of seven interdependent components:

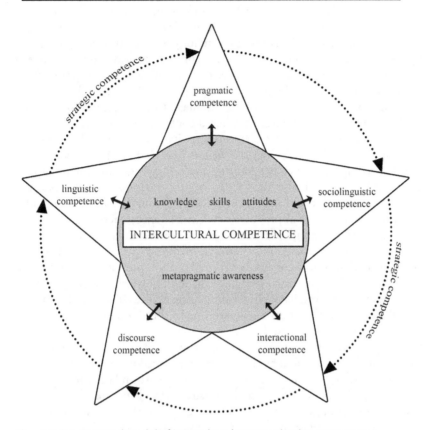

Figure 1.2 Integrated model of intercultural communicative competence

intercultural competence, at the center of the figure, and six competencies that aim to foster communication and assessments of intercultural interactions: linguistic, pragmatic, sociolinguistic, discourse, interactional and strategic. These competencies interact with each of the four components of intercultural competence, namely, knowledge, skills, attitudes and metapragmatic awareness.

The six components surrounding intercultural competence refer to the communicative component of intercultural competence. Of these, strategic competence serves as a support for the other competencies, connecting them for successful intercultural interaction.[3] A learner with strategic competence can make clarifications, reformulate, rephrase, or repair in conversation. Over time and with frequent reflective activities and sociopragmatic awareness, the learner develops the ability to interact effectively and appropriately according to the sociocultural expectations of intercultural speakers from different cultures and various languages.

Linguistic competence encompasses knowledge of the various components of the grammatical system of a standard version of the language, such as knowledge of the rules of phonology (sound structure), morphology (structure and function of words), syntax (formation and structure of the sentence) and semantics (propositional meaning of words, phrases and sentences). It refers to the ability to apply conceptual knowledge of the rules of the standard version of the language to produce and understand spoken and written language in isolated contexts of language use.

Pragmatic competence refers to the ability to produce and understand explicit and implicit meanings, as well as intended or unintended meaning. It encompasses both pragmalinguistic (lexico-grammatical conventions) and sociopragmatic knowledge (appropriateness and perception of contextual variables) (Leech, 1983, 2014; Thomas, 1983). It includes declarative knowledge of pragmatic routines or speech acts (e.g. greetings, requesting, refusing, apologizing), deictic expressions (e.g. social, place, time deixis), comprehension of implicit meaning through inference (e.g. conventional and non-conventional implicature, humor and irony), and an understanding of non-verbal cues through gesture, eye gaze or body movement. Since pragmatics is about making choices in situated contexts, this ability also includes an understanding of three contextual variables – social distance, power, and degree of imposition – and the dynamics of the intercultural encounter that is co-constructed by at least two interlocutors, a speaker/user and a hearer/observer engaged in social action.

Discourse competence refers to the ability to use and interpret stretches of monologic or dialogic connected text, such as the structure of paragraphs, stories, essays, political speeches and conversations that follow the conventions of the culture of the participants in situated contexts (Johnstone, 2018). It includes the ability to negotiate meaning using language to construct joint action, to create and comprehend cohesion (i.e. connecting sentences to create paragraphs, including conventions for the use of reference [anaphora/cataphora]), and expressing coherence in spoken and written discourse, such as managing old and new information or maintaining organizational schemata. Coherence expresses meaning that 'is greater than the sum of its parts' (Schiffrin, 2006: 171). Thus, discourse competence is the ability to use language beyond the sentence level according to the conventions and sociocultural expectations of the target culture in intercultural interactions.

Sociolinguistic competence includes knowledge of register variation, knowledge of cultural references and figures of speech, situational variation and knowledge of macro-social variables such as region (e.g. knowledge of dialects of a language), age, sex, education and social status (Schneider & Barron, 2008). It also refers to an awareness of linguistic, regional and social variations. For example, learners demonstrate an awareness of and reflection on the regional variation of the Spanish language across Spain, Africa (Equatorial Guinea) and across 19 regions in Latin America (18 countries and Puerto Rico) that use Spanish as an official language. Similarly, learners of English develop awareness of regional and social variation among varieties of English spoken in the United States, Canada, the United Kingdom and Australia, as well as English as a *lingua franca* in regions of Africa.

Interactional competence includes the learner's ability to co-construct social action with others through the deployment of interactional resources in spoken interaction. For example, it includes the learner's ability to negotiate speech acts in interaction and knowledge of how to take turns, how to respond to an interactional trouble (repair), how to open and close an interaction (boundaries), how to interrupt, how to introduce, change and abandon new topics, and how to get, hold and abandon the floor in conversation. Interactional competence refers not only to knowledge of how to deploy interactional resources in social action, but also the ability to co-construct social meaning, including the management of nonverbal resources such as gaze, gesture and body movements to express meaning (Young, 2019) and 'through the collaborative efforts of the interactional partners' (Kramsch, 1986: 367).

Strategic competence refers to the ability to compensate for breakdowns in communication (communication strategy), to calibrate for missing or partial knowledge during the delivery of a speech act, or to compensate for missing grammatical information or vocabulary (metacognitive strategy [Cohen, 1998; Oxford, 2011]). In Figure 1.2, this competence is displayed by connecting with the other competences, serving as a support system 'that is available as a resource in case of insufficient knowledge and/or communicative breakdown' (see also Timpe-Laughlin *et al.* [2015: 18] and Celce-Murcia *et al.* [1995]). Intercultural speakers use strategic competence by rephrasing the intended message (circumlocution), self-monitoring to allow for self-repair (e.g. 'I mean...'; 'That's not what I mean..'), style-shifting (e.g. switching from informal to formal address forms), code-switching from one language to another, planning what to say first, selecting the language of thought and delivery or challenging the interlocutor's perspective by adopting one's own cultural norms and identity preferences. Thus, through strategic competence, the learner serves as a mediator and acts as an agent.

Intercultural competence is placed at the center of Figure 1.2. It refers to the ability to communicate effectively and appropriately in intercultural situations with individuals who are culturally and linguistically different from one's self. It incorporates five dimensions included in previous models (Byram, 1997, 2021; Deardorff, 2006; Fantini, 2020): knowledge, skills, attitudes and metapragmatic awareness. I adopt the first three from Byram (1997, 2021) in foreign and study-abroad contexts:

- *Knowledge* refers to what the individual brings to the interaction, including knowledge from one's culture about social groups, specific social practices, history, geography, education, the dynamics of interaction in formal and informal contexts, diversity, transnational representation of current issues in a country and identity. Since knowledge is relational, the intercultural speaker will analyze these elements in relation to those of the host culture to increase their level of intercultural awareness (see Risager [2022] for transnational representation of knowledge).

- *Skill* references to the ability to discover, interpret texts or social behavior, relate with others and interact. Intercultural speakers engage in interaction with members from the host culture or participate in discussions of cultural diversity in the FL classroom. For example, it comprises the ability to interpret and relate to a document (essay, novel, poetry, newspaper, ad, etc.) or a particular intercultural interaction that may be perceived as polite or impolite, humorous or sarcastic. Skill also includes the ability and willingness to discover and engage in conversation about everyday topics (e.g. personal, friendship, education, politics); this could be during a conversation with a person from the host culture or in an interaction with an instructor or a classmate in the FL classroom.
- *Attitudes* refer to the intercultural speaker's curiosity, openness, readiness, willingness to engage with others and reduce prejudice and stereotypes, and to suspend beliefs and values.
- *Metapragmatic awareness* appears in the center of Figure 1.2, below intercultural competence, because it connects the other dimensions (knowledge, skills, attitudes) through reflection, retrospection and critical understanding. According to McConachy (2018: 33), metapragmatic awareness 'denote[s] the learner's awareness of how choice of particular pragmatic realization patterns (such as speech acts, honorifics, etc.) tends to be influenced by particular features of context'. Specifically, 'awareness of the various layers of meaning which are brough to bear for the purposes of interpreting and using language as a form of social action' (2018: 47–48). In Chapter 2, I develop this concept further.

It should be noted that the four dimensions of intercultural competence are interdependent, and each one should be analyzed in relation to the others. Of these, metapragmatic awareness is fundamental to maximize ICC in the FL classroom and in study abroad settings (see Liddicoat & McConachy, 2019; McConachy, 2018, 2022; McConachy & Spencer-Oatey, 2020; [also see Chapters 4 and 6]).

In sum, the dimensions of ICC equip the learner with the ability to communicate effectively and appropriately in formal and informal situations. It is also useful for teachers to become aware of and reflect on the importance of the construct of ICC and its interconnected components that can be used in the FL classroom. While the assessment and testing of ICC are beyond the scope of this book, however it is crucial for language teachers and researchers to understand how to incorporate it into the classroom, and, ultimately, in the curriculum (Byram, 2021: Chapters 3–5; Scarino & Kohler, 2022).

Conclusion

This chapter offered an assessment of the various dimensions of ICC from a pragmatic perspective in order to examine language use in action and to foster reflection and cultural understanding among learners in FL and study abroad contexts. The two settings in which the development of ICC takes place include the FL classroom and study abroad contexts. Overall, ICC should be viewed as multifaceted and interactive, with the central component being intercultural competence, and six components that define the communicative dimension of FL and study abroad learners: linguistic, pragmatic, sociolinguistic, discourse, interactional and strategic. Of these, strategic competence serves as a support system for the other components (Figure 1.2). One key premise of this model is for teachers to engage learners in reflection, metapragmatic awareness, collaborative activities and an evaluation of contextual variables, such as social distance, power and degree of imposition. A pragmatic perspective on intercultural language learning aligns with current research exploring revisions and extensions of ICC. This perspective can be applied to other sociocultural contexts, different pedagogical approaches and diverse student demographics. Additionally, it contributes to a broader understanding of crucial topics, such as intercultural citizenship, intercultural development, student mobility (McConachy *et al.*, 2022 [also McConachy, 2018]), and performative competence (Beecroft, 2022).

In the next chapter, I offer a critical appraisal of and extensions to two fundamental concepts of our understanding of ICC: pragmatic competence and metapragmatic awareness.

Notes

(1) Although Huang (2017a) makes a strong case for the Anglo-American school of thought (cognitive and philosophical pragmatics), he highlights the benefit of using both approaches to examine broad topics within macro-pragmatics: (i) cognitively oriented macro-pragmatics; (ii) socially and/or culturally oriented macro-pragmatics; and (iii) topics that do not fall in any of the aforementioned categories, such as historical sociopragmatics, clinical pragmatics, literary pragmatics, second-language pragmatics, variational pragmatics or legal pragmatics.
(2) In their Festschrift to Michael Byram, Golubeva *et al.* (eds., 2022), offer a state-of-the-art appraisal and extensions of Byram's work to foreign language education. In particular, the following chapters are worth reading: Introduction, Chapters 1 and 10. The 17 chapters offer outstanding theoretical and empirical contributions to our understanding of ICC in foreign and study-abroad settings.
(3) Following Timpe-Laughlin *et al.* (2015), strategic competence serves to support the intercultural speaker's other five competencies (linguistic, sociolinguistic, pragmatic, interactional, discourse), including intercultural competence.

2 Pragmatic Competence and Metapragmatic Awareness in Intercultural Understanding

Introduction

The construct of pragmatic competence has been debated, defined and extended from different theoretical and methodological research traditions. Pragmatic competence depends on how the construct of pragmatics is defined by either the narrow or broad view (see Chapter 1, Situating Pragmatics from a Social and Interactional Perspective). Under the narrow view (or the cognitive-philosophical perspective), pragmatics is viewed as a component of mental grammar, following Gricean's (1975, 1989) pragmatics as an *a priori* mental state of the speaker and a cognitive-context orientation. In contrast, under the broad view (or the sociocultural-interactional perspective), pragmatics interfaces with other research traditions such as sociology, anthropology and psychology; the notion of context is approached from a cognitive, social and cultural perspective (Verschueren, 1999: 7). Under this view, intention is considered as *post factum*, jointly co-constructed by the speaker and the hearer in social interaction. Following previous research on pragmatic competence from different views (Culpeper, 2021; Ifantidou & Schneider, 2020; Schauer, 2004), in this book, I adopt the broad perspective of pragmatics with select concepts from the narrow view (e.g. speaker's intention, cognitive context) to examine pragmatic competence from an intercultural perspective in order to examine intercultural understanding through the lens of L2 pragmatics with an emphasis on reflection, interaction and metapragmatic awareness.

This chapter is organized as follows: first, I review 10 definitions of pragmatic competence that have been proposed since the early 1980s to examine what dimensions of pragmatic knowledge researchers have prioritized. Second, I compare and problematize four current perspectives of pragmatic competence from different research traditions: interlanguage pragmatics (or L2 pragmatics), relevance and communication, sociocultural pragmatics and intercultural pragmatics. In each of these perspectives, I examine how the notions of pragmatic awareness and metapragmatic awareness are conceptualized; specifically, I focus on the scope of metapragmatic awareness to engage learners in reflection, discussion and collaborative speech. I conclude with my understanding of pragmatic competence from an intercultural pragmatic perspective with multilingual language users (learners/speakers/writers and hearers/observers) who use language to communicate effectively and appropriately and in a variety of modalities, such as in-person, virtual interactions or intercultural interactions through social media (Facebook, Reddit, YouTube, etc.).

Defining the Construct of Pragmatic Competence

Pragmatic competence has been analyzed from at least three perspectives: development of pragmatic competence in a native language (NL), pragmatic development in a non-native language and pragmatic development in clinical and atypical conditions. While the first two perspectives examine the development of pragmatic knowledge (production and interpretation) with healthy individuals, the third view looks at various aspects of pragmatic and discourse knowledge among individuals with varying conditions of developmental disabilities, such as those with autism (Colle, 2020) or down syndrome (Foster-Cohen & van Bysterveldt, 2020). The third perspective adopts the broad view of pragmatics to analyze speech acts in interaction, politeness, turn-taking in conversation and the comprehension of irony and humor. While the development of pragmatic competence in individuals in clinical contexts is a *research desideratum*, in this chapter I focus on the production and comprehension of pragmatic competence from a discourse and multilingual perspective among adult individuals who are learning a second/additional (Lx) language in the foreign-language (FL) classroom or study-abroad contexts. I adopt the broad view to examine different dimensions of pragmatic knowledge from a discursive and intercultural perspective.

What kind of pragmatic knowledge do competent language users need to communicate effectively and appropriately in an L2 or Lx sociocultural context? Researchers in L2 Pragmatics identify the core topics of pragmatics as follows: production and comprehension of speech acts (e.g. complimenting, refusing, apologizing, complaining), knowledge of deictic expressions (e.g. T/V, here/there, go/come, take/bring or discourse markers [*well, then, now*]), understanding of implicature/humor/irony, and the realization and perception of polite and impolite behavior. The intention of the speaker and contextual factors (e.g. social distance, power and degree of imposition) may influence the outcome of the interaction during the negotiation of pragmatic meaning at the micro- (single speech act) or macro-level of discourse (joint discourse through speech acts in interaction or identity construction).

Table 2.1 includes 10 selective definitions that are often cited in the literature of L2 pragmatics, sociology, discourse analysis, intercultural and cross-cultural pragmatics, pragmatic variation and cognition. These definitions aim to show how the scope of pragmatic competence has evolved to examine other dimensions of pragmatic knowledge in each research tradition. The definitions are presented in chronological order to show how pragmatic competence has been conceptualized since the early 1980s. In the next section, they will be organized and explained in four categories: L2 pragmatics, inference, co-constructed and sociocultural view and variation.

Table 2.1 Defining pragmatic competence

Author (Year)	Definition of pragmatic competence
Thomas (1983)	'The ability to use language effectively in order to achieve a specific purpose and to understand language in context'. (1983: 92)
Bachman (1990)	'comprises knowledge [...] employed in the contextualized performance and interpretation of socially appropriate illocutionary acts in discourse'. (1990: 98)
Kasper (1996)	'nonnative speakers' (NNS) use and development of L2 pragmatic knowledge'. (1996: 103)
Barron (2003)	'knowledge of the linguistic resources available in a given language for realizing particular illocutions, knowledge of the sequential aspects of speech acts and finally, knowledge of the appropriate contextual use of the particular languages' linguistic resources'. (2003: 10)
Koike (2009)	'how the grammatical knowledge is used to convey and interpret speakers' intentions, and how it is used to respond to utterances in the context in which they occur. [...] pragmatic knowledge entails knowledge of the target society and culture - for example, values and perspectives on social issues, rules for interaction, and social hierarchies'. (2009: 38)
Fraser (2010)	'ability to communicate your intended message with all its nuances in any socio-cultural context and to interpret the message of your interlocutor as it was intended'. (2010: 15)
Kecskes (2014)	'a very dynamic and flexible phenomenon whose development and functioning depends on several different variables including, among others, age, individual motivation, quality and quantity of input, and socio-cultural environment'. (2014: 80)
Ifantidou (2014)	'the ability to a. identify relevant linguistic indexes (*Linguistic Awareness/LA*); b. retrieve relevant pragmatic effects (*Pragmatic Awareness/PA*); c. explicate the link between lexical indexes and pragmatic effects retrieved (*Metapragmatic Awareness/MA*)'. (2014: 130)
Timpe-Laughlin et al. (2015)	'[r]epresents one dimension of communicative language ability. Includes five interrelated dimensions of knowledge: sociocultural knowledge, pragmatic-functional knowledge, grammatical knowledge, discourse knowledge, and strategic knowledge'. (2015: 16)
Taguchi and Roever (2017)	Pragmatically competent speakers are individuals who can 'adapt and calibrate their linguistic resources for the benefit of their interlocutors, communicative needs, and goals of interaction, and use their resources to mediate across cultural and linguistic boundaries'. (2017: 275)

Five authors examined different aspects of pragmatic competence from an L2 pragmatic and teaching perspective. Their understanding of pragmatic competence follows Grice's (1975) notion of the speaker's intention and Searle's (1975) cognitive view of the illocutionary act. From a classroom teaching perspective, Thomas's (1983) conceptualization of pragmatic competence refers to how L2 learners will develop the ability to use language effectively as to achieve a specific purpose and understand language in context. The author notes that any deviations from the expected norm will be attributed to pragmatic failure, following Leech (1983), which results in two types: pragmalinguistic and sociopragmatic. While the former refers to a negative transfer of the conventional linguistic resources (i.e. differences in the linguistic encoding of pragmatic force) or when speech act strategies are inappropriately transferred from L1 to L2, the latter – sociopragmatic transfer – refers to cross-cultural perceptions of what constitutes inappropriate behavior, as in not following the expected sociocultural expectations of what constitutes socially appropriate polite or impolite behavior. It should be noted that the pragmalinguistic and sociopragmatic distinction has been assessed and revised by researchers in L2 pragmatics (Marmaridou, 2011).

The second definition adopts an assessment and teaching perspective through the work of Bachman, who defines pragmatic competence as knowledge that is 'employed in the contextualized performance and interpretation of socially appropriate illocutionary acts in discourse' (1990: 98). His understanding of pragmatic competence comprises speech acts, language functions, rules of appropriateness, cultural references and figures of speech. Situated in the field of interlanguage pragmatics, Kasper (1996) viewed pragmatic competence as the non-native speakers' (NNSs) use and development of L2 pragmatic knowledge. To complement this view, Kasper and Rose (2002) and Bardovi-Harlig (2013) examined how learners develop the ability to perform and understand communicative action in the target language, such as speech acts, pragmatic routines, politeness and understanding of implicature. From a study-abroad perspective, Barron (2003) expanded the scope of pragmatic competence to include knowledge of appropriate contextual use (sociopragmatic knowledge) and knowledge of the linguistic resources to perform actions such as the sequential aspects of speech acts at the discourse level. Furthermore, Timpe-Laughlin *et al.* (2015) adopted a language teaching perspective in analyzing pragmatic knowledge as a component of communicative language ability, required for comprehension and production of speech act intentions. According to this perspective, pragmatic knowledge is accomplished based on three dimensions (context, meaning and interaction) and five interrelated components: sociocultural knowledge, pragmatic-functional knowledge, grammatical knowledge, discourse knowledge and strategic knowledge (2015: 16). Finally, adopting an inferential view of utterance interpretation, Ifantidou (2014) views pragmatic knowledge from a cognitive perspective, where pragmatically competent learners have to infer both explicit and implicit meaning from the linguistic and cognitive environment. Given the complexity of understanding implicit meaning and the role of metapragmatic awareness in fostering the learner's knowledge of pragmatics in an L2 or Lx, this perspective will be explained in more detail below.

As shown in Table 2.1, three authors defined pragmatic competence according to how the speaker's intentions are co-constructed and negotiated at the discourse level and in specific sociocultural contexts. Adopting a revised version of the Gricean (1975) view of speaker intention embedded in sociocultural settings, Fraser (2010) defined pragmatic competence as the speaker's ability to communicate their intended message 'with all its nuances in any socio-cultural context and to interpret the message of your interlocutor as it was intended' (2010: 15). For this author, hedging, also known as attenuation, represents one aspect of pragmatic competence (e.g. *I think/believe; unfortunately; perhaps*, etc.). Koike (2009) takes a dialogic view of pragmatic knowledge and focuses on 'how the grammatical knowledge is used to convey and interpret speakers' intentions, and how it is used to respond to utterances in the context in which they occur. [...] pragmatic knowledge entails knowledge of the target society and culture - for example, values and perspectives on social issues, rules for interaction, and social hierarchies' (2009: 38). This perspective takes into account the speaker's expectations from prior experience that influence performance and comprehension of speech acts and other communicative functions at the discourse level. Further, from an intercultural pragmatic perspective, Kecskes (2014) views pragmatically competent speakers as the result of socialization; that is, interlocutors (speaker and hearer) engage in frequent intercultural encounters where they produce and understand a variety of speech acts, pragmatic routines, implicit meaning and formulaic expressions. For Kecskes (2019), impoliteness represents one component of pragmatic competence. Overall, these authors view pragmatic competence as the negotiation of meaning in specific sociocultural settings, including both social, physical and cognitive contexts that are dynamic and negotiable based on the speaker's intentions. Under this view, individual factors may influence the development of pragmatic competence, such as motivation, age, gender, the sociocultural environment and the quality and quantity of input received in foreign or study-abroad contexts.

Taguchi (2017) and Taguchi and Roever (2017) adopt a discursive and intercultural perspective of pragmatic competence from the lens of interactional competence and pragmatics. For these authors, pragmatically competent language learners 'adapt and calibrate their linguistic resources for the benefit of their interlocutors, communicative needs, and goals of interaction, and use their resources to mediate across cultural and linguistic boundaries' (2017: 275). This view of pragmatic competence takes an interactive view and focuses on the learner as an intercultural speaker who negotiates meaning in social interaction and one who mediates between languages and cultures. Given the popularity of pragmatic competence within the field of ILP, this perspective will be explained in more detail below.

The aforementioned definitions illustrate how researchers interested in L2 pragmatic use and development have conceptualized the construct of pragmatic competence from different research traditions. Some take the narrow view to examine the learner's pragmatic knowledge to include speech acts at the utterance level (micropragmatics, mainly production), implicature and politeness, from a cognitive and non-interactive perspective. Others take the broad view to examine the pragmatic targets at the discourse level, taking into account sociocultural expectations and norms, sequential context and the speaker's expectations of the prior experience (macropragmatics). A global perspective on pragmatic competence should go beyond the pragmalinguistic and sociopragmatic distinction, and consider other dimensions such as discourse and interaction, awareness of sociocultural expectations and cultural norms of the L1 and the target culture, the co-construction of meaning in social interaction using both linguistic and non-verbal cues, and an understanding of pragmatic variation. The concept of the 'intercultural speaker', either as a learner, mediator or agent, is crucial to understanding pragmatic competence from an intercultural pragmatic perspective.

Perspectives of Pragmatic Competence

In this section, I focus on four perspectives that conceptualize the construct of pragmatic competence from different theoretical and methodological traditions: L2 pragmatics, pragmatics and relevance, sociocultural theory and intercultural pragmatics. I look at the following dimensions that each perspective offers or lacks: the scope of pragmatic targets, the learning context, the inclusion of speaker and hearer in isolated or interactive contexts, the inclusion or absence of variation, pragmatic awareness, the cultural dimension and the speaker's identity to negotiate meaning. Lastly, I present my understanding of pragmatic competence from an intercultural pragmatic perspective.

Second language pragmatics

In the early stages of interlanguage pragmatics (ILP) research, pragmatic competence was defined in the narrow sense as speech act competence, with a focus on nonnative language use and learning. Pragmatic competence was initially defined as the NNSs 'comprehension and production of speech acts, and how their L2-related speech act knowledge is acquired' (Kasper & Dahl, 1991: 216). From a study-abroad perspective, Barron (2003) extended the scope of pragmatic competence to include other areas of language use and interaction:

> knowledge of the linguistic resources available in a given language for realizing particular illocutions, knowledge of the sequential aspects of speech acts and finally, knowledge of the appropriate contextual use of the particular languages' linguistic resources. (Barron, 2003: 10)

Lastly, with a focus on second language learning, pragmatic competence investigates 'how L2 learners develop the ability to understand and perform action in a target language' (Kasper & Rose, 2002: 5). Bardovi-Harlig (2013) made the case for L2 pragmatics as the study of how learners acquire or develop pragmatic knowledge in a second language.

What kind of pragmatic knowledge do learners need to develop to communicate effectively and appropriately in an L2 or Lx? Researchers in L2 pragmatics generally point to two types of pragmatic knowledge that allow learners to develop pragmatic competence over time (incidental learning) or to improve as a result of pedagogical intervention (for an overview, see Bardovi-Harlig, 2001, 2013; Félix-Brasdefer, 2017a; Kasper & Rose, 2002; Taguchi, 2017). *Pragmalinguistic competence* refers to knowledge about and performance of the conventions of language use or the linguistic resources available in a given language that convey 'particular illocutions' (Leech, 1983: 11). It includes knowledge of strategies (e.g. directness, conventional indirectness) and the linguistic and non-linguistic resources (e.g. prosody in phrase final intonation, loudness and duration) used to convey pragmatic meaning. The second component, *sociopragmatic competence,* refers to knowledge about and performance consistent with the social norms in specific situations in a given society, as well as familiarity with assessments of (im)politeness and variables of social power, social distance, and the degree of imposition. For example, to issue a request, learners not only need knowledge of the various lexicogrammatical options available in the grammar (e.g. I need/want a letter of recommendation, Can/could/would you write a letter of recommendation?, I was wondering if you would have time to write a letter of recommendation), they should also have knowledge of the *where/who/when/how* these requests are used in particular situations. For example, they should understand appropriate degrees of directness and indirectness, politeness and impoliteness, as well as the sociocultural expectations of when to use a particular request.

Research on ILP is based on three main models: Grice's (1975) notion of speaker intention, the traditional view of speech act theory (Searle, 1975), and Brown and Levinson's (1987) model of linguistic politeness. With these models, L2 pragmatics adopts a cognitive view and a learner's focus on pragmatic competence, while little attention is given to social and interactional aspects of language use in social interaction. The notion of context is non-dynamic. Under this view, pragmatic competence is mainly understood as speech act competence, especially during the early stages of development. It is generally defined with a narrow focus as the 'learner's ability to produce and understand speech acts, pragmatic routines, or implicature; while the broad view takes other pragmatic targets such as implicature, politeness, irony/humor, and recent studies take a pragmatic-discursive approach to examine speech acts at the discourse level' (Félix-Brasdefer, 2019b; Kasper, 2006). Most work in L2 pragmatics research adopts the ethnocentric – universal – approach to linguistic politeness, with a focus on the speaker, conventional linguistic politeness and politeness as realized in speech acts produced in isolated contexts (Félix-Brasdefer, 2017a; Félix-Brasdefer & Koike, 2014). Furthermore, research on L2 pragmatics mainly focuses on the NNS or the learner who produces communicative action at the utterance level, such as the production of speech acts, pragmatic routines or L2 implicature with little attention to interaction (Kasper & Rose, 2002). The line of research has mainly focused on language use and development of L2 pragmalinguistic knowledge, but few researchers have analyzed various aspects of sociopragmatic knowledge (Bardovi-Harlig, 2014; Bardovi-Harlig & Dörnyei, 1998; Bardovi-Harlig & Griffin, 2005; Takahashi, 2013).

With regard to pragmatic awareness, ILP research has adopted two models of language processing. From a Second Language Acquisition (SLA) perspective, Schmidt's (1993, 1995) model specifies the conditions for pragmatic learning to take place. Specifically, for learning to take place, learners have to pay attention to some aspects of the input, among other things, which later becomes *intake* and leads to acquisition, if learners notice the input. He proposed the notion of noticing (observation) and awareness of pragmatic features. For pragmatic learning to take place, noticing aspects of the pragmatic target is a necessary condition for language learning. Schmidt (1993) pointed out that for pragmatic information to be *noticed* and therefore available for further processing, the learner has to attend to the selected input and store it in short-term memory. Metapragmatic instruction (Kasper & Rose, 2002) includes explicit instruction of pragmatic features, that is, the learner's ability to explicate the pragmatic factors (e.g. context, social power, distance and degree of imposition) when performing a speech act. The noticing hypothesis goes beyond attention to linguistic forms: learners need to pay attention to linguistic forms, functional meanings and relevant textual features. According to this model, noticing is a prerequisite for learning, but it does not guarantee acquisition. For example, DiBartolomeo (2022) used a revised version of this model to teach L2 apologies using an explicit/implicit instructional format, accounting for explicit metapragmatic instruction.

The second model (Bialystok, 1993) of language processing was initially proposed to examine how bilingual children process language, and it has been adopted for adult learning of pragmatic features. The author proposed two aspects of language ability: analysis of knowledge and control of processing. While analysis of knowledge refers to the learner's ability to access grammatical knowledge of the linguistic representations (declarative knowledge), control of processing concerns the learner's ability to structure and organize linguistic knowledge. For example, learners have to learn pragmalinguistic knowledge (analytical representations) and how to use the pragmalinguistic forms and sociopragmatic knowledge in appropriate contexts in the target culture. Incidentally, L2 learners have difficulty accessing their linguistic representations to accomplish linguistic functions, such as speech acts. Using this model to examine learning of L2 speech acts, the learners in Hassall's (1997) study successfully used linguistic representations but had difficulty controlling their knowledge in real-time interactions.

Overall, while Schmidt's model focuses on noticing the initial conditions of input selection, the two-dimensional model centers on the intermediate stages of development. The noticing hypothesis cannot fully be used to examine learning among learners in intercultural encounters because it must be revised to include reflection and metapragmatic discussion of sociopragmatic and cultural aspects of the L1 and L2 cultures. Additionally, the two-dimensional model does not account for how learners of L2 or Lx can develop the learning of pragmatic targets through awareness or a reflection of the pragmatic features to further their automaticity or control in appropriate situations.

In sum, ILP adopts a monolingual perspective and relies on NS baseline data to compare and contrast with learner data. The aim is to compare and contrast the learner's production and comprehension to NSs' knowledge in comparable situations. The scope of L2 pragmatic awareness is limited and restricted to explicating some pragmatic functions of grammatical concepts, focusing on what the speaker notices in the input. It also offers little attention to the reflection of the learner's choices and the impact that these choices have on the hearer. However, which social conventions and pragmatic norms should we adopt in the classroom with pluricentric languages such as English, French, Arabic, Chinese, or Spanish? For example, the pragmatic norms, social conventions, and sociocultural expectations of English-speaking countries (US, UK, Canada, Australia, etc.) or Spanish-speaking countries (Argentina, Mexico, Guatemala, Ecuador, the Dominican Republic, or Spain) vary across different varieties of the language (Schneider & Félix-Brasdefer, 2022). Finally, ILP explains issues of pragmatic transfer (positive and negative) from the native language and appears to overlook issues of pragmatic resistance, that is 'L2 user's *deliberate* divergence from perceived pragmatic norms and language uses they are aware of and linguistically capable of producing' (Ishihara, 2019: 165 [see Chapters 4–6 for more information on agency and pragmatic resistance]). While researchers in

ILP focus on the learner and the NS as the target model, the concept of the intercultural speaker, as mediator and agent, is not the center of attention. L2 pragmatic researchers largely engage in the analysis of single utterances in oral or written modalities at the production level, and little attention is given to comprehension or perception of speech acts.

Pragmatics and relevance

When adopting a cognitive perspective to language learning, few researchers have analyzed the construct of pragmatic competence from a relevance theory perspective to examine how learners develop pragmatic knowledge through pragmatic inferences and awareness (Ifantidou, 2014, 2021). Relevance Theory (Sperber & Wilson, 1995; Wilson, 2017) is a theory of utterance interpretation through which human communication is achieved through the speaker's intentions and the hearer's recognition of that intention. Under this view, learners have to draw inferences from the input available in the environment, including linguistic, prosodic (low or final intonation, loudness, pauses), or non-verbal cues (eye gaze, body movement). Context is based on the hearer's assumptions about the world, beliefs, and presuppositions.

Under this view, pragmatic competence concerns the learner's ability 'to engage in pragmatic inferences and on their awareness of how lexical indicators are used as evidence for interpretations retrieved' (Ifantidou, 2014: 149). Pragmatic competence is achieved through three processes through which learners develop awareness (2014: 149–50):

(1) **Linguistic awareness** concerns the ability to identify relevant linguistic indexes, or linguistically encoded phenomena. For example, a knowledge of the meaning of words through decoding and inferences, explicatures as shared assumptions, such as knowing that the meaning of *yet* can be retrieved by means of the meaning of the word and an explicit assumption via inference. In this example, 'The students have not arrived *yet*,' the learner has to know the conventional meaning of the adverb 'yet' (decoding) and via inference, the students will arrive *soon*. Other examples include decoding and inferring the procedural meaning of epistemic modals or evidentials (e.g. *I think/believe; should*) or discourse markers (e.g. *well, actually, so*).
(2) **Pragmatic awareness** refers to the ability to retrieve relevant cognitive effects, such as contextual implications. For example, understanding the intended meaning of a humorous joke, an ironic remark, or a disrespectful comment. Learners also have to be aware of the degree of social status, power and degree of imposition between the speaker and hearer according to the expectations of the target speech community. Since pragmatic awareness focuses on production, it centers on the speaker's ability to infer characteristics from the cognitive context.

(3) **Metapragmatic awareness** concerns the learner's ability to explicate and reflect linguistically encoded meaning (linguistic awareness) and to draw contextual effects from an inference. It focuses on the hearer's reception to understand meaning as a result of explication and reflection.

According to this view, learners who perform successfully in all three types of awareness are considered highly competent learners of L2 or Lx. Pragmatic competence is measured in terms of degree, that is, based on what the learner can produce and infer during the understanding of meaning as a constructed process between speaker and hearer.

Due to the cognitive focus of this model, pragmatic competence relies on the learner's ability to understand pragmalinguistic knowledge with various degrees of linguistic complexity (both conceptual and procedural meaning), an understanding of social variables of the target culture (power, social distance, degree of imposition), and a knowledge of the sociocultural expectations of what is considered polite and impolite behavior. To develop levels of pragmatic awareness, the learner needs to infer the speaker's intended meaning to achieve a contextual pragmatic effect, such as an understanding of implicit meaning which requires an advanced level of linguistic proficiency, as well as a knowledge of sociocultural expectations.

While this perspective explains how learners interpret explicit and implicit meaning using relevant cues from the cognitive environment, it does not offer ways to analyze joint action. The cognitive aspect will be adapted to my understanding of pragmatic competence from a discursive perspective with intercultural speakers who co-construct meaning in social interaction. Due to the focus on developing the learner's ability to infer explicit and implicit meaning such as irony and metaphors (Ifantidou, 2021), the following concepts will be used in my understanding of pragmatic competence: contextualization cues, prior context, metapragmatic awareness and contextual implications as a result of successful pragmatic inferences (see Chapter 3, Figure 3.1).

Sociocultural theory

Pragmatic competence has also been conceptualized through the lens of sociocultural theory (SCT) in FL classrooms and study-abroad contexts. Based on previous tenets of SCT (Lantolf & Thorne, 2006; van Compernolle, 2014; Vygotsky, 1997), L2 pragmatic development is viewed fundamentally as a conceptual process, as culturally-constructed concepts mediate cognition. According to this view, pragmatics is mediated by social interaction through a gradual process as the learner acquires social knowledge and linguistic resources for mental development. A key concept of SCT is the assumption that (pragmatic) learning occurs through scaffolded learning, known as the zone of proximal development (ZPD) (Vygotsky, 1978), as in learners interacting with advanced learners, tutors, or with NSs of the target language. With regard to L2 pragmatic learning, pragmatics is mediated by social interaction with learners reflecting on their own linguistic and social choices. Social actions (e.g. T/V distinction, apologizing, requesting, complaining) are mediated by pragmalinguistic choices (i.e. the grammar for the service of pragmatics), and these choices are mediated by the speaker's sociopragmatic knowledge (i.e. knowledge of the social conventions and appropriate or inappropriate behavior that regulates sociocultural expectations).

Pragmatic learning improves as a result of 'metapragmatic awareness' defined as 'the knowledge of the social meaning of variable second language forms, how they mark different aspects of social contexts or personal identities, and how they reference broader language ideologies' (van Compernolle & Kinginger, 2013: 284). Metapragmatic awareness is realized through either monologic or dialogic verbalized reflection. Of these, metapragmatic awareness through dialogical verbalized reflection fosters collaborative dialogue through an engaged reflection of the learner's pragmalinguistic choices which mediate how language is used in appropriate settings, thus, emphasizing awareness of sociocultural knowledge. Henery (2015) represents one study that examined the development of metapragmatic awareness abroad exploring the role of expert-mediation. The two participants abroad received metapragmatic awareness at the beginning and end of the program in the form of journal discussions and language awareness interviews comparing and contrasting two texts in formal and informal registers. The students' explanations revealed an awareness of the language choices, a discussion of the sociocultural expectations (e.g. social power, social distance), and evidence of pragmatic development from the beginning to the end of the semester. Using the model of sociocultural theory, Kinginger and Carnine (2019) analyzed the sociopragmatic development of two learners during dinner interactions with the host family in France. The data was collected from two students through interviews (perception data), field notes and audio mealtime interactions over one semester and one academic year, respectively. The results suggested the relevance of interacting with the host family members during mealtime interactions to increase participation and reflection of sociocultural topics in the target community of practice. The input provided by the host family also influenced the conversational development of each student, reflecting on their linguistic choices and the sociocultural expectations with members of the target community, which increased the learners' awareness of social topics and their ability to interact with them at the discourse level.

The aforementioned studies highlight the importance of homestays as recurring language practices, including dinner interactions with the host family and with members of the target culture. These recurrent events not only support integrated learning of language and culture but also highlight the importance of reflection and individual differences of learners who interact with different types of host families and with members of the host community in a variety of formal and informal settings. While both pragmalinguistic and sociopragmatic knowledge are crucial for L2 pragmatic development, SCT emphasizes sociocultural knowledge and metapragmatic awareness. Despite the focus on various aspects of sociopragmatic practices mainly in study-abroad contexts, there is a preference for NSs to engage with the learner to promote learning through scaffolding. Similar to ILP which focuses on bilingual learners and the NS as the ideal target language norm, SCT tends to favor the monolingual view, with little attention to the multilingual perspective and regional or social variation. Finally, the emphasis on metapragmatic awareness, with reflection, analysis, discovery and collaboration, is an important aspect to expand the construct of pragmatic competence.

Intercultural pragmatics

An intercultural perspective to pragmatic competence takes a dynamic view of context and speaker intention constructed through interaction (Kecskes, 2014, 2020), the negotiation of meaning, sociocultural norms/expectations and a reflection of contextual factors (social distance, power, degree of imposition). Unlike ILP, which adopts a monolingual view, intercultural pragmatics focuses on intercultural speakers who engage in social interaction and co-construct meaning according to the demands of the interaction. Intercultural pragmatics has its own sociocultural foundation, social nuances and shared assumptions, beliefs, attitudes and behavioral expectations. Intercultural pragmatics focuses on intercultural interaction as a cultural practice, with speakers and hearers negotiating their intentions through the emerging situational context. The assumption is that bilingual and multilingual speakers already have 'an L1-governed pragmatic competence in place, which will be adjusted to accommodate the socio-cultural requirements of the new language(s)' (Kecskes, 2014: 61).

From an ILP view, the pragmalinguistic (lexico-grammatical resources used for the service of pragmatics) and sociopragmatic knowledge (e.g. appropriateness of social norms, discourse practices and social conventions, perceptions of social power and social distance, etc.) can be used to examine the development of intercultural communicative competence among L2 and FL learners. However they must be adapted to the intercultural language learning view, which considers learning as a process both collaborative and reflective (Liddicoat & Scarino, 2013; McConachy, 2018). Further, research on interactional competence (Young, 2019) complements the construct of pragmatic competence with learners using the pragmalinguistic resources that are deployed mutually and reciprocally through social interaction. Some of these resources include turn-taking practices (when to hold the floor, when to overlap and when to interrupt), repair in conversation (how to recognize and repair trouble), how to open and close interaction, how to deploy these resources to convey assessments of polite or impolite behavior, and the process to produce and comprehend speech acts in interaction. More importantly, according to Young, interactional competence 'is co-constructed by all participants in a discursive practice' (2019: 96). Discursive practices include recurring episodes of social interaction, such as asking a professor for a letter of recommendation, negotiating service in intercultural service encounters (e.g. buying coffee at a café or buying food at a supermarket), or issuing an invitation and accepting or declining.

Overall, since intercultural speakers do not often share common ground (i.e. shared knowledge about the world, presuppositions, beliefs, social norms, social expectations, behaviors, etc.), mutual understanding has to be negotiated through social interaction and mediation. This perspective adopts fundamental concepts of the sociocognitive approach (Kecskes, 2014): speaker's intentions as emergent in interaction, prior knowledge and the negotiation of common ground, attention and intention, and a multi-faceted view of the context, including cognitive, social and interactive dimensions.

Pragmatic Competence from an Intercultural Pragmatics Perspective

What kind of pragmatic knowledge do competent language learners need to communicate effectively and appropriately in an L2 or Lx? In this book, I adopt an interactive intercultural perspective to pragmatic competence that encompasses four dimensions: first, given the increasing number of students engaging in intercultural communication in a global world, learners are viewed as bilingual or multilingual speakers who interact with either NSs or learners of different linguistic and cultural backgrounds through various modalities, such as oral, written, or technology-mediated communication (Bou-Franch, 2021; Herring & Androutsopoulos, 2015). Under this view, the NS is not considered the ideal base of comparison to social norms and established social conventions of the target culture. Instead, the focus is on the learner as an intercultural speaker. Second, pragmatic competence develops through socialization with other interlocutors in L2 or FL contexts, engaging with others in a variety of formal and informal intercultural situations. The acquisition of linguistic and sociocultural knowledge is interdependent and learners develop sociocultural expectations of social conventions through their participation in language activities (Ochs, 1988: 14). Moreover, pragmatic development takes place through interaction in oral or written mode, including technology-mediated communication and through 'the use of language to encode and create cultural meaning' (Poole, 1994: 594). Third, unlike ILP where learners are expected to behave like NSs of the target language, bilingual and multilingual speakers develop pragmatic resistance to target pragmatic norms and expectations; that is, cases in which learners may know the target language norms and sociocultural expectations, but deliberately choose not to act accordingly (Adamson, 1988; Ishihara, 2019; Li, 2008). Fourth, metapragmatic awareness is the result of reflection, discovery and analysis of sociocultural concepts that foster intercultural understandings (Liddicoat & Scarino, 2013; McConachy, 2018; McConachy & Spencer-Oatey, 2020). Specifically, language learners 'need to engage in processes of reflection and mediation between languages and cultures' (McConachy, 2022: 37).

Reflection and pragmatic awareness take place when the learner and the instructor discuss pragmatic concepts (e.g. social distance, power, degree of imposition) or when the learners engage in conversations where they have to assess sociopragmatic norms, such as polite and impolite behavior and understandings of implicit meaning such as irony or humor. Overall, the view of pragmatic competence – from an intercultural pragmatics perspective – is adopted in this book because it encompasses both understandings of sociocultural norms (e.g. beliefs, conventions, behaviors) and the use of pragmalinguistic choices to convey social and pragmatic meaning (see also Kecskes, 2019).

Three studies examined various aspects of pragmatic competence from an intercultural pragmatic perspective. Using frameworks of intercultural pragmatics and intercultural language learning, McConachy (2018) analyzed how Japanese learners of English as a FL engage in reflection, collaborative talk, and metapragmatic development of requests, apologies, and compliments over a 10-week communicative EFL course taught by the author as part of a study-abroad preparation institute in Japan. He analyzed roleplay interactions as collaborative dialog to examine learning practices of interacting, noticing, comparing and reflecting. The analysis showed that engagement in reflective and metapragmatic interpretations improved the learner's ability to notice, compare and reflect on how NSs and intercultural speakers negotiate speech acts at the discourse level. In a different study, Liddicoat and McConachy (2019) examined perceptions of politeness as one component of pragmatic competence, followed by collaborative talk and metapragmatic reflection. They examined learning practices of gratitude in intercultural encounters, and reflection of pragmatic expectations during classroom interaction. The authors found that intercultural learning took place as a result of students' reflection, metapragmatic awareness and collaborative discussion. With regard to impoliteness, Kecskes (2019) made a strong case to show how the comprehension and realization of impolite behavior represent one dimension of pragmatic competence. Furthermore, adopting the main tenets of the socio-cognitive approach, Kecskes (2014) convincingly showed how norms, standards and conventions of politeness and impoliteness are the product of prior experience and repeated prior contexts. Thus, the understanding and negotiation of impolite behavior is the result of repeated intercultural encounters, motivation and a 'willingness to accept L2 politeness and impoliteness conventions' (Kecskes, 2019: 65).

In this book, I adopt a perspective of pragmatic competence that goes beyond the traditional view of ILP. It is situated within intercultural pragmatics and ILP of intercultural speakers (learners, mediators, or agents) who negotiate meaning during emergent situational contexts. **Pragmatic competence** is understood as the learner's ability to produce and understand meaning in social interaction, such as the negotiation of speech acts at the discourse level (joint action), understanding both conventional and non-conventional meaning (e.g. indirect requests or suggestions, humor, irony), and the ability to communicate in a variety of formal and non-formal contexts, among other topics. The negotiation of pragmatic meaning also includes interactional competence, such as the ability to understand and produce social action in intercultural contexts (Félix-Brasdefer, 2019b; Kasper, 2006), competence to open and close interaction, the ability to repair misunderstandings in social interaction, and the ability to deploy interactional resources to co-construct social action across multiple turns. Intercultural speakers should develop an awareness of social conventions, variation, and expected sociocultural norms of what is considered appropriate behavior in both the first and the target culture. It encompasses a multilingual perspective with intercultural speakers engaging in intercultural interaction, understanding social norms and conventions in the L1 and L2 cultures, and achieving mutual intersubjectivity. Moreover, researchers in L2 pragmatics should focus on the prosodic resources (e.g. final intonation, loudness and duration) that learners use to produce and comprehend meaning in learner-NS speaker interactions. For a recent analysis of prosody and pragmatics, see Escandell-Vidal and Prieto (2021) and Kang and Kermad (2019).

The notion of variation has been added as a dimension of pragmatic competence, where learners communicate effectively and appropriately taking into account macro- (region, age, gender, socioeconomic status) and micro-social factors, such as the situation, social power and social distance. Adopting a variational perspective, Schneider (2017: 317) proposed two components that should be included within pragmatic competence, a distinction between 'utterance-based micropragmatic competence (knowing how to perform a communicative act) and discourse-oriented macropragmatic competence (knowing how to behave in interaction or, more generally, in discourse)'. From a variational pragmatic perspective, Barron's (2020) conceptualization of pragmatic competence encompasses different levels of analysis, such as formal (discourse markers, epistemic expressions), actional (speech acts), interactive (speech act sequences), stylistic (register variation and forms of address) and organizational (turn-taking in conversation). Schauer (2024) analyzes pragmatic competence through the lens of intercultural competence, variational pragmatics and intercultural understanding as a learning process. Overall, the variational dimension of pragmatic competence highlights the relevance of language use at micro- and macro-levels of analysis.

Finally, to achieve pragmatic competence in an L2 or multilingual contexts, the following dimensions should be considered. Drawing on previous research on pragmatic competence and the intercultural speaker (Ishihara, 2019; Ishihara & Cohen 2010; Liddicoat & McConachy, 2019; Schauer, 2024; Taguchi & Roever, 2017); in the FL or study-abroad contexts, learners should be able to:

- perform and understand communicative action in social interaction (e.g. speech acts, conventional and non-conventional meaning, humor, irony, politeness and impoliteness);
- adjust and calibrate their intentions during the course of the interaction;
- pay attention to verbal and non-verbal features of the interaction;
- be mindful of pragmalinguistic and sociopragmatic variation in their own and the target cultures;
- engage in metapragmatic awareness through reflection, analysis, discussion, and collaborative dialogue;
- develop agency to make their own choices, such as conforming or challenging the interlocutor's point of view, adjusting to social norms, or choosing to deviate from the sociocultural expectations of the target culture in order to maintain their own identity and preference of social interaction.

Conclusion

This chapter reviewed the main components of the construct of pragmatic competence from different research traditions, beginning with the inception of pragmatic competence in the field of interlanguage pragmatics. Subsequently, it assessed four research traditions that conceptualize pragmatic competence: intercultural pragmatics, inference and communication, sociocultural theory and intercultural pragmatics. In this book, I argue that the construct of pragmatic competence should be expanded to encompass the learner's ability to negotiate communicative action in spoken, written or technology-mediated discourse (Bou-Franch, 2021; Herring & Androutsopoulos, 2015), as well as the ability to negotiate joint actions in formal and informal contexts. At the end of this chapter, I presented my understanding of pragmatic competence from an intercultural pragmatic perspective, which includes a focus on the intercultural speaker as a learner, a mediator and an agent (Ishihara, 2019; Liddicoat

& McConachy, 2019). It also encompasses intercultural interaction, negotiation of emergent situational contexts at the discourse level, analysis and reflection of pragmalinguistic and sociopragmatic norms, and the development of agency to mediate between languages and cultures. The concept of mediation as problem-solving and as an intermediary position will be addressed in Chapter 6 (see also Liddicoat, 2022).

The next chapter describes the main concepts and proposes a pragmatic-discursive approach to intercultural communicative competence.

3 Pragmatic-Discursive Perspective on Language Use and Intercultural Understanding

Introduction

Chapter 2 took a close look at how the notion of awareness is conceptualized in three areas of research, namely: interlanguage pragmatics, sociocultural theory and intercultural pragmatics. Awareness represents a central component for the development of intercultural communicative competence (ICC) through mediation, reflection, agency and collaboration between members of different cultures (Liddicoat & McConachy, 2019; McConachy, 2022). This chapter describes the main tenets of an integrative pragmatic-discursive approach to examine language use in intercultural action and cultural understanding in the foreign language (FL) classroom and study abroad contexts. Intercultural interaction is analyzed from a pragmatic-discursive perspective with speakers and hearers in spoken interaction, writers, or users in technology-mediated discourse, who execute agency when they agree or disagree, reply politely or impolitely, agree to mediate or not, or take a stance regarding a controversial issue (Ishihara, 2019). Pragmatics centers on language use in context from the perspective of the speaker's actions and the effect that those actions (linguistic and non-verbal) have on the intentions and emotions of the interlocutor. Discourse looks at stretches of talk beyond the sentence, and it is defined as 'the way in which people construct social reality through their linguistic behavior' (Jones, 2017: 371). This definition is important because it paves the way to examine the blending of two or more cultures during an intercultural encounter in order to examine the construction of identities and social action.

In this chapter, I focus on intercultural interaction among language learners – as agents and mediators – who mediate between two or more languages and cultures and who speak a different language in two contexts, namely, the FL classroom and study abroad contexts. It is divided into two main sections; in the first, I outline the key elements of a pragmatic-discursive approach for examining the intercultural understanding and the negotiation of meaning between learners who engage in collaborative interaction and assess social action such as polite or impolite behavior. The second part draws on concepts and methodological frameworks from the field of ICC including extended discourse, collaboration, contextualization cues, and levels of pragmatic analysis to examine variability through intercultural understanding.

Pragmatic-Discursive Approach to Intercultural Interaction

The pragmatic-discursive approach to intercultural interaction that I take is based on fundamental concepts of pragmatics theory, discourse approaches to language use, interactional sociolinguistics, language awareness and approaches to (im)politeness. Some of these are influenced by philosophical concepts, such as language games (Wittgenstein, 1958), the intentionality and perlocutionary effect of communicative acts (Austin, 1962; Searle, 1969), inferential communication, for example, conversational implicature (Grice, 1975), and an inferential approach to utterance interpretation (Sperber & Wilson, 1986 [1995]). Other foundational concepts that can be adapted to examine intercultural interaction include language use as a joint action (Clark, 1996), speech acts in interaction in L2 pragmatics (Félix-Brasdefer, 2019b; Kasper, 2006)[1], an integrative approach to pragmatics that emphasizes (im)politeness in social action and metapragmatic awareness (Culpeper & Haugh, 2014; Haugh & Culpeper, 2018; Verschueren, 1999, 2021), pragmatic variation (Barron, 2019, 2020; Félix-Brasdefer & Yates, 2020; Schneider & Barron, 2008), interactional sociolinguistics (Gumperz, 1982; Schiffrin, 2006: 187), and the socio-cognitive approach to intercultural pragmatics that highlights concepts of prior and emergent context in intercultural interaction (Kecskes, 2014, 2020, 2023). My approach focuses on intercultural speakers who engage in social action, execute agency to agree or disagree with the interlocutor, co-construct contexts during the interaction and maintain awareness of variation in discourse to convey intended or initiated actions.

Based on the aforementioned approaches to integrative pragmatics (Culpeper & Haugh, 2014; Haugh & Culpeper, 2018; Verschueren, 2021),[2] Figure 3.1 illustrates the pragmatic-discursive approach to intercultural interaction that I adopt. It includes nine components, which will be discussed individually in the upcoming sections.

The interlocutors (user/speaker and addressee/hearer) appear on each side in spoken, written or technology-mediated modalities. At the center of the figure is 'intercultural interaction', which refers to the interaction between members of different cultures who engage in joint action. 'Intention/attention' and 'emergent common ground' (Kecskes, 2014, 2020; see also Kecskes, 2023) are placed on opposite sides of 'intercultural interaction'. 'Pragmatic

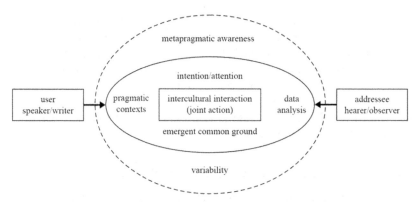

Figure 3.1 Pragmatic-discursive approach to intercultural interaction

contexts' are placed to the left of 'intercultural interaction', including the notion of contextualization cues. During the negotiation of meaning, the interlocutors construct pragmatic contexts, based on cognitive (prior experience), social and actual situational contexts. A key element of this approach is the analysis of data from different methods. Metapragmatic awareness and variability are placed on opposite sides, connected through broken lines to both the user and addressee. Metapragmatic awareness refers to the cognitive process through which interlocutors (speaker/hearer or observer) reflect on their language use through interaction and evaluation of social action. It focuses on reflexive awareness, intercultural understanding, awareness of contextual factors (power, social distance) and awareness of sociocultural expectations (Liddicoat & McConachy, 2019; McConachy, 2018). Variability (linguistic, social, regional) is placed on the periphery of the circle, connecting to the interlocutors and their awareness of variation through intercultural interaction.

Overall, this approach to intercultural interaction and cultural understanding will be used to examine the production and evaluation of speech acts and cultural understanding in Chapters 4–6. Each component is explained below.

Intercultural Interaction through Joint Action

In Figure 3.1, intercultural speakers/hearers engage in interaction to negotiate meaning through joint action. Inspired by Austin's (1962) original classification of illocutionary acts, Searle (1976) proposed a five-way taxonomy of speech acts: representatives (asserting, describing, reporting), directives (requesting, suggesting, asking questions), commissives (promising, refusing an invitation, taking an oath), expressives (apologizing, blaming, congratulating) and declarations (christening, naming or declaring a marriage official). While speech act theory (Austin, 1962; Searle, 1969) was not conceptualized to examine stretches of talk, it provides the foundation for the analysis of speech acts in interaction, such as compliment-response sequences, offer-acceptance or disagreement sequences. Speech act theory makes fundamental contributions to our understanding of extended units of discourse, beyond the traditional analysis of isolated strategies that comprise a speech act (Levinson, 2017). Notions such as uptake, illocutionary force, conventionality, felicity conditions and indirectness have been adopted to examine a wide range of speech act sequences among native and non-native speakers and in different languages. The uptake is crucial for promoting joint action among learners in FL and study abroad contexts, as well as during intercultural interactions. Streeck (1980) and Edmondson (1981) were some of the first researchers to focus on the speaker's use of sequential resources during the co-construction of exchanged verbal messages. Edmondson's (1981) model of spoken discourse focused on sequences of speech acts. The notion of 'speech act sequence' (originally introduced by van Dijk in 1979) represents the foundation for the analysis of social action.

Further, Clark (1996: 3) offers a discursive approach to language use that can be adapted to examine intercultural interaction. He uses the concept of joint action, that is, action 'carried out by an ensemble of people acting in coordination with each other'. The author emphasized the need to analyze natural social interactions in face-to-face conversation, which has the following features: immediacy (copresence, visibility, audibility and instantaneity), the medium of how meaning is expressed in interaction (evanescence, recordlessness and simultaneity) and control of the interaction (extemporaneity, self-determination, and self-expression) (1996: 9–10). Following Levinson's (1992) notion of *activity type*, Clark employed the concept of *joint activity* to refer to the social setting or speech event in which social action takes place (e.g. a family dinner, a classroom or a supermarket). A joint activity is defined by the setting (e.g. a service encounter), the participants' roles (e.g. a clerk and a customer) and the allowable contributions for each activity (e.g. the rights and obligations of the interlocutors during the interaction). Clark adopts an extended version of speech act theory (Austin, 1962; Searle, 1969) and key methodological concepts from Conversation Analysis (CA) to examine individual communicative acts performed by at least two participants who engage in joint actions. In sum, Clark's model of joint action can be used to examine joint activity during the creation of social identity, the creation of new intercultures and the negotiation of meaning in intercultural encounters.

The pragmatic-discursive approach to intercultural interaction adopts analytical concepts from CA for examining how intercultural speakers construct their identities and develop intercultural understanding. CA offers a rigorous methodological framework for the analysis of talk-in-interaction. It has been employed to examine sequential organization (e.g. openings, closings, speech act sequences, pre-/post-sequences), the organization of turn-taking (e.g. overlap), the organization of preference or dispreference, the concept of repair, the organization of laughter and the organization of topic development (see Schegloff [2007] and Sidnell [2010]). CA tools (e.g. adjacency pair, turn-taking patterns, repair and preferred and dispreferred actions) are essential for the analysis of intercultural interaction with respect to how individual actions are organized into sequences in openings, closings, request-response sequences, and turn-taking mechanisms. (Adapted from Félix-Brasdefer, 2015: 10–11, 28–30.)

Overall, the conceptualization of intercultural interaction through joint action is central to the analysis of the speech-data, the negotiation of speech acts in interaction and the evaluations of polite and impolite behavior in the FL classroom (Chapter 4) and in study abroad settings (Chapters 5 and 6).

Intention and Attention

During an intercultural encounter, interlocutors require both intention and attention to manage a successful interaction. In this section, I present a selective account of three perspectives (Grice's model of intentionality, Austin/Searle's speech-act theory account of illocutionary intentions and Sperber and Wilson's inferential model of utterance interpretation), followed by an evaluation of how these concepts contribute to our understanding of meaning in intercultural interaction.

Speaker's communicative intentions

According to Grice's model of conversational implicature, communication is the product of the speaker's communicative intentions alongside the inferential abilities of the hearer(s) to recognize those intentions. Grice's (1975, 1989) theory of meaning describes how people use language based on the speaker's intended meaning and the inferential abilities of the hearer(s) to recognize those intentions. The author noted that conversational exchanges consist of cooperative efforts which encompass the speaker's intention and the hearer's recognition of that intention (by inference) in specific situations. As a result, he proposed the Cooperative Principle (CP): 'Make your conversational contribution such as is required, at the stage at which it occurs, by the accepted purpose or direction of the talk exchange in which you are engaged' (1975: 45). In addition, Grice proposed four conversational maxims governing the rules of conversation: quantity (informativeness), quality (truthfulness), relation (relevance) and manner (clarity). According to him, adhering to the CP and abiding by the maxims represents the normal assumption in the production and interpretation of utterances, namely, that interlocutors produce and interpret utterances that are satisfactorily informative, true, relevant and perspicuous. Grice's account represents a cognitive/inferential perspective on how communication takes place but leaves aside the interpersonal and co-constructed meanings that emerge during intercultural interaction. For a revised conceptualization of Grice's model (neo-Gricean pragmatics), see Huang (2017b).

Illocutionary act and perlocutionary effects

The notion of speaker intention takes a normative and conventional perspective in speech-act theory. The main tenet of the theory is that when a speaker utters a sentence, they perform an action within the framework of social institutions and conventions; that is, saying is part of doing. Austin proposed a three-way taxonomy of speech acts: (1) a locutionary act refers to the act of saying something meaningful in the literal sense (referring and predicating); (2) an illocutionary act is performed by saying something that has an intentional and conventional force such as informing, ordering, warning, complaining, requesting and refusing (the speaker's intention); and (3) a perlocutionary act refers to what we achieve '*by* saying something, such as convincing, persuading, deterring, and even, say, surprising or misleading' (Austin, 1962: 109 [emphasis in original]). Specifically, the illocutionary act refers to the action intended by a speaker according to the conventional force associated with the linguistic expression. As stated in Huang (2014: 128), the illocution generally refers to 'the type of function the speaker intends to fulfill or the type of action the speaker intends to accomplish in the course of producing an utterance'. The concept of 'speech act' is generally used to refer to illocutionary acts. Finally, the perlocutionary act refers to the effect the utterance may have on the addressee; that is, the perlocution represents a consequence, intentional or not, of what is said.

Further, Searle (1969) proposed a set of felicity conditions that must be met before an utterance can be considered successful: the propositional content focuses only on the textual or content (literal meaning); the preparatory conditions emphasize the background circumstances or the requisites prior to the execution of the speech act; the sincerity condition reflects the speaker's psychological state; and, the essential condition centers on the illocutionary point of what is said (the speaker's intention). Searle focused on the illocutionary force to refer to the speaker's intention to perform a speech act, which is intended to be recognized by the hearer.

Overall, while the illocutionary act is intended by the speaker and is under the speaker's control, the perlocutionary act is not always intended by the speaker and is not always under the speaker's control. Both concepts are fundamental for the negotiation of meaning in social interaction (language use) and intercultural understanding (metapragmatic awareness). I take a discursive perspective on speech acts in social interaction. It includes both the illocutionary act (speaker's intention) and the perlocutionary effect, that is, the impact that the speaker's utterance (what is said) has on the hearer's thoughts, emotions and feelings. As I mention in the section of 'emergent common ground', the speaker and the hearer co-construct their intentions during the course of the interaction.

Communicative intentions, attention and relevance

Relevance theory (Sperber & Wilson, 1986 [1995]; Wilson, 2017; Wilson & Sperber, 2004) offers an alternative view of communication (or speaker's meaning) to account for how the hearer infers information based on the evidence provided in the environment. The main tenet of relevance theory is that 'any external stimulus or internal representation which provides an input to cognitive processes may be relevant to an individual at some time' (Wilson & Sperber, 2004: 608). For communication to take place, interlocutors must pay attention to the input available in the environment such as a sign, a sound, an utterance, a memory, a smell, and so on. Accordingly, there are two types of intention during the management of inferential communication (2004: 611): (i) informative intention (the intention to inform others of something) and (ii) communicative intention (the intention to inform others of one's informative intention). According to this model, understanding is accomplished when 'the communicative intention is fulfilled', that is, when the others recognize the informative intention. Under this model of communication, hearers need to pay **attention** to the stimuli during the communicative exchange. One example of paying attention to characteristics of the linguistic and cognitive context is through contextualization cues.

Contextualization cues

From an anthropological point of view, Gumperz (1982, 2001) proposed Interactional Sociolinguistics (IS) as an approach to discourse analysis that analyzes the ability to interpret participants' meaning in situated communicative practices. Gumperz's model is based on (shared) background knowledge that allows the participants to infer meaning through verbal or non-verbal information. He used the term *contextualization cue* to refer to verbal and non-verbal signs that can be inferred from the situation, in co-occurrence with other lexico-grammatical information. Examples include prosodic cues (e.g. intonation, stress, duration), pronunciation, non-verbal signs (e.g. eye gaze, strong handshake), and code-switching to negotiate meaning in two or more languages, as in bilingual (Callahan, 2009) or multilingual intercultural interactions during the negotiation of service (Solon, 2013; Torras & Gafaranga, 2002).

During the construction of intercultural meaning, interlocutors often pay attention to verbal and non-verbal cues to advance meaning construction. For example, they can pay attention to how certain words or formulaic expressions (e.g. it's raining cats and dogs), pragmatic routines (e.g. No, thanks, I'm just looking), or code-switching between two or more languages are used to achieve mutual understanding. Thus, to achieve a successful interaction, the intercultural speaker must focus their attention on verbal and non-verbal cues available during the interaction.

The notions of intention and attention to achieve human communication vary in each of the aforementioned perspectives. For Grice, communication is fulfilled according to the speaker's expression and recognition of communicative intentions, along with the inferential abilities of the hearer. In contrast, in relevance theory, communication is accomplished through the speaker's intentions that are informative to others based on the evidence or input available. According to the latter view, interlocutors pay attention to cues and how hearers infer the speaker's meaning based on the evidence provided. Finally, speech-act theory accounts for communication based on the illocutionary intentions to perform speech acts, 'which are those that modify the normative status (rights and obligations) because they are constituted by socially instituted rules' (Navarro, 2017: 221). While the Gricean 'speaker's intention model' and relevance theory account for communication from a cognitive and inferential perspective of communication, the speech-act theory alternative focuses on the illocutionary intention to perform speech acts under the appropriate circumstances and the right conditions. However, the notions of intentionality do not seem to fully account for the negotiation of meaning in intercultural interaction with speakers who may not share common ground and need to co-construct meaning during the interaction.

Taken together, the notion of the speaker's intention and attention should be revised to account for intercultural communicative competence. Following the fundamental tenets of the socio-cognitive approach (Kecskes, 2014, 2020, 2023), the notion of intention should be understood as **emergent** during meaning construction, with interlocutors (speakers and hearers) negotiating meaning during the course of the interaction. During the co-construction of the interaction, interlocutors negotiate and renegotiate their intentions and hearers may have to pay attention to verbal and nonverbal cues to achieve successful understanding. In addition, following Kecskes's socio-cognitive approach, intention is considered 'a dynamically changing phenomenon that is the main organizing force with attention in the communicative process' (2014: 50). Further, in intercultural interaction, the construction of meaning is influenced by the interlocutors' prior experience and the emergent situational contexts, yielding 'blending' as the main force during intercultural communicative competence (2014: 49). Previous work on im/politeness is consistent with the view that intentions emerge through interaction (Arundale, 2009; Haugh, 2009; see also Chapter 6 of this book). Thus, the concepts of intention/attention and contextualization cues should be viewed from an interactive and dynamic perspective, with interlocutors engaged during the co-construction of meaning in intercultural interaction.

Pragmatic Contexts

The concept of *context*, derived from Latin *contextus* meaning 'connection, coherence', has been analyzed from different perspectives. For

Austin (1962), the notion of context refers to the appropriate circumstances within a theory of social pragmatics. On the other hand, according to Searle (1969), the nature of context is cognitive because the felicity conditions must hold prior to the performance of a speech act (i.e. illocutionary force). The notion of 'context' is viewed as predetermined, unchangeable, cognitive and as knowledge that is not subject to the negotiation of face in social interaction. From a relevance theory perspective (Sperber & Wilson, 1986 [1995]; Wilson, 2017; Wilson & Sperber, 2004), context is cognitive and refers to the 'set of premises used in interpreting an utterance'. Context 'is a psychological construct, a subset of the hearer's assumptions about the world' (Sperber & Wilson, 1995: 15). For Levinson (1992), context falls under an *activity type*, in which the situation is determined. For example, a family dinner: the roles of the participants are specified, and their contributions are constrained by the sociocultural expectations of the situation.

Sbisà (2002) proposed that three criteria should apply to the context of a speech act: namely, it should be constructed, limited and objective. The context of a speech act is first constructed and renegotiated during social interaction and is not necessarily determined prior to the performance of a speech act, as previously posited by Searle (1969). Sbisà asserted that context is constructed by the participants during the ongoing flow of conversation. Second, the context of a speech act is limited to a specific situation and evaluated by the speaker and interlocutor within a particular communicative event. That is, to obtain a limited or specific evaluation of a speech act, 'it should be clear or ascertainable what belongs to context and what does not' (Sbisà, 2002: 427). Third, the author stated that the context of a speech act is objective if it is determined by various external social or material circumstances or 'relevant states of affairs occurring in the world, of which participants might not even be aware' (2002: 428). In general, the context of a speech act is seen as dynamic and changeable during the course of social interaction.

From a linguistic anthropological perspective, Duranti and Goodwin (1992) observed that context comprises two components: a focal event and the field of action. Context includes information that goes beyond the event, such as the cultural setting, speech situation and shared background assumptions (1992: 3). Additionally, according to Goffman, context is determined by both the 'rules of the group and the definition of the situation' (1967: 6). Since Goffman (1961, 1981) is concerned with encounters as 'focused gatherings' in face-to-face interactions, his notion of context takes place in social situations that frame and organize talk in situated settings. From an interdisciplinary perspective, Fetzer (2012) conceptualized a dynamic context as both process and product. For this author, context is 'more or less (un)bounded, it is invoked in and through the process of communication, it is imported in and through the process of communication, and it is entextualized in and through the process of communication and thereby assigned the status of a bounded object' (2012: 125).[3]

Finally, from an intercultural pragmatics view, Kecskes (2014, Chapter 6), proposed a dynamic perspective that includes both the individual's prior context and actual situational context. He argued that the notion of 'context' in intercultural interaction is viewed as dynamic, created and co-constructed. His dynamic model of meaning includes both prior context (the individual's prior experience) and the current situational context, where the interlocutors' actions are interpreted, created and negotiated.

The notion of 'context' should include a dynamic and co-constructed perspective for the analysis of meaning in intercultural interaction. Intercultural speakers bring different types of knowledge to the interaction, including their prior experience which is blended with the actual situational context. Another concept which is needed to understand the notion of 'context' is emergent common ground, as seen in Figure 3.1.

Emergent Common Ground

The concept of *common ground* is fundamental for the negotiation of meaning in intercultural interaction, which is placed below 'intercultural interaction' in Figure 3.1. Common ground has been called shared knowledge, mutual knowledge or belief, common knowledge, joint knowledge, background knowledge shared by the participants in a communicative situation or familiarity with the interlocutor's beliefs (see Clark, 1996 [Chapter 4]; Kecskes, 2014 [Chapter 7], 2023; Stalnaker, 2002). In social interactions, people predetermine common beliefs or certain things about the speakers and the situation, that is, 'the mutually recognized shared information in a situation' (Stalnaker, 2002: 704). Clark (1996) refers to joint or coordinated mutual knowledge that participants share in conversation, which includes both communal and personal common ground. Communal common ground generally refers to the facts, beliefs and assumptions about sociocultural norms of behavior, conventions and procedures that are accepted by the members of a community of practice. For example, when two speakers from the same community get together, they assume that they share the following information prior to the interaction: language, nationality, education, gender, politics, religion. In contrast, in personal common ground, people bring their individual experiences to the interaction, resulting in joint common ground or joint perceptual experiences (Clark, 1996: 112). However, while these shared assumptions may be familiar to individuals from the same community of practice, interactions with interlocutors of distant familiarity and limited contact (e.g. strangers) have limited or no personal common ground. In the context of intercultural interactions where interlocutors have limited or no common ground, they must, in accordance with Clark (1996), build up common ground through the negotiation of joint actions, including various attempts to elaborate, rectify, or clarify misunderstandings. Under this view, 'common ground' is a form of self-awareness (Clark, 1996: 120); in intercultural interactions, observers are not necessarily aware of the information they share and thus their understanding is obtained through inferences.

While Clark's (1996) notion of 'common ground' was mainly proposed for interactions among native speakers, Kecskes (2014, 2020, 2023) proposed a dynamic concept of common ground among intercultural speakers, *emergent common ground*. It is based on the individual's prior experience (core common ground) which is negotiated and co-constructed during the actual situational context (emergent common ground). This represents a dynamic view of communication with multilingual speakers from different first languages and different cultures.

Overall, during an intercultural encounter in a FL context, such as the classroom, or in study abroad contexts, students interacting with members of a different culture negotiate an emergent common ground, yielding a new interculture that is created, calibrated and co-constructed during the course of the interaction. In the FL classroom, students and instructors may begin with limited to no personal and communal common ground, but through interactive pedagogical activities and meaning construction in face-to-face or virtual interactions, their common ground emerges over time (see Chapter 4). On the other hand, in a study abroad context, where students communicate in a different language in different situational contexts (e.g. host family, school, friends, strangers), they may need to be aware of the information they share and the new information they need to share to achieve mutual understanding (see Chapter 6). In general, learners in FL or study abroad contexts need to be aware of the previous information they bring to the interaction, as well as the need to gain new information that is blended in a new interculture during the course of the interaction.

Data Analysis

Data analysis is included to the right of 'intercultural interaction' (Figure 3.1). The integrative approach to intercultural interaction is data-driven through methods that examine different aspects of social interaction, pragmalinguistic and sociopragmatic knowledge, evaluation of politeness and impoliteness and instruments that assess different aspects of intercultural competence such as cultural and value orientations. Traditional data collection methods in pragmatics have been shown to have some degree of validity and reliability. These include authentic and experimental data (Félix-Brasdefer & Hasler-Barker, 2017; Kasper, 2000; Koike, 2021; Schneider, 2018). Authentic methods that examine different dimensions of intercultural interaction include natural conversations in face-to-face interaction or online interactions, such as computer-mediated discourse, through platforms such as Zoom, Facebook, YouTube, Reddit and Twitter (X), among others. Experimental data include roleplays, which can examine interactive aspects of the interaction, such as open roleplays, or pragmalinguistic aspects of pragmatic routines, such as production questionnaires (also called closed roleplays) (Félix-Brasdefer, 2018). In Chapters 4 and 5, I use roleplays and metapragmatic reflection to examine both pragmalinguistic and sociopragmatic aspects of speech act production and intercultural understanding.

Other instruments are commonly used to assess different dimensions of intercultural competence, such as knowledge, skills, attitudes, reflexivity and evaluations of polite and impolite behavior (Spencer-Oatey & Franklin, 2009 [Chapter 8]). Politeness events, also known as critical incidents (Bennett, 1995; Culpeper, 2011; Culpeper *et al.*, 2010), have been used to examine evaluations of politeness and impoliteness. Other instruments that measure different dimensions of intercultural communicative competence (Chapter 1, Figure 1.2) include the Cross-Cultural Adaptability Inventory (Kelley & Meyer, 1993), which is based on a 50-item self-assessment of cultural values and skill sets. Likert-Scales (Kasper, 2000; Schauer, 2024) and verbal reports (Cohen, 2012) are also employed to assess different aspects of sociopragmatic awareness, as well as the relationship between intercultural competence and pragmatics. Another instrument that assesses different dimensions of cultural values, skills, and knowledge is the Intercultural Development Inventory (IDS) (Bennett & Bennett, 2004). This instrument is mainly used to assess dimensions of diversity, sensitivity and cultural awareness. The aim of this tool is to evaluate cultural sensitivity and diversity, as well as how to transition from a monocultural to an intercultural mindset. In Chapters 4 and 5, I examine methods for assessing intercultural understanding through metapragmatic awareness and reflexivity, and in Chapter 6, I use impoliteness events, Likert-Scales and portions of the Cross-Cultural Adaptability Inventory to examine dimensions of intercultural communicative competence, such as pragmatic knowledge and intercultural competence (Chapter 1, Figure 1.2).

The last two components of a pragmatic-discursive approach to intercultural interaction (Figure 3.1) are metapragmatic awareness and variability, which connect the user (speaker/writer) and addressee (hearer/observer) during the negotiation of meaning in intercultural and global contexts.

Metapragmatic Awareness

In Chapter 2, I examined the role that awareness, in general, and metapragmatic awareness play in the development of pragmatic competence. From a discourse and cognitive view, Meier (2015) extended Schmidt's (1993, 1995) concept of 'noticing' to refer to awareness during the negotiation of social action, including an awareness of social norms and sociocultural expectations, such as polite and impolite behavior or perceptions of contextual variables such as social distance, power, and degree of imposition (see Chapter 4). From a pedagogical view, critical cultural awareness is generally defined by Byram as the 'ability to evaluate critically and on the basis of explicit criteria perspectives, practices and products in one's own and other cultures' (1997: 53). Others used the term 'critical intercultural awareness', which entails a philosophical, pedagogical and political attitude (Guilherme, 2022: 109). From the perspective of intercultural understanding, researchers take a broader view of metapragmatic awareness as a way to help learners understand language use through reflection, mediation and agency with members of different cultures (Liddicoat, 2022; Liddicoat & McConachy, 2019; McConachy, 2018). Further, based on previous accounts of mindfulness as a state of conscious awareness and salience (Kecskes, 2014 [Chapter 8]; Meier, 2015; Sternberg, 2000), Žegarac et al. (2014: 8) proposed the notion of mutual mindfulness as 'the awareness of each participant of their own as well as of other participants' levels and directions of active attention'. Finally, for Verschueren (1999: 187–197; also 2021), metapragmatic awareness refers to indicators of language use through consciousness or reflexive awareness of the choices as a range of options. Metapragmatic indicators 'guide the listener's or reader's interpretations' (2021: 129). Some of the indicators that promote reflection of language use include discourse markers (e.g. *but, actually, then, so*) and contextualization cues (e.g. prosodic, code-switching).

Overall, metapragmatic awareness takes place when students are engaged in critical intercultural awareness and social interaction through collaboration and reflexivity of the language choices they select to communicate effectively and appropriately in each situation. Based on the aforementioned accounts of metapragmatic awareness (e.g. Liddicoat & McConachy, 2019; McConachy, 2019; Verschueren, 1999), in this book metapragmatic awareness is defined as a cognitive process through which interlocutors (speaker/hearer or observer) reflect on their language use during a joint and collaborative interaction. Metapragmatic awareness focuses on reflexive awareness of various dimensions of language use: attention to the interactional strategies necessary to construct joint action (e.g. repair, turn-taking, opening and closing an interaction); awareness of the contextual factors, such as social power, social distance, and the degree of imposition; awareness of the sociocultural expectations of both the speaker's own culture and the other's culture, including an understanding of the norms of im/politeness; and, awareness of cultural differences that allow the intercultural speaker to engage in global citizenship in topics that affect our understanding of the world such as education, economy, politics, etc.

Instructors should encourage and teach students to develop metapragmatic awareness and explicit understanding of the sociocultural values and interactional strategies necessary to engage in social interaction in the

FL classroom and study abroad contexts. The development of intercultural communicative competence is accomplished through the negotiation of discourse and constant reflection and analysis of the relevant contextual variables in a situation, the participants' status, the communicative goals of the interaction, as well as the prior knowledge that participants bring to the interaction in order to be co-constructed collaboratively.

Variability

In Figure 3.1, variability is placed at the opposite end of metapragmatic awareness in a circular mode since variation is inherent in language use. Interaction and variability should be viewed as dynamic elements that are constantly changing. According to Verschueren (1999: 59), variability is 'the property of language which defines the range of possibilities from which choices can be made'. The ways in which linguistic forms and non-verbal resources are used based on the context in which they occur are variable across individuals, groups, situations, speech acts, languages and varieties of the same language. Variation may be conditioned by social (e.g. age, gender, social status) and discourse factors that determine how social action is negotiated in written and spoken modalities. Variability occurs at the pragmalinguistic (inventory of language forms used to express social action) and sociopragmatic levels (perception of sociocultural expectations and contextual factors). At the sociopragmatic level, speakers make evaluations of the actions of im/politeness of others engaged in social interaction. Overall, variability is a fundamental component of intercultural interaction because the choice of linguistic forms in different situations is attached to the context in which the forms are used and should be seen as dynamic and negotiable throughout the course of the interaction.

Levels of pragmatic analysis

I adopt a revised version of the variational pragmatics approach to examine language use in intercultural interaction between individuals from different cultures who speak different languages either in an FL or study abroad context; that is, intercultural speakers who interact with an instructor or peers in the classroom or with native or multilingual speakers while living in the host culture. Variational Pragmatics (VP) was initially proposed to examine variation across varieties of a language (intra-lingual variation or Fried's [2010] local perspective of linguistic variation). It has also been used to examine cross-cultural pragmatic and interlingual variation in the context of service encounter interactions across varieties of Spanish (Félix-Brasdefer, 2015; Félix-Brasdefer & Placencia, 2020), and recently in study abroad contexts to examine social interaction among students (Barron, 2019, 2020).

Variational pragmatics adopts an integrative model of spoken discourse (Barron & Schneider, 2009; Schneider, 2010, 2020; Schneider & Barron, 2008: 19). Félix-Brasdefer (2021b: 272–276) added other levels of analysis to analyze other dimensions of language use such as the non-verbal and prosodic level. Macrosocial factors interact with microsocial factors, such as the situation and the degree of social distance and power between the interlocutors. The VP approach for the analysis of intercultural interaction consists of seven levels of pragmatic analysis: (taken from Félix-Brasdefer, 2021a: 274–277).

The *formal level* includes form-function/function-form analysis, given that a linguistic form may convey different functions and that a single function may be realized through different forms (Barron, 2020: 433). Examples at this level include discourse markers (e.g. *well, so, then, OK*), backchannels, epistemic expressions such as *I think, I believe, I guess*, or other mitigating devices such as hedges, tag questions and diminutives.

The *actional level* is concerned with the analysis of the pragmalinguistic strategies used in speech acts (e.g. requests, offers, greetings). In addition, it includes levels of directness and indirectness. The aim at the actional level is to analyze the pragmalinguistic expressions used to convey the illocutionary force of the action.

The *interactional level* focuses on the analysis of speech act sequences and joint-social action throughout the interaction (e.g. compliment-response, invitation-acceptance/refusal). This level employs tools of conversation analysis (see Sacks *et al.*, 1974; Schegloff, 2007) to examine the sequential patterns for the organization of speech actions jointly produced by interlocutors.

The *organization level* involves the organization of turn-taking in conversation and is influenced by conversation analysis (Sacks *et al.*, 1974; Schegloff, 2007). It addresses aspects of turn-taking, overlap, interruption, silence and preference organization. This level is concerned with turn-taking procedures in openings, closings, as well as other joint-actions such as request-response sequences, bargaining sequences, agreement and disagreement responses.

The *stylistic level* focuses on the stylistic aspects of an interchange. It includes choice of tone (e.g. serious or joking), shifting from a business talk (e.g. buying and selling) to a friendly tone (e.g. joking or small talk), politeness and impoliteness styles, and the appropriate selection of address forms to open, close and negotiate a colloquial or business transaction.

The *topic level* is concerned with discourse content throughout the interaction. It includes topic selection, topic management, topic extension, topic abandonment, topic shift and the introduction of new topics. It focuses on knowing which topics are appropriate or inappropriate to bring up in a conversation, as well as the choice and management of sensitive topics.

The *prosodic level* is a pragmatic resource used to express interpersonal or marked meaning. This level focuses on a pragmatic meaning that is conveyed through prosodic information: intonation (e.g. low or high pitch), stress, loudness, duration and timing (e.g. rhythm and rate of speech). These prosodic resources function as 'contextualization cues' (Gumperz, 1982, 2015): signals that allow the interlocutor to draw an inference from the speaker's message. For example, Félix-Brasdefer (2015, Chapter 6) examined prosodic resources used during the realization of requests for service with a falling tone or rising intonation that signaled polite requests. The interpretation of social action (e.g. requests for service, offers, greetings, clarification requests, payment sequence, closing, etc.) is frequently contingent upon the interlocutor's understanding of the prosodic cues that accompany the utterances.

Finally, the *non-verbal level* (Spencer-Oatey, 2000) consists of social actions performed through gestures. Kendon refers to gestures as 'visible acts' when uttering actions (2010: 1), such as body movement, hand movement, or gaze direction. Gesture accompanies the kinds of actions we are taking with our utterances; with gestures, we can show, among other things, agreement or disagreement, affirmation or denial. We can show that we are asking a question or begging for another's indulgence, that we are doubtful of something or that what we are saying is hypothetical (Kendon, 2010: 1). For example, Dorai and Webster (2015) offered a conceptual model of non-verbal communication in service encounter contexts. The model shows that both verbal and non-verbal elements between the service provider and the service seeker influence the service seeker's affect or subjective feelings, which, at the same time, impact the evaluation of the service encounter. In institutional discourse (e.g. doctor-patient, attorney-client), nodding, smiling, and frequent eye contact show understanding, empathy, and friendliness. These non-verbal features can vary across languages and across varieties of the same language. For example, in the United States, the circle hand finger means OK. In Germany and Brazil, it represents an obscene gesture; in Japan it means money, while in France it usually means zero or useless. In Arab countries this is also an offensive gesture. What does this sign hand gesture mean in your culture?

Taken together, these levels of pragmatic analysis allow the researcher to examine different aspects of an intercultural interaction. While the actional, interactional, and stylistic levels have been widely analyzed (Félix-Brasdefer, 2021a; Placencia, 2011; Schneider & Placencia, 2017), other dimensions should be examined to complement our understanding of language use in intercultural interaction, such as turn-taking, prosodic meaning, and non-verbal aspects of the interaction. Finally, intercultural speakers should be aware of regional variation across varieties of a language, such as an awareness of the social norms and sociocultural expectations of varieties of English (Australia, Canada, United Kingdom, United States, as well as other varieties spoken in Africa, among others), including English as a lingua franca.

Overall, the integrative approach to intercultural interaction (Figure 3.1) offers an alternative for examining the negotiation of meaning in FL and study abroad contexts. The focus is on how learners – as mediators and agents – construct social meaning at the discourse level: paying attention to the linguistic and non-verbal features of the interaction and developing an awareness of the pragmatic contexts so they can calibrate their conversational contributions. It also includes a reflection on metapragmatic awareness through reflection and evaluations of social action. In particular, emergent common ground (Kecskes, 2014, 2020, 2023) is crucial during the co-construction of the interaction. Finally, variability in language use is a key component of the proposed model, as learners vary their negotiation of meaning and assessments of discursive practices according to linguistic and social factors, including the geographic origin of the learners, age and gender, among others.

Conclusion

The proposed pragmatic-discursive approach analyzes different dimensions of intercultural interactions with learners in FL (classroom) and study abroad contexts. The nine components illustrated in Figure 3.1, with intercultural interaction in the center, should be seen as interactive, dynamic, emergent, and interdependent. The goal of this approach is to examine language use and intercultural understanding among speakers interacting in various written and spoken modalities, including users writing through technology-mediated discourse (e.g. email, chat, FaceBook, Reddit, YouTube, etc.) or speakers negotiating pragmatic meaning in spoken interaction, face-to-face or through online platforms such as Zoom (Herring *et al.*, 2013; Tecedor, 2023). The roles of the interlocutors, namely the user (speaker or writer) and the addressee (hearer or observer) are fundamental for mediating social meaning through the understanding of im/politeness and contextual variables such as social distance, power, and degree of imposition. Intercultural interaction, manifested through joint action, focuses on social interaction at the discourse level. Intention/attention and emergent common ground are used to foster awareness during the construction of intercultural interaction through the negotiation of meaning and cultural understanding. Pragmatic contexts include cognitive and social contexts, as well as contextualization cues that allow the intercultural speaker to draw inferences from the linguistic and non-verbal stimuli available during the construction of the interaction. Finally, metapragmatic awareness and variability, connected to the user (speaker/writer) and the addressee (hearer/observer), are fundamental for negotiating meaning through collaboration and the learner's agency to guide the direction of the interaction. These concepts equip the intercultural speaker with reflexivity to select an appropriate linguistic form that matches the context in which it is used, including an awareness of regional and social variation (Guilherme, 2022). This approach to intercultural interaction and cultural understanding engages the researcher in the analysis of data from natural and experimental sources using qualitative and quantitative analysis.

Chapters 4, 5 and 6 incorporate the pragmatic-discursive approach in order to examine language use and intercultural understanding of im/politeness and social norms in FL and study abroad contexts.

Notes

(1) Kasper (2006) reviewed previous approaches to the analysis of social action, including differences between rationalists and discursive approaches to speech acts in interaction, including research by conversation analysis (see also Salaberry *et al.*, 2019).
(2) My proposed model of intercultural interaction follows Culpeper and Haugh's (2014) and Haugh and Culpeper's (2018) integrative pragmatic approach to im/politeness.
(3) This information is taken from Félix-Brasdefer (2015: 11–13), and adapted to explain the construct of intercultural interaction.

4 Pragmatic Learning and Intercultural Understanding in the Foreign Language Classroom

Introduction

This chapter adopts an intercultural perspective to examine language learning of pragmatic knowledge and the effects of teaching pragmatics in the foreign language (FL) classroom. Successful language learning requires both knowledge and awareness of pragmatic and intercultural competence. While pragmatic competence concerns the learner's ability to produce and comprehend linguistic and non-verbal actions in socially appropriate communicative settings such as speech acts (e.g. apologies, requests, refusals), intercultural competence refers to 'the ability of a person to behave adequately and in a flexible manner when confronted with actions, attitudes and expectations of representatives of foreign cultures' (Meier, 2015: 29; see also Chapters 2 and 3). This chapter contributes to our understanding of pragmatic competence through the lens of intercultural pragmatics, with learners engaging in collaboration, negotiation of speech acts, contextual analysis and discussion and reflection of issues of language use, contextual factors and sociocultural expectations (Liddicoat & McConachy, 2019; McConachy, 2018; McConachy & Spencer-Oatey, 2020). The chapter focuses on pragmatic language learning among learners of Spanish who engage in metapragmatic reflection of speech act production and interaction in the FL classroom. Some of the sociopragmatic concepts include the notion of insistence, directness and indirectness, politeness and impoliteness and awareness of regional pragmatic variation across varieties of Spanish. Adopting a one-group pre-posttest design, I showcase the development of sociopragmatic awareness with a group of 22 FL Spanish students as they produce requests, apologies and refusals at the beginning and end of the semester (16 weeks), followed by pragmatic instruction and metapragmatic reflection of their speech act performance. The group, divided into those with and without exposure to studying abroad, received metapragmatic instruction (awareness-raising activities, awareness of contextual factors, discussion of politeness practices, regional variation across varieties of Spanish), followed by production, reflection, collaboration and discussion of pragmalinguistic expressions and social norms. I also include an interactive analysis during the negotiation of social action through roleplays in the classroom. I will use some of the concepts presented in Chapter 1 (Figure 1.2) regarding the components of Intercultural Communicative Competence (ICC). The pragmatic-discursive approach to intercultural interaction (Chapter 3, Figure 3.1), will be used to examine the negotiation of speech acts and intercultural understanding, including intercultural interaction (joint action), metapragmatic awareness and variability.

This chapter is organized as follows: After an overview of the concept of pragmatic competence in the FL classroom, I explain the effects of pragmatic instruction and metapragmatic awareness to observe whether instruction (implicit and explicit) produces a change in the learners' pragmatic and intercultural knowledge at the end of the semester. Then, I offer an intercultural perspective to examine language teaching and learning in the FL classroom. This is followed by an analysis of a classroom-based study that looks at development of pragmalinguistic and sociopragmatic awareness among FL learners of Spanish. Finally, the analysis focuses on the development of pragmatic and intercultural competence in the FL classroom, including metapragmatic awareness, reflection of pragmatic variation and cultural norms, and the learners' ability to make informed linguistic and social choices that may or may not conform to the target culture.

Developing Pragmatic Competence in the Foreign Language Classroom

What kind of pragmatic and intercultural knowledge do learners in the FL classroom need to communicate effectively in an L2, L3 or Lx language? The classroom 'is a genuine context for social interaction, but it is also a place where the teacher has an explicit warrant to provide guided opportunities as well as direct feedback to help learners develop sociopragmatic knowledge' (Riddiford & Holmes, 2015: 131; see also Ohta, 2001). In this chapter, it will be argued that learners not only need pragmatic and intercultural knowledge to maximize their ability to produce and comprehend communicative action (pragmatics), but they also need to develop metapragmatic awareness and partake in reflective discussions in the classroom from an intercultural perspective (sociocultural expectations of one's and others' cultures). As mentioned in Chapter 2, researchers in L2 pragmatics generally adopt two types of pragmatic knowledge that allow learners to develop pragmatic competence over time (incidental learning) or to improve learning as a result of pedagogical intervention (for an overview, see Bardovi-Harlig, 2001, 2013; Félix-Brasdefer, 2017a; Kasper & Rose, 2002; Taguchi, 2017). *Pragmalinguistic knowledge* refers to knowledge about and performance of the conventions of language use or the linguistic resources available in a given language that convey 'particular illocutions' (Leech, 1983: 11). It includes knowledge of strategies (e.g. directness, conventional indirectness) and the linguistic and non-linguistic resources (e.g. prosody in phrase final intonation, loudness and duration) used to convey pragmatic meaning. In contrast, *sociopragmatic knowledge* refers to knowledge about and performance consistent with the social norms in specific situations in a given society, as well as familiarity with assessments of (im)politeness and variables of social power and social distance. For example, to issue a request, learners not only need to know the various lexico-grammatical options available in the grammar (e.g. I need/want a letter of recommendation, Can/could/would you write a letter of recommendation?, I was wondering if you would have time to write a letter of recommendation), they must also have knowledge of the *where/who/when/how* these requests are used in particular situations. For example, the learners should understand appropriate degrees of directness/indirectness, politeness/impoliteness, norms of interaction and sociocultural expectations of the target culture regarding when to use a particular request.

As explained at the end of Chapter 2, I adopt a broad perspective on pragmatic competence that goes beyond the pragmalinguistic and sociopragmatic distinction, and considers other dimensions such as discourse and interaction, awareness of sociocultural expectations and cultural norms of one's and others' cultures, the co-construction of meaning in social interaction using both linguistic and non-verbal cues, and an understanding of pragmatic variation. The concept of the intercultural speaker either as a learner, an individual, or agent is crucial to the understanding of pragmatic competence from an intercultural pragmatic perspective (Liddicoat & Scarino, 2013 [Chapter 4]). Finally, as mentioned in Chapter 2, to achieve pragmatic competence in an L2 or Lx, the following dimensions should be considered. Learners in the FL classroom should be able to:

- perform and understand communicative action in interaction (e.g. speech act sequences, conventional and non-conventional meaning, humor, irony, politeness and impoliteness);
- adjust and calibrate their intentions during the course of the interaction;
- pay attention to verbal and non-verbal features of the interaction;
- be mindful of pragmalinguistic and sociopragmatic variation and the choices they make in their own and the target culture(s);

- engage in metapragmatic awareness through reflection, discussion and collaborative dialogue;
- and develop agency to make their own choices, such as to conform to or deviate from the sociocultural expectations of the target culture.

As a result, research has shown that while incidental learning of speech acts such as requests (Achiba, 2003; Ellis, 1992) and refusals (Bardovi-Harlig & Hartford, 1993) takes time to develop in natural settings, there are some aspects that take longer to develop and may benefit from pedagogical intervention. Instruction of pragmatics in FL contexts facilitates learning and, therefore, should be integrated into the curriculum from the beginning levels of instruction (Alcón & Guzmán, 2010; Félix-Brasdefer & Hasler-Barker, 2012; Ishihara & Cohen, 2010; Rose, 2005).

The learning of pragmatic knowledge in the FL classroom is different from the input learners receive in a study abroad context. Unlike intercultural learners who are exposed to input in the target environment (e.g. Americans studying Spanish in Mexico City), learners studying in the FL classroom (e.g. Americans learning Spanish at Indiana University) do not have the same experiences and opportunities to receive pragmatic input and to interact with speakers of the target culture. Following Rose (2005) and Ohta (2001), learners in the FL classroom:

- do not have immediate and frequent access to NSs of the target language;
- are not afforded sufficient input that is frequent, varied, or natural as in the target culture(s);
- are often exposed to modified and structured input in the textbook;
- do not have access to formal and informal settings where pragmatic input is necessary to develop the skills to negotiate speech acts in interaction (e.g. invitation-refusal sequence), conventional and non-conventional meaning, or lack opportunities to interact in intercultural encounters to produce and comprehend appropriate polite and impolite behavior;
- lack opportunities to participate in authentic situations outside of the classroom context;
- are often exposed to input in the textbook that is mainly restricted to simulated scenarios with little (or no) information directed toward developing the learner's pragmalinguistic and sociopragmatic knowledge.

Overall, as noted in previous work on pragmatic instruction, 'pragmatically appropriate authentic language samples are only rarely presented in English as a second language (ESL)/English as a foreign language (EFL) textbooks' (Bardovi-Harlig et al., 2015). Other researchers make a strong case for the need for pragmatic instruction in the FL classroom, highlighting the amount of pragmatic input, the modality of pragmatic instruction, attention to pragmatic input, metapragmatic awareness, collaborative activities, contrastive analysis and intercultural interactions (Félix-Brasdefer, 2012; Ishihara & Cohen, 2010; McConachy, 2018; McConachy et al., 2022). Other key issues include the amount and the quality of pragmatic input in the FL classroom, how collaborative practice is delivered, as well as the modality in which pragmatic input should be delivered.

Teaching Pragmatic and Intercultural Competence

The topic of instruction of pragmatics has received significant attention in the L2 pragmatics literature. Research shows that learners who receive instruction in pragmatics develop different pragmatic systems from learners who do not receive instruction (Bardovi-Harlig, 2001; Bardovi-Harlig et al., 2015; Félix-Brasdefer, 2006b, 2007; Kasper & Roever, 2005; Taguchi & Roever, 2017 [Chapter 8]). Pragmatic development as a result of pedagogical intervention indicates that a consciousness-raising approach (Schmidt, 1993, 1995), followed by meta-pragmatic instruction, is more efficient than input alone (Kasper & Rose, 2002). In L2 pragmatics research, explicit instruction is often delivered through metapragmatic information (i.e. explicit instruction of pragmalinguistic rules and explicit teaching of sociopragmatic expectations) and production activities. In addition, Schmidt's (1993) noticing hypothesis is essential, with pragmatic input delivered through input enhancement or any other means to direct the pragmatic target to the learner's attention. Explicit pragmatic knowledge is declarative and rule-based, whereas implicit knowledge is generally memory-based and depends on general exposure to input (oral, aural, written) with some degree of attention on the part of the learner. Moreover, in her analysis of 58 studies that examined the effect of explicit and implicit instruction, Taguchi (2015) concluded that pragmatic instruction is more effective than non-instruction, and that explicit teaching (delivered through noticing activities, metapragmatic information, and production activities) is more effective than implicit instruction. Other researchers argued for both implicit and explicit instruction for lasting effects of pragmatic development (Alcón-Soler, 2015; Martínez-Flor, 2016).

The type of instruction – implicit, explicit, or both – influences the type of learning about the pragmatic target. Although learners who are exposed to pragmatic input in naturalistic settings acquire certain aspects of pragmatics over long periods, adding an instructional component facilitates learners' ability to produce and interpret linguistic action and develop reflection and critical awareness of both linguistic and sociopragmatic norms of the L1 and L2 cultures. That is, learners who receive instruction in pragmatics and participate in activities which raise their awareness of communicative actions are observed to outperform those who do not receive instruction (Bardovi-Harlig, 2001; Hasler-Barker, 2016). Further, many instructional targets of pragmatics can be taught in the classroom, but teachers need to incorporate elements of pragmatics that are appropriate to the students' proficiency level. For instance, some speech acts that are not linguistically complex (e.g. greetings, compliments) can be taught at the beginning levels of instruction in the classroom by means of making input salient (e.g. bolding [in written materials] certain elements necessary to make a request), followed by communicative activities that help the learner notice both the form and function of particular expressions used in a specific context. Other concepts in pragmatics that require sophisticated linguistic knowledge can be taught at more advanced levels of proficiency at the discourse level, such as issuing and declining invitations, which require negotiation across multiple turns.

Research on L2 pragmatics should go beyond speech acts as single units of analysis and expand our understanding of Schmidt's (1993) noticing hypothesis. Instead, instructors should focus on the analysis of communicative action at the discourse level using a variety of metapragmatic instruction elements. Some of these include explicit teaching of pragmalinguistic and sociopragmatic knowledge, collaborative activities, and discussion of pragmatic targets that allow the intercultural speaker to compare, contrast and reflect on both their own pragmatic knowledge and the target culture (Félix-Brasdefer, 2017a, 2017b; McConachy, 2018; McConachy & Spencer-Oatey, 2020). Awareness of pragmatic variation should also be included in effective metapragmatic instructional treatments, including an analysis of regional variation of the pragmalinguistic and sociopragmatic norms used in different regions where the target language is used as an official language (e.g. production of pragmatic routines) such as English (United States, United Kingdom, Australia), French (France, Canada, Senegal), and Spanish (Spain, Equatorial Guinea, and the 18 countries in Latin America, in addition to Puerto Rico) (for an overview of regional pragmatic variation across varieties of Spanish, see Félix-Brasdefer, 2021a). Instructors should not only focus on the provision of declarative (explicit) knowledge of the target feature, but also on how those pragmatic targets are used through frequent practice and feedback, in communicative language use, and with input and practice of intercultural interactions.

In this chapter, I focus on the analysis of intercultural language learning in the FL classroom through the lens of pragmatics, including contextual analysis, pragmalinguistic and metapragmatic awareness, reflection of pragmatic variation and collaborative activities that include analysis, comparison and contrast of the pragmatic targets.

Intercultural Perspective on Teaching and Learning

Principles of teaching and learning

As mentioned in Chapter 1, in this chapter I adopt an intercultural perspective to examine language learning and the effects of teaching pragmatic knowledge and fostering intercultural understanding in the FL classroom. I adopt Liddicoat and Scarino's (2013) five principles of teaching and learning languages from an intercultural perspective, but adapt them to the FL classroom:

- *Active construction*: The FL classroom is the place where teachers provide opportunities to reflect on and analyze the concept of culture and language use; teachers are facilitators and engage the students in the interpretation and creation of meaning through collaborative reflection of the L1, L2, L3 (or Lx) languages and cultures. Students are constantly reflecting upon and exploring their own interpretations based on the teaching opportunities afforded in the classroom.
- *Making connections*: For language learning to take place, students connect their prior knowledge to their current experiences outside and inside the classroom, connecting knowledge of prior cultures to the target communities. The intercultural speaker mediates their identity as a learner, user and individual by 'connecting the intraculturality of others to one's own' (Liddicoat & Scarino, 2013: 57). Connections in the FL classroom are intercultural because learners 'are required to engage beyond their own intracultural positions and interpret meanings across linguistic and cultural boundaries' (2013: 57). Learners make connections to their previous identities and knowledge of previous diverse cultures and connect them to their culture knowledge, by establishing 'similarities and differences that are perceived' across cultures (2013: 57).
- *Social interaction*. Effective intercultural speakers communicate, create and develop pragmatic and intercultural competence in the FL classroom. Interaction takes place by engaging the language learner as a language user to interpret and negotiate meaning. Social interaction is the result of interpretation and negotiation of linguistic and social meaning through the use of collaborative dialog, negotiation of meaning and metapragmatic reflection (interactions about language) with other learners, the teacher and other intercultural speakers.
- *Reflection*. Effective communicative and interpretative skills are the result of constantly using the language to create meaning; reflecting about language use; and engaging in metapragmatic reflection about how language is used inside and outside of the classroom. Following Liddicoat and Scarino (2013: 58), the process of reflection in the FL classroom is both cognitive and affective. It is cognitive because the intercultural speaker explores attitudes and assumptions that they bring during language use in intercultural encounters, and how those assumptions affect the learners' cognitive state of mind. It is affective because the act of communication in intercultural encounters may bring a positive or negative impact on the feelings and emotions of the learners, and this emotional impact has to be 'considered and

interpreted by the learners' (2013: 58). The process of interpreting and negotiating assumptions and prior knowledge may affect how intercultural speakers calibrate their emotions and attitudes when negotiating social meaning in the FL classroom.
- *Responsibility.* Learning in the FL classroom is the result of the intercultural learner's 'attitudes, dispositions, and values developed over time (…); the intercultural speaker has the responsibility to develop intercultural sensitivity and intercultural understanding' (Liddicoat & Scarino, 2013: 58). Intercultural speakers with their multiple identities – as a learner, user, or person – have the 'ethical commitment' to connect their prior knowledge and assumptions with diverse cultures, to engage in reflection about their own and others' cultures, and to communicate effectively with speakers who share similar and different backgrounds and who create new meanings as a result of blended interactions.

To examine the effects of instruction in the FL classroom from an intercultural perspective, I follow Liddicoat and Scarino's (2013) four practices for intercultural learning, which I adapt to teach pragmatic knowledge and intercultural understanding in the FL classroom: noticing, comparing, reflecting, and interacting (see also McConachy [2018], which used these principles in his study). These intercultural learning practices are displayed in a circular fashion, but the main idea is that these practices are interconnected, and no practice represents a beginning or end point. Teachers should provide information so that learners notice specific pragmalinguistic and sociopragmatic features in the input (Schmidt, 1993, 1995). They can also compare and contrast differences and similarities of cultural norms when noticing specific cultural practices, norms, or values. By exercising the cognitive strategy of comparison, learners exert reflection and agency through interaction (Liddicoat & McConachy, 2019). In the FL classroom, interaction takes place in different ways: teacher-learner question-answers, learner-learner discussions about guided topics, production and comprehension of speech acts using production questionnaires and roleplay interactions (e.g. apologizing, requesting, refusing), and teacher-learner interactions inside and outside the classroom.

Overall, the aforementioned principles and the social practices allow the teachers to direct their teaching with guided instruction and feedback and include pedagogical activities to raise awareness about cultural norms and expectations such as polite and impolite behavior, identity and stereotypes. Teachers should engage learners in metapragmatic reflection to develop ethical commitment, to raise awareness of diversity and social variation in intercultural interaction, and to promote critical awareness about making personal choices such as agreeing, disagreeing, or challenging sociocultural expectations (L2 agency).

Pragmatic instruction and sociopragmatic reflection in the classroom

In this section, I describe and assess three studies that examined the effects of teaching pragmatics and developing sociopragmatic awareness in both comprehension and production of speech acts in the classroom. The three studies were selected because they teach one or more aspects of pragmatics from an intercultural perspective in study abroad (Riddiford & Holmes, 2015) and FL context using a pre-posttest design in the classroom (Dávila-Romero, 2022; McConachy, 2018). Riddiford and Homes (2015) examined the development of sociopragmatic awareness and intercultural development of refusals in the workplace of one migrant learner who arrived in New Zealand from the Philippines and was provided with explicit pragmatic instruction and opportunities to interact inside and outside of the classroom during a 12-week period. The data were taken from multiple sources including a refusal scenario (refusing a boss's request to move a box) from production questionnaires (Discourse Completion Task [DCT] and roleplays), at the beginning (week 1), middle (week 6), and end of the program (week 13). Retrospective reports were also collected three times and were collected immediately after the roleplay task to encourage the learner to reflect on his refusal behavior, sociocultural norms and behavioral expectations. Explicit instruction of sociopragmatics was delivered during five weeks in the classroom through the following method: explicit instruction of and attention to identification of refusal strategies, comparing pragmalinguistic and sociopragmatic norms, and reflection and awareness of contextual factors (social distance, power, and social setting).

The final component included data collection of recordings of natural interactions in various settings in the workplace. The learner was asked to carry a tape recorder to record his experience in intercultural settings. Data collection took place during the first two weeks and again during the last two weeks of the program. Results showed evidence of sociopragmatic and pragmalinguistic development at the end of the 12 weeks when refusing a boss's request to move books: brief exchanges, reduction in the amount of apologizing, developing more confidence in the acceptability of stating the problem, and change of the expression of willingness to help. The results from the retrospective verbal reports showed that the learner attributed the changes in his refusal behavior to the instruction and reflective activities provided in class. Overall, the following factors contributed to the development of sociopragmatic knowledge in the classroom: analysis and comparison of authentic workplace interaction; opportunities to receive explicit sociopragmatic instruction and feedback; opportunities to reflect and to develop awareness of contextual factors; and opportunities to practice the negotiation of speech acts at the discourse level.

The second study by McConachy (2018) examined the effects of explicit instruction and metapragmatic awareness, and the role of reflection on interlanguage language learning in the FL classroom. He analyzed the learning opportunities that four Japanese learners of English received during 10 weeks of classroom instruction: the first seven weeks focused on the metapragmatic instruction of speech acts (greetings, requests, apologies, compliments, invitation-refusals), contextual analysis of roleplay samples in English, and collaborative reflection on the speech acts at the discourse level (teacher-learner and learner-learner interactions). Week 8 focused on learner-learner roleplay performance, and post-roleplay analysis; week 9 engaged learners in dialog analysis and production in the classroom; and week 10 focused on a discussion on cultural generalizations in learner-learner and teacher-learner interactions. Through classroom interaction, the qualitative analysis showed that learners were able to notice pragmalinguistic and sociopragmatic features of the interactions, reflect on sociocultural norms in both their L1 (Japanese) and L2 (English), and reflect on their experiences and classroom practices to facilitate intercultural language learning and collaborative reflection. Most importantly, reflection on performance 'creates affordances for learning through the way it facilitates learners' explorations of their own emotional reactions to aspects of interaction' (2018: 147). This study shows the importance of creating reflective and interactive activities to foster production and intercultural understanding between the teacher and the student and through learner-learner roleplay interactions.

Finally, Dávila-Romero (2022) examined the effects of pedagogical intervention for the teaching of the concepts of culture and intercultural conflict among beginning German students of Spanish as a FL in a university in Southern Spain. Using Byram's (1997) model of intercultural communicative competence (knowledge, attitudes, skill, awareness), the author examined perceptions of the notion of cultural awareness and intercultural conflict before and after pedagogical intervention. Using a pre-posttest design, he conducted a survey at the beginning and end of the class to examine the students' awareness of culture and associations of the following concepts: humanistic (e.g. literature, art, music), anthropological (e.g. everyday routines, beliefs, attitudes), closed (e.g. race, religion, history), relational (e.g. extroverted, conflict, interpersonal relations, respect), and negative (e.g. intolerance, conflict, misunderstanding, discrimination) and positive attitudes (e.g. friendship, tolerance, reflection). Instruction included metapragmatic discussions and reflection of the concepts of culture and intercultural conflict. Students also practiced dialogues and activities outside of class. Later, the students were assigned to prepare a final paper to present at the end of the class, based on their interpretations and reflections of the concept of intercultural conflict. Results showed positive change on their understanding and awareness of culture based on positive attitudes, associations of conflict, racism, respect, misunderstandings, tolerance, acceptance, respect and interpersonal relations. However, no change was noted on the posttest after pedagogical intervention on the perception and association of the first three concepts: humanistic, anthropologic, and close concepts. Overall, as mentioned by the author, the lack of change in the perception of the concepts of culture (humanistic, anthropologic, and closed) may be due to the beginning proficiency level and the selection of the topic of intercultural conflict.

The aforementioned studies show that the FL classroom provides intercultural learning opportunities to raise metapragmatic awareness and reflection of speech acts through the following learning practices. Metapragmatic awareness and reflection:

- directs the learners' attention (noticing) to specific aspects of language use, comparing the learners' previous experiences to current ones (previous assumptions, identity, beliefs);
- allows the learners to compare and contrast speech acts in the L1 and target languages;
- engages learners in collaborative reflection of their experiences;
- provides feedback and interactive activities through roleplay practice;
- engages the learners in critical metapragmatic reflection of the negotiation of speech acts in learner-learner and teacher-learner interactions.

Classroom-Based Study of Learning Spanish as a Foreign Language

In this section, I provide an analysis of the effects of instruction and metapragmatic reflection in the FL classroom from the lens of intercultural language learning (Liddicoat & Scarino, 2013; McConachy, 2018). To do this, I examine how FL learners of Spanish develop sociopragmatic awareness of different aspects of pragmatic knowledge (requesting, apologizing, refusing), complemented by metapragmatic awareness and reflective activities, as a result of instruction. See Chapter 1 (Figure 1.2) for the description of the pragmatic component as part of the learner's intercultural communicative competence. For the negotiation of meaning and intercultural understanding, see the pragmatic-discursive approach in Chapter 3 (Figure 3.1), in particular, the components of metapragmatic awareness and variability.

Participants

Twenty-two learners of Spanish as a FL language participated in this study. They were between 20–22 years old (18 females; 4 males) and they varied according to their study abroad experience. They were enrolled in an upper-division class over the course of one semester in Hispanic pragmatics that is offered for advanced-level undergraduate students majoring in Spanish at a Midwestern university (all students had a second major). Situated in classroom-based research (Rose & Kasper, 2001 [Chapter 3]), no proficiency test was used to measure their proficiency in Spanish. To enroll in this course, the students took their last requirements to complete the major in Spanish, at least two courses in linguistics (Phonetics, Syntax, Pragmatics, Sociolinguistics or Second Language Acquisition). Of these, 21 learners reported English as L1 and Spanish as an L2 (one L3 Portuguese; one L3 French and L4 Italian); one learner had Tamil as L1, English as L2, and Spanish as L3. Eleven students (8 females; 3 males) had never studied abroad (learners 1–11) and eleven had studied in one or more regions of the Spanish-speaking world with different lengths of residence (LoR) (10 females; 1 male [learners 12–22]), Table 4.1.

Seven students studied in various regions in Spain (one studied in both Spain and Mexico), two in the Dominican Republic, one in Chile and one in Argentina. Regarding the LoR, two students studied for one semester abroad; six studied abroad for 1–3 months; three students studied abroad for 2–3 weeks. Finally, seven students chose to live with a host family and four in an apartment with other international students.

Table 4.1 Learner characteristics with and without previous study abroad experience

Participants	Native Language	Other Languages	Region Abroad	Duration Abroad	Living Condition Abroad
1–11	English (learner #5 had Tamil as L1)	Spanish (learner #5: English as L2, Spanish as L3)	No	N/A	N/A
12	English	Spanish	Argentina (Buenos Aires)	2 months	Host family
13	English	Spanish	Mexico (Yucatán); Spain (Alcalá)	3 months	Host family
14	English	Spanish	Spain (Barcelona)	6 weeks	Host family
15	English	Spanish	Dominican Republic (Santiago)	3 weeks	Apartment
16	English	Spanish	Spain (Salamanca)	2 weeks	Host family
17	English	Spanish, Portuguese	Spain (Oviedo)	2 months	Host family
18	English	Spanish, French, Italian	Dominican Republic (Santiago)	3 weeks	Apartment
19	English	Spanish	Spain (Madrid)	1 semester	Apartment
20	English	Spanish	Spain (Madrid)	1 semester	Host family
21	English	Spanish	Chile (Santiago)	2 months	Host family
22	English	Spanish	Spain (Murcia, Sevilla)	1 month	Apartment

Instrument and procedures of data collection

To examine production and awareness of pragmatic and cultural norms, the data was triangulated using an oral DCT, reflection and awareness of the learner's speech-act performance, and open-ended roleplays, followed by reflective analysis and awareness of the learner's negotiation of speech acts. The production data was collected twice using a computer-delivered production questionnaire (oral DCT) in a pretest (beginning of semester) and posttest design (end of semester). To examine the negotiation of speech acts at the discourse level, roleplay data from one learner was examined at the beginning and end of the semester (five months after pretest). The oral DCT elicits experimental speech-act data under controlled conditions with the aim of measuring pragmalinguistic or sociopragmatic knowledge in a non-interactive format. That is, this instrument measures what the participants know, rather than how they use their ability to interact with an interlocutor. This instrument has been used to examine various speech acts in different learning contexts and with different learner populations (Félix-Brasdefer & Hasler-Barker, 2017; Schauer, 2004). Some limitations have been noted regarding the validity of the data and the non-interactive format, among others (Kasper & Dahl, 1991; Ogiermann, 2018; Schneider, 2018). Despite these limitations, an oral DCT was used in the present study to examine pragmalinguistic and sociopragmatic knowledge of these speech acts under controlled conditions in a pretest-posttest design and with responses delivered orally. At the end of the semester, learners were asked to transcribe their responses and to examine their speech-act performance with metapragmatic reflective analysis (see section 'Pragmatic instruction and metapragmatic reflection').

Learners were asked to read 16 situations in a PowerPoint and respond orally to different speech acts (apologies, requests, refusals, compliments). Each situation included written, visual and oral input.

For this study, I examined five situations: two requests, two apologies, and one refusal to an offer of food (Table 4.2).

After students read the description of each situation, they responded orally with what they would say according to the contextual description.

Table 4.2 Roleplay situations: Requests, apologies, refusal to an offer

Role-play situation	Social Distance	Social Power
Requesting water from flight attendant on plane en route to a Spanish-speaking country	+D	+P
Requesting to borrow shampoo from roommate abroad	-D	-P
Apologizing to professor for arriving late to appointment	+D	+P
Apologizing to classmate for damaging a car	-D	-P
Refusing host mother's offer to eat more	+/-D	+P

The refusal to the offer of food included two prompts: offer-response and insistence response. While the first response represents an ostensible refusal, the response to the insistence can include a direct or indirect refusal to the offer (reason, alternative, apology, indefinite reply) or an acceptance. According to previous research, an insistence in Spanish (and in Asian cultures [Chinese], Indian and Pakistani), represents a sociocultural expectation, an appropriate behavior; not insisting is viewed as inappropriate behavior and gives the impression to the hearer that the offer is not sincere (Félix-Brasdefer, 2008, 2019a [Chapter 7]; García, 1992; Isaacs & Clark, 1990; Su, 2020).

Finally, learner #6 volunteered to participate in two roleplay interactions at the beginning of semester and five months later (apologizing to professor for arriving late; refusing offer of food). Roleplay interactions (Félix-Brasdefer, 2018; Kasper, 2000) were used to analyze the negotiation of meaning of an apology and a refusal to an offer, followed by metapragmatic awareness of the student's performance.

Instruction and meta-pragmatic reflection

Using a classroom research design (Rose & Kasper, 2001 [Chapter 3]), the 22 students took an introductory course on Hispanic pragmatics during one semester (16 weeks). Instruction, teacher-student discussions, reflective activities, and student collaborative activities occurred in Spanish. The 35 hours of class instruction (75 minutes each session [implicit instruction]) were followed by the instructional component and posttest at the end of the semester. The aim of the class was to offer an overview and analysis of the fundamental topics in Hispanic pragmatics, such as the scope of pragmatics, context, speech acts, deixis, indirect meaning, discourse, politeness and impoliteness, pragmatic variation, and second language pragmatics and the effects of instruction in speech act production and comprehension. Table 4.3 includes the pragmatic topics discussed during the 16 weeks instruction, metapragmatic discussion, reflection, production and collaborative practice. Learners completed the pretest in week 1 and the posttest in week 16.

Pragmatic instruction and metapragmatic reflection

As mentioned above, the students completed the pretest at the beginning (week 1) and the posttest at the end of the semester (week 16). One day prior to the posttest (week 16), the students read two articles that contained information on the pragmalinguistic and sociopragmatic aspects of speech acts (requests, apologies, refusals), including a description of the forms and pragmatic functions used to mitigate or upgrade these speech acts (Félix-Brasdefer & Cohen, 2012; Fuentes Rodríguez, 2010). A 75-minute class (taught in Spanish) was devoted to explaining

Table 4.3 Instructional treatment, pretest and posttest

Length	Pretest	Topics discussed	Metapragmatic information	Reflection	Production / collaborative practice	Posttest
Week 1	X	Defining pragmatics, context and contexts				
Weeks 2–3		Pragmalinguistic and sociopragmatic knowledge; context; and deixis		X		
Weeks 4–5		Compare and contrast speech acts in different varieties of Spanish (requests, refusals, compliments, apologies)	X	X	X	
Weeks 6–8		Indirect speech acts and implicit meaning; humor (implicature)		X	X	
Week 9		Discourse analysis		X	X	
Weeks 10–11		Politeness and impoliteness	X	X	X	
Weeks 12–13		Variation of speech acts and polite behavior across regions of Spanish-speaking world	X	X	X	
Weeks 14–15		Intercultural competence; L2 pragmatics	X	X	X	
Week 16		Reflection of pragmatic topics covered during semester; pedagogical intervention; posttest		X		X

and discussing the pragmatic functions of grammatical forms and structures used for the service of pragmatics: the conditional and imperfect to express respect and distance, the subjunctive to convey doubt or hesitation, lexical forms to express an apology in Spanish and English (*lo siento* 'I'm sorry'; *disculpa/e* 'I apologize [T/V]', *perdona/e* or *perdona/eme* 'forgive me [T/V]', *qué pena* 'I regret'), strategies to express direct and indirect requests and refusals, request perspective (speaker oriented [can I have…?] vs hearer oriented (*me da…* 'can you give me [V]'), and mitigating forms to soften a request or a refusal. Instruction also included the importance of contextual factors that condition the selection of pragmalinguistic forms in formal and informal situations, namely, social distance and power and degree of imposition. Finally, given the regional pragmatic variation that exists across regions in Spain and Latin American (19 countries that speak Spanish as an official language, and Puerto Rico as a US territory) and in Africa (Equatorial Guinea), a discussion of regional differences in speech act production and comprehension was provided to raise awareness (Félix-Brasdefer, 2021a; Félix-Brasdefer & Placencia, 2020; Schneider & Placencia, 2017). At the end of the session, students were engaged in roleplay practice of these speech acts. Three students roleplayed the speech acts in front of the class, followed by a metapragmatic analysis and reflection of the forms and strategies used during the interaction (opening, speech-act response, closing). The session was recorded. The pedagogical intervention, feedback and all reflective activities were conducted in Spanish.

The students completed the posttest (week 16) one day after the instructional treatment and were asked to do the following in Spanish:

- Record your responses for the posttest (same situations and same order as the pretest).
- Transcribe your responses for the pretest and posttest for all 16 responses. Only the five situations were included in the present analysis.
- Engage in metapragmatic reflection by comparing and contrasting their responses from the pretest to the posttest:

    Reflection based on your responses for each speech act in the pretest and posttest, reflect on each response at the beginning (pretest) and end of the semester (posttest). You can comment on the following: do you observe any similarities and differences in the choice of forms and strategies you used in each response? Do your responses follow the expected sociocultural expectations of the Hispanic culture that you learned in this class? (politeness and impoliteness norms, degrees of directness and indirectness, the notion of the insistence after refusing an offer or an invitation), do you observe any positive or negative transfer in your responses from the pretest to the posttest?

- At the end of the metapragmatic reflection, the students were asked to write a final reflection: 'Do you think that your responses reflect an improvement of your pragmatic competence at the end of the semester? Do you feel that you changed your responses to conform to the expected sociocultural norms of the region(s) of the Hispanic culture with which you identify? How did this class help you improve your pragmatic and intercultural competence and become more aware when negotiating speech acts in Spanish?

Research on metapragmatic reflection has been used to examine the language learning process of learners from an intercultural perspective with a focus on sociopragmatics (Henery, 2015; McConachy, 2018; McConachy & Spencer-Oatey, 2020; van Compernolle & Kinginger, 2013). Specifically, an intercultural perspective to language learning promotes the development of sociopragmatic awareness through metapragmatic reflection of their oral speech act performance, collaborative classroom discussion, scaffolding of speech analysis at the discourse level and contextual analysis of social distance, power and degree of imposition.

Data analysis

The data was analyzed in two parts:

(a) analysis of the classification of pragmalinguistic strategies used to produce requests and apologies (Blum-Kulka *et al.*, 1989) and refusals (Beebe *et al.*, 1990). The selected strategies for each speech act and expressions of internal modification will be described in the Results section when analyzing the data for each speech act;
(b) content analysis. The metapragmatic reflective students' comments were analyzed qualitatively following Saldaña's (2015, 2021) notation for transcribing and annotating qualitative data. As mentioned in Chapter 5, by analyzing qualitative data,

[o]ur brains synthesize vast amounts of information into symbolic summary (codes); we make sense of the world by noticing repetition and formulating regularity through cognitive schemata and scripts (patterns); we cluster similar things together through comparison and contrast to formulate bins of stored knowledge (categories); and we imprint key learning from extended experiences by creating proverb-like narrative memories (themes). (Saldaña, 2015: 11)

The following codes were used to examine the metapragmatic reflective analysis of the pretest and posttest data:

- pragmalinguistic awareness of speech act performance;
- awareness of pragmatic variation;
- sociopragmatic awareness: sociocultural and interactional norms;
- awareness of lack of pragmatic competence.

The next section presents the quantitative analysis regarding the frequency and distribution of the pragmalinguistic strategies used to perform requests, apologies and a refusal of food, supplemented by a qualitative analysis of the learners' metapragmatic reflection of their speech act performance during the posttest and after the pedagogical intervention. As mentioned in the Method section, the 22 learners who took a Hispanic Pragmatics course over the course of one semester (16 weeks) were divided into two groups according to learning context: 11 learners who had never studied abroad (learners #1–11) and 11 who had studied abroad in different regions in Spain and Latin America with various LoR (learners #12–22) (Table 4.1). In the examples below, I use the following pronominal forms: 'T' for informal address (-D, -P) and 'V' for formal and deferential address (+/-D, +P).

Requesting in the Foreign Language Classroom

Requests belong to the speech act of directives because they direct the hearer to do something for the benefit of the speaker (Searle, 1977). As noted in Table 4.2, the two request situations varied according to social distance and power: a student passenger asks the flight attendant for water (+D, +P) and a student asks their roommate to borrow shampoo (-D, -P). Following Blum-Kulka *et al.* (1989), the requests were analyzed according to the degree of directness and internal modification to soften the request. The direct requests observed in the data included the use of imperatives (Give me water), ellipticals (Water please), want statements (I want water), I'd like statements (I'd like water), and assertions of the hearer's course of actions (*me da / me pone / me trae agua* [V] 'you give me / you put me / you bring me water'). Conventional indirect requests included the following variants with the intention of directing the hearer to do something for the speaker (requesting water or shampoo): Can I have water? / Do you have water? Is it possible to borrow your shampoo?). In addition, internal modifiers to soften the request were classified as follows: No mitigator, one mitigator, two or more mitigators (e.g. please, diminutives, hedges [a little bit, some, the conditional or imperfect to express distance or request]).

Since no major situational variation was noted in each group, the frequencies for the request type, request perspective, and internal modification were analyzed for both situations. Each participant contributed twice, one for each request situation (22 cases overall; 11 cases per situation). Table 4.4 displays the frequencies for the preference for request type in both situations and in both learning contexts (study abroad [SA] vs no study abroad). Both groups were studying Spanish in the FL classroom at an institution in the United States.

Of the six request strategies used, conventional indirectness predominated in the pretest in the SA (82%) and no SA group (91%), and a decrease in conventional indirectness was evident at the end of the semester (50%–54.5%). Towards the end of the semester, the no SA group chose imperative forms (18%; 2 cases in each situation). Two infrequent strategies included 'I'd like' and 'I want statements' (1 case in each group). Both groups selected assertions of the hearer's course of action, a strategy that is frequent in Spanish and was part of the instructional treatment (*me da / me pone / me prestas...* 'Can you give me...[V]'/ 'Can you put me...[V]'/ 'Can you lend me...[T]'). One learner in the no SA group, changed from conventional indirectness (*puedo tener agua* 'Can I have water') to the use of an

Table 4.4 Frequency of request type by learning context

Request type	Study Abroad		No Study Abroad	
	Pretest	Posttest	Pretest	Posttest
Conventional indirect	82% (18)	50% (11)	91% (20)	54.5% (12)
Imperative	4.5% (1)	4.5% (1)	4.5% (1)	18% (4)
I'd like	0% (0)	0% (0)	4.5% (1)	0% (0)
Want	4.5% (1)	0% (0)	0% (0)	0% (0)
Elliptical	0% (0)	0% (0)	0% (0)	4.5% (1)
Assertion	9% (2)	45.5% (10)	0% (0)	23% (5)
Total	100% (22)	100% (22)	100% (22)	100% (22)

Table 4.5 Request perspective by learning context

Request perspective	Study Abroad		No Study Abroad	
	Pretest	Posttest	Pretest	Posttest
Speaker	68% (15)	27% (6)	82% (18)	27.3% (6)
Hearer	32% (7)	73% (16)	18% (4)	68.2% (15)
None	0% (0)	0% (0)	0% (0)	4.5% (1)
Total	100% (22)	100% (22)	100% (22)	100% (22)

elliptical request, a frequent request in Spanish (*agua, por favor* 'water, please'). This strategy, which reflects the effects of instruction (absent during the pretest), predominated in the SA group (45.5%) and was less frequent among the learners who had no exposure to SA (23%).

Change in the learner's request perspective was also observed in the preference for speaker-perspective. As shown in Table 4.5, the majority of learners in both groups and in both situations changed from a speaker's perspective (e.g. *Puedo tener...* 'Can I have...'; *Es posible que yo tenga...* 'Is it possible that I have...') to a hearer's perspective, as explained during the pedagogical intervention (*me puede traer* 'Can you bring me [V]'; *me pone* 'Can you put...[V]'/ *da* 'Give [T]'; *deme* 'Give me [V]') (SA group: 73%; no study abroad: 68%).

Finally, as displayed in Table 4.6, most learners changed from no mitigation to mitigation of the request at the end of the semester, with a predominance in the SA group. Most learners (60% or higher) increased

Pragmatic Learning and Intercultural Understanding in the FL Classroom   93

Table 4.6 Frequency of mitigators by learning context

Mitigator	Study Abroad		No Study Abroad	
	Pretest	Posttest	Pretest	Posttest
None	54.5% (12)	9% (2)	32% (7)	13.6% (3)
One mitigator	41% (9)	82% (18)	50% (11)	63.4% (14)
Two or more	4.5 (1)	9% (2)	18% (4)	23% (5)
Total	100% (22)	100% (22)	100% (22)	100% (22)

the use of one or more mitigators when issuing a request to the flight attendant or the classmate at the end of the semester.

As noted in the examples (1) and (2), most learners in each group changed their request preference from the pretest to the posttest, decreasing use of conventional indirectness. In some cases, there was no change. The metapragmatic reflection for each example (from pre- to posttest) is also included to account for pragmalinguistic and sociopragmatic awareness in each situation:

(1) Requesting development in the FL classroom (no study abroad experience)

Requesting water from flight attendant (+D, +P)

a. Female learner #1
   Pretest: Hola, ¿*puedo tomar* una botella de agua?
                 'Hi, can I have a bottle of water?'
   Posttest: Agua, *por favor*
                 'Water, please'
   Reflection: I don't use *puedo* ('I can') at the end of the semester because it's more indirect.

b. Female learner #10
   Pretest: ¿*Puedo tener* un poco de agua por favor?
                 'Can I have some water, please?'
   Posttest: Hola, señora, **deme** una botella de agua *por favor*
                 'Hello, ma'am, give me a bottle of water, please'
   Reflection: There's a change in the structure. On the pretest, it uses the form that is transference from English; on the posttest, it uses the form that is more common in Spanish.

Requesting shampoo from classmate (-D, -P)

c. Female learner #2
   Pretest: ¿*Puedo usar* un poco de tu champú, *por favor*?
                 'Can I use a little of your shampoo, please?'

Posttest: *¿Me prestas <u>un poco</u> de tu champú?*
'Will you lend me a little of your shampoo?'
Reflection: There are two differences in these responses: 1. I excluded 'please' in my second response and, as a result, my answer at the end of the semester is more direct. 2. I changed the verb from 'can I use' to 'will you lend me'. This change is important because, again, Spanish is a hearer-oriented language. For this reason, in my second response, I corrected my error from the pretest, and I used a more acceptable verb according to Spanish norms.

d. Male learner #6
Pretest: *Hola amigo, ¿**es posible que puedo** usar un poquito de tu champú? Olvidé traer mía. <u>Si no, no es un problema</u>.*
'Hello friend, is it possible that I can use a little bit of your shampoo? I forgot to bring mine. If not, it's no problem'
Posttest: *Hola amigo, ¿**es posible que puedo** usar tu champú <u>por una vez</u>?*
Lo olvide, si no, puedo comprar algo el próximo día.
'Hello friend, is it possible that I can use your shampoo one time? I forgot it, if not, I can buy some the next day'
Reflection: They are almost the same as other examples. My English has transferred.

(2) Requesting development in the FL classroom (study abroad experience)

Requesting water from flight attendant (+D, +P)

a. Male learner #15
Pretest: *¿**Puedo tener** un vaso de agua?*
'Can I have a glass of water?'
Posttest: *Hola, **me da** una botella de agua por favor?*
'Hi, give me a bottle of water, please?'
Reflection: The first response is 'overpolite' and the second is closer to a native speaker, but you can still see my English politeness with 'please'

b. Female learner #19
Pretest: *Hola perdona, es que tengo sed. **Quiero** una botella de agua <u>por favor</u>.*
'Hi, excuse me, the thing is I'm thirsty. I want a bottle of water, <u>please</u>'
Posttest: *Es **posible** que pueda tener una botella de agua <u>por fa</u>?*
'Is it possible that I can have a bottle of water <u>please (informal)</u>?'
Reflection: In both responses, I think I used politeness as we are going to use it in the United States.

The thing is that in Spanish-speaking countries, it's likely that they will be more direct and use grammar similar to a command. I think that in the second response you can see the idea of pragmatic transfer with the use of 'can I have.' It's something that can work and that people in Mexico will understand, but really it's just something I said because it's what I'd say in English. In my opinion, it's an example of negative pragmatic transfer.

Requesting shampoo from classmate (-D, -P)

c. Male learner #13
   Pretest: ¿*Está bien si* uso yo tú champú? Es que...<u>creo</u> que lo mío está en el hotel.
   'Is it okay if I use your shampoo? The thing is...I think mine is in the hotel'
   Posttest: Oye amiga, **préstame** <u>un poco</u> de tu champú, es que no tengo lo mío.
   'Hey friend, lend me a little of your shampoo, the thing is that I don't have mine'
   Reflection: There is a notable change between the first answer and the second. My first response totally represents transfer from English (Is it okay if I use...?) My second response is more appropriate according to Spanish use and the informal context of speaking with an acquaintance or a friend. In comparison with English (in general), Spanish is more direct – and this can be seen with the use of a command to make a request. In both responses, I use supporting elements to soften the obligation for the hearer.

d. Female learner #16
   Pretest: Um oye, me olvidé el champú en mi casa y creo que la tienda esta cerrada, um, puedes, **puedo usar** un poco de tu champú <u>por favor</u>? Muchas gracias porque tengo de la champú y quiero lavar mi, la cabello, muchas gracias.
   'Um hey, I forgot my shampoo at home and I think the store is closed, um can you, can I use a little of your shampoo, <u>please</u>. Thanks a lot because I have shampoo and I want to wash my hair, thank you'
   Posttest: Um, perdon, **me prestas** <u>un poco</u> de tu champú porque no tengo más y necesito comprar un poco de champú pero la tienda está cerrado. <u>Un poquito</u>, es porque tengo un poco de arena en el pelo, muchas gracias.
   'Um, sorry, will you lend me a little of your shampoo because I don't have any more and I need to buy a little shampoo but the store is closed. A little, it's because I have a little sand in my hair, thank you.'

Reflection: This response was interesting because at the beginning I made a conscious effort to be more focused on my request, but after I continued speaking, I was thinking less about how I was speaking and I returned to speaking Spanish with sentence structures in English. This situation was also interesting because when I read this message I wasn't sure how direct I should speak because my answer is in Spanish, but my roommate is American like I am. In general, I was more direct, but either one of my answers would have been accepted due to the fact that the speaker as well as the hearer were American.

Change of pragmatic and intercultural knowledge was noted in both groups at the end of the semester. Regarding pragmatic knowledge of requesting, most learners changed conventional indirectness and speaker perspective to different strategies with a focus on the hearer's perspective at the end of the semester. For example, in the examples in (1), learners with no previous SA experience changed from conventional indirectness and speaker's perspective to hearer's perspective (1a–c). These learners changed to elliptical (1a), imperative (1b) and assertion (1c) with a focus on the hearer's perspective. In the metapragmatic reflection, these learners were aware of the preference of direct request from a hearer's perspective. They showed awareness of transfer from the native language (NL) from the pretest to the posttest in both the selection of request strategies and the request perspective (1b and 1c). The learner's metapragmatic reflection in (1c) showed explicit knowledge of the information learned in the pedagogical intervention session, awareness of the assertion request strategy (from *puedo usar* 'Can I use' to *me prestas* 'Borrow me'), which, according to the learner, followed the norms of the Hispanic culture. In contrast, in (1d), no change was noted from the pretest to the posttest, using the same strategy, which is more common in request strategies in English. In the metapragmatic reflection, the learner was aware of his influence from the NL in both responses ('[my responses] are almost the same as in the other examples. My English has transferred'). Since this learner was aware that this strategy represents a direct transfer from English ('Is it possible that I can use...?'), with more practice and understanding of contextual analysis, he could choose either other request strategies according to the sociocultural expectations of the Hispanic culture, or his own strategies, which may or may not conform to the target culture.

The learners in the SA group showed a higher degree of pragmalinguistic and sociopragmatic awareness than the learners with no exposure to previous study abroad. In examples (2a, c-d), learners changed from using different forms of conventional indirectness with a speaker's perspective (*Puedo usar...* 'Can I use'; *Está bien si...* 'Is it okay if...') to assertions (*me da...* 'can you give me...'; *me prestas...* 'can you lend me...') and an imperative when requesting shampoo from the classmate (*préstame..* 'lend me...').

Regarding the metapragmatic reflection, these learners showed awareness of influence from English to Spanish (2a) when overusing 'please' in the posttest. The metapragmatic reflections in (2c-d) showed sociopragmatic awareness of requesting in an informal situation (-D, -P). For example, in (2c), the learner explained that he used the L1 English form ('Is it OK if I use...') on the pretest, and then changed to an appropriate response at the end of the semester, according to the pragmatic instruction she read in the textbook and the intervention, a direct form (*Préstame un poco de champú* 'Lend me a little bit of shampoo'). Similarly, in (2d), the learner explained that she was aware of the use of directness and a hearer orientation in this informal request (pretest: *Puedo usar...* 'Can I use...': Posttest: *Me prestas...* 'will you lend me...'). The response in the posttest shows markers of politeness (*perdón* 'sorry', *un poco* 'a little', *un poquito* 'a little bit of'), and a longer explanation than the pretest. This learner explained that she was aware of the request perspective oriented towards the hearer. In contrast, no change was observed in the response in (2b) from the pretest (I want) to the posttest (Is it possible that I can have...), both with a speaker's perspective. In the metapragmatic reflection, the learner explained that she was aware of the negative pragmatic transfer of this L1 strategy commonly used in English (Félix-Brasdefer, 2020a).

The learners in both groups showed development of both pragmatic and intercultural competence at the end of the semester. Pragmatic change occurred with a preference to the hearer's request perspective, preference for use of assertions of the hearer's course of action and use of imperative, especially in the informal situation. A higher level of pragmalinguistic variation was noted in the learners with previous SA experience, especially since they could connect their responses to their experience abroad. The data from the **metapragmatic reflection** showed explicit awareness of sociopragmatic norms used from the beginning and end of the semester, acknowledging the information they received during the intervention and the readings in class, such as knowledge of the norms and sociocultural expectations of directness and indirectness, politeness and impoliteness, and a reflection of the social factors of social distance, power and degree of imposition in the L1 and L2 cultures (intercultural competence). Further, as seen from the examples in (1–2), a higher frequency and varied inventory of mitigators were used on the posttest (*un poco* 'a little', *un poquito* 'a little bit', *por favor/por fa* 'please', *si no es un problema* 'if it is not a problem'). Finally, there were a few learners that noticed their influence from the L1 at the end of the semester, using forms used in English.

Overall, while the request responses show evidence of the preferred pragmalinguistic expressions used at the end of the semester, the learners' metapragmatic reflections demonstrate the learners' awareness of sociopragmatic norms and their agency to make informed decisions when making formal and informal requests in Spanish. Some learners were aware that they used their L1 norms to express a request in Spanish to sound direct and according to their L1 identity norms. Thus, instead of choosing the expected L2 norms, the learners reported feeling more comfortable using their L1 sociocultural norms of directness and knowledge of the imposition of the request in formal and informal situations.

Apologizing in the Foreign Language Classroom

Apologies, like requests, represent a complex speech act for language learners because they require the appropriate selection of pragmalinguistic strategies and the understanding of sociopragmatic norms based on situational factors. Apologies are expressive speech acts (Searle, 1975) which are performed when the speaker acknowledges that social norms have been violated, and there is an attempt to repair the severity of the offense. According to previous research (Blum-Kulka et al., 1989; Olshtain & Cohen, 1983), the strategies observed in the data included an expression of apology (head act 'I apologize / I'm sorry'), acknowledgement of responsibility ('It was my fault'), an explanation or account ('I had to call my parents'), an offer of repair ('I'll pay for it'), and a promise of non-recurrence ('It won't happen again'). Apologies also vary according to the speaker or hearer perspective: speaker-oriented as in English ('I'm sorry') or hearer-oriented, as in varieties of Spanish (*perdóname* [T] 'forgive me'; *discúlpame* [T] 'I apologize') (Cordella, 1990; Márquez Reiter, 2000). Moreover, due to the severity of offense, intensification of the apology is often necessary based on the demands of the situation ('I'm really / so / terribly sorry'). While not all strategies occurred in the data, I focus on the variants used to express an apology, the learner's perspective, and the expressions used to intensify the severity of offense. As noted in Table 4.2, the two situations included: apologizing to the professor for arriving late to the appointment (+D, +P) and apologizing to a friend for damaging the car (-D, -P).

Table 4.7 displays the distribution of the apology choices used by the 22 learners in both learning contexts (11 for each situation). Since no major situational differences were observed, the results for both situations are analyzed together.

Although both learning groups changed from a speaker-oriented to a hearer-oriented perspective and expanded their pragmalinguistic forms on the posttest, the learners with SA experience improved the most at the end of the semester. The SA group decreased the use of speaker-oriented perspective (yo) *lo siento* 'I'm sorry' from the pretest (72.7%) to the posttest (45.5%). Other forms were infrequent during the pretest (forgive me, I regret [27.3%]) and increased during the posttest altogether (49.9%, columns 1–2, rows 2–4); of these, the hearer perspective *disculpa/disculpe* 'forgive me' (T/V) was most frequent among these learners. In contrast, most of the learners with no SA experience reduced the frequency of *lo*

Table 4.7 Frequency of apology type by learning context

Apology	Study Abroad		No Study Abroad	
	Pretest	Posttest	Pretest	Posttest
lo siento 'I'm sorry'	72.7% (16)	45.5% (10)	86.4% (19)	22.7% (5)
disculpa/e (T/V) 'forgive me/I apologize'	13.7% (3)	27.2% (6)	9% (2)	27.2 (6)
Perdóname (T) 'forgive me'	9% (2)	13.7% (3)	0% (0)	45.5% (10)
Lo lamento/me da pena 'I regret'/ 'I feel bad'	4.6% (1)	9% (2)	0% (0)	0% (0)
None	0% (0)	4.6% (1)	4.6% (1)	4.6% (1)
Total	100% (22)	100% (22)	100% (22)	100% (22)

Table 4.8 Frequency of intensifiers in apology by learning context

Intensifier used	Study Abroad		No Study Abroad	
	Pretest	Posttest	Pretest	Posttest
Yes	54.5% (12)	77.3% (17)	41% (9)	68% (15)
No	45.5% (10)	22.7% (5)	59% (13)	32% (7)
Total	100% (22)	100% (22)	100% (22)	100% (22)

siento 'I'm sorry' with a speaker-oriented perspective from the pretest (86.4%) to the posttest (22.7%). These learners also expanded their repertoire of pragmalinguistic forms with a hearer-oriented perspective, using *disculpa/e* 'forgive me' and expressions of forgiveness (72.7%) in the posttest (column 4, rows 2–4).

Change was also noted in the use of intensification of the severity of offense in both situations. Table 4.8 (11 learners per situation) shows that approximately 50% of the learners in each learning group increased both the frequency and repertoire of these forms from the pretest to the posttest (*lo siento mucho* 'I'm really sorry'; *de verdad, me siento muy mal, perdóneme* 'really, I feel terrible, forgive me'). By the posttest, a few learners chose zero intensification in the SA group (22.7%) and in the no SA group (32%).

Altogether, while the learners with previous SA experience changed from a speaker-oriented to a hearer-oriented perspective and expanded their use of apology forms using the T/V distinction to express formality and informality (*disculpa/e* 'I'm sorry'; *Me da pena* 'I feel bad'), the learners with no SA experience displayed a higher degree of change in the reduction of *lo siento* 'I'm sorry', and a preference for *disculpa/e*; *perdona/e, perdóname* 'forgive me [T/V]' at the end of the semester, as noted on the posttest. However, the learners with previous SA experience often used two apology forms in their responses on the posttest with a hearer perspective and a deferential tone (*Disculpe, perdóneme, por favor, no vuelve a pasar* 'I'm sorry, forgive me, please, it won't happen again'). The new forms used by the learners with no SA experience were part of the pedagogical intervention prior to the posttest (*perdóname* 'forgive me' [T] and *disculpa/e* 'forgive me' [T/V]). With regard to sociopragmatic variation, most learners used the form of respect *usted* (you-formal) and other markers of formality when apologizing to the professor (e.g. *discúlpeme, professor* 'Forgive me [V], professor'; *lo siento mucho, por favor* 'I'm very sorry, please'), and the *tú* form (you-informal) and other markers of affiliation when apologizing to the friend (*amigo/a* 'friend'). Finally, by the end of the semester, both groups improved on the use and repertoire of intensification. Some learners, however, didn't select any form of intensification in both groups on the posttest (22%–32%).

Examples (3) and (4) show metapragmatic awareness and reflection of the learners' choices from the pretest to the posttest.

(3) Apologizing in the FL classroom (no study abroad experience)

Apologizing for arriving late at professor's appointment

  a. Female learner #2

    Pretest: *Buenas tardes, profesor. **Lo siento <u>mucho</u>** por llegar tarde. Gracias por su paciencia.*
'Good afternoon, Professor. **I'm <u>very</u> sorry** for arriving late. Thank you for your [V] patience.'

    Posttest: ***Disculpe**, profesor. Gracias por su paciencia y su ayuda. Sólo tengo dos o tres preguntas.*
'**Pardon me** [V], Professor. Thank you for your patience and your [V] help. I only have two or three questions.'

    Reflection: My apology from my answer at the end of the semester is more appropriate than my apology from the beginning of the semester because 'I'm so sorry' (*lo siento mucho*) is too serious for this specific situation. In both answers, I thanked the professor for his patience. I used these thanks to show respect and to soften the error. Although my responses are formal, I think they follow the sociocultural norms because there is distance and a power imbalance between the professor and I.

  b. Female learner #3

    Pretest: *Hola profesor, **lo <u>mucho</u> siento** por llegar tarde a sus horas de oficina. Muchas gracias por
quedarse en oficina para hablar conmigo. muchas gracias y lo siento*

	'Hello, Professor. **I am** <u>very sorry</u> for arriving late to your office hours. Thank you so much for staying in the office to speak with me. Thank you and I'm sorry.'
Posttest:	*Hola profe,* **perdóname** *por estar tarde a nuestra reunión.* <u>*Mucho siento,*</u> *no tengo teléfono y no puedo llamar para informar.*
	'Hello Prof, **forgive me** (T) for being late to our meeting. <u>Sorry very</u>, I don't have a telephone and I can't call to inform.'
Reflection:	In the first recording, I make a word change oriented to the speaker (*lo siento*) to a word oriented toward the hearer (forgive me (T) [*perdóname*]). In the first recording, there is **transfer** because of this, but not in the second. In the second, I provide a justification to add respect and minimize the imposition. I don't know why I say sorry very (*mucho siento*).

c. Female learner #7

Pretest:	*Lo siento mucho por mi atendencia en clase y esta hora.*
	'I am very sorry about my attendance ((transfer from the English word)) in class and at this time.'
Posttest:	*Perdóname, mi profesor, no tengo mi teléfono celular para comunicar que estoy y tarde a su conferencia.*
	'**Forgive me, my professor,** I don't have my cell phone to communicate that I am late to your meeting.'
Reflection:	*Usé perdóname porque aprendí que es más común.*
	'I used "forgive me" because I learned that it is more common.'

Apologizing for damaging friend's car

d. Female learner #2

Pretest:	*Lo siento mucho por el daño a tu coche. Voy a pagar todos los gastos de arreglo.*
	'**I am** very **sorry** for the damage to your [T] car. I am going to pay all repair expenses.'
Posttest:	*Perdona, amigo. Puedo pagar por los daños.*
	'**Pardon**, friend. I can pay for the damages.'
Reflection:	My apology changes between the recordings at the beginning and the end of the semester. In my pretest response, I used 'I'm very sorry' (*lo siento mucho*) because I believe that damaging someone else's car is a very serious act. Nevertheless, I changed this apology to 'Pardon, friend' in my response on the posttest. I am not sure whether my response on the pretest justified the use of *lo siento* (I'm sorry), but I was cautious in my second response because I know that that apologies normally are less formal in Spanish than in English, using the form toward the hearer, 'perdona.'

e. Female learner #8
   Pretest: *Lo siento mucho por el daño a su carro (.) puedo pagar para tenerlo uh: reparado.*
   'I am <u>very</u> sorry for the damage to your [V] car (.) I can pay to have it uh: repaired.'
   Posttest: *Lo siento <u>mucho</u>, pero el carro se chocó con un poste y le hice daño - te puedo pagar lo que cuesta arreglarlo*
   'I am <u>very</u> sorry, but the car ran itself into a post and I caused damage to it - I can pay what it costs to repair it.'
   Reflection: In the two recordings, I used the form *lo siento*, which is reserved for more serious things and it is also oriented toward the speaker; a transfer from English

In the examples in (3), the learners with no SA experience changed from a speaker to a hearer perspective, using other forms beyond *lo siento* 'I'm sorry'. When apologizing to the professor, the learners in (3a-c) used *disculpe* (V) and *perdóname* (T) (I apologize). While in (3a) the learner used the appropriate formal form of address using the V form in both pre- and posttest (*disculpe* [V] 'pardon me'), in (3b-c), the learners used the informal form (*perdóname* 'forgive me' [T]) in the posttest. The responses in the posttest are more deferential than on the pretest, using markers of formality and respect (e.g. Professor, V form).

The metapragmatic reflections of these learners show awareness of their pragmatic development; they chose a deferential style and hearer-oriented apologies on the posttest. The learner in (3b) selected two forms on the posttest, *perdóname* and an ungrammatical form with an intensification *mucho siento* ('a lot sorry'). In her metapragmatic reflection, the learner reported that she was unaware of her influence from English to Spanish, but also an improvement in her use of formality and intensification. She also reported that she did not know why she selected the ungrammatical form *mucho siento* 'too much sorry'. When apologizing to the friend, the learner in (3d, same as in 3b), changed from a speaker-oriented (*lo siento* 'I'm sorry') to a hearer-oriented request (*perdona* 'forgive me') and the vocative *friend* 'amigo'. In (3e), no change was noted, using the same speaker-oriented form with intensification in both responses (*lo siento* 'I'm sorry'). During the metapragmatic reflection, the student noted that her responses reflect influence from English, or perhaps her preference for apologizing in L2 Spanish.

In the examples (4a-f), the learners with previous SA experience showed some evidence of change, but also demonstrated agency to use forms in Spanish that are the result of transfer from English.

(4) Apologizing in the FL classroom (Study abroad Experience)

Apologizing for arriving late at professor's appointment

a. Male learner #14
   Pretest: *Lo siento <u>mucho</u> profesor por llegar tarde. Sé que esto no me parece bien porque yo también he*

faltado a clases. ¿Hay alguna manera de compensarlo con trabajo extra?

'**I am** <u>very</u> **sorry**, professor, for arriving late. I know that this doesn't seem good to me because I have also missed classes. Is there a way to make up for this with extra work?'

Posttest: *Disculpas, profesor. Sé que llego tarde y es mi culpa, asumo la responsabilidad. He estado lidiando con muchas cosas en este momento y he estado luchando. Prometo hacerlo mejor en el futuro.*

'**Apologies**, professor. I know that I arrived late and it's my fault, I accept responsibility. I have been dealing with a lot of things at the moment and I have been struggling. I promise to do it better in the future.'

Reflection: In the second response, I tried to demonstrate more respect than in the second using common strategies from the speech act of apologies, such as accepting responsibility and giving reasons why I arrive late.

b. Female learner #21

Pretest: *Hola, Profe- Profesor. Lo siento para llegar tarde'*
'Hi, Prof -, Professor. **I am sorry** for arriving late.'

Posttest: *Perdón profesor, **discúlpame** por mi tardanza*
'**Pardon**, Professor, **excuse me** [V] for my lateness.'

Reflection: Yes, I use vocatives and a more appropriate form (pardon instead of I'm sorry).

c. Female earner #13

Pretest: *Hola profe, **discúlpame** por llegar tarde. No tengo un teléfono y no podría llamarle.*
'Hi prof, **excuse me** [V] for arriving late. I don't have a phone and I wouldn't be able to call you.'

Posttest: ***Lo siento** muchísimo por llegar tarde a la cita para hablar sobre la clase. Sé que no he asistido a muchas de las clases este semestre y quiero hablar consigo sobre mi asistencia y la clase. **Lo siento** muchísimo.*
'**I'm** <u>very</u> **sorry** for arriving late to the appointment to talk about the class. I know that I haven't attended many of the classes this semester and I want to talk with you about my attendance and the class. **I'm** <u>very</u> **sorry**.'

Reflection: There is a notable change between the two responses. In the first response I used 'excuse me' (*discúlpame*) and in the second one I used 'I'm sorry' (*lo siento*). I know that it's more common to use 'excuse me' (*discúlpame*), but if I remember correctly, the context is important here. The situation, in my opinion, demands more than just saying 'excuse me.' With this idea, my second response can represent my identity as an intercultural speaker. I have to use my pragmatic system from English and Spanish - which combine to form a pragmatic system in development (interlanguage). Also, my second response has more movements/elements of support than the first. There is a use of *usted* [V] of formality here.

Apologizing for damaging friend's car (Study abroad experience)

d. Male learner #14
Pretest: *Lamento <u>mucho</u> haber dañado tu auto. Te pagaré todos los daños y te compraré algo de cena para compensarlo. ¿Hay algo más que pueda hacer para compensarte?*
'**I'm <u>very</u> sorry** to have damaged your [T] car. I will pay you for all of the damage and I'll buy you [V] some dinner to make up for it. Is there something more than I can do to make it right?'
Posttest: *Oye amigo, **lo siento <u>mucho</u>**, pero rayé tu auto. Pagaré los daños y te lo llevaré a la tienda, **lo siento**. ¿Qué tal si te invito algo de almuerzo para compensarlo también?*
'Hey friend, **I'm <u>very</u> sorry**, but I scratched your [T] car. I will pay for the damages and I'll take it to the shop for you. **I'm sorry**. How about if I invite you to lunch to make up for it as well?'
Reflection: I apologize a lot in both responses, but the second response is more formal and with less social distance, since I still call him friend and I speak informally.

e. Female learner #18
Pretest: *Me siento horrible, **lo siento <u>mucho</u>**. No sé lo que pasó, pero yo choqué tu carro con otro carro. Yo puedo pagar, yo puedo hacer lo que quieras para resolver la situación, **lo siento otra vez**.*
'I feel horrible, **I'm <u>really</u> sorry**. I don't know what happened, but I crashed your [T] car into another car. I can pay, and I can do whatever you'd like to resolve the situation, **I'm sorry again**.'
Posttest: *Ay es mi culpa, no sé lo que pasó con tu carro, es que lo choqué con otro, pero es mi culpa, **lo siento <u>mucho</u>, perdóname**.*
'Oh, it's my fault, I don't know what happened with your car, it's that I ran into another car with yours, but it's my fault, **I'm <u>very</u> sorry, forgive me** [T].'
Reflection: In both instances, I accept the blame for the situation before apologizing, but in the first, I offer reparations for the offense. In both phrases, I use 'I'm sorry' (*lo siento*), and although it is not the typical grammatical form used to apologize, it could be that I felt that this was a more serious situation that required the use of 'I'm sorry' (*lo siento*), but it could also be that this is

just another example of negative pragmatic transfer that makes reference to the speaker.

f. Female learner #19
Pretest: *Amigo **lo siento muchísimo** es que hay daño al lado del coche porque he puesto el coche tan cerca de algo y pues por eso hay daño. **Lo siento muchísimo** y voy a pagar para arreglarlo.*
'Friend, **I'm very sorry**, the thing is that there's damage to the side of the car because I put the car so close to something and because of that there's damage. **I'm very sorry** and I'm going to pay to fix it.'

Posttest: ***Lo siento muchísimo** es que he destruido una parte del coche cuando…**lo siento muchísimo** es que he dañado su coche cuando…contra un poste. Voy a pagar y puedo pagar para todo que necesita ayuda."*
'**I'm very sorry**, the thing is that I have destroyed a part of the car when …**I'm very sorry**, the thing is that I have damaged your car when… against a post. I'm going to pay and I can pay for everything that needs help.'

Reflection: In both responses, I think I followed politeness in English. I know that I should apologize for the damage that I have made, but I think that my responses are still too formal for a friend. The apology does not follow the sociocultural norms. Because of this, I think that there is negative pragmatic transfer because I have used things that I would say in English. I think that this is a result of it being a very specific situation and I didn't know what was the best and most appropriate response.

When apologizing to the professor, the learners in (4a-c) used a hearer-perspective, changing from *lo siento* 'I'm sorry' to *disculpas / disculpe / discúlpame* 'forgive me [T/V]' and *perdón* 'sorry', and various markers of formality. The learner in (4b), used two different forms at the end of the semester (*perdón* and *discúlpame*), using the T form. The metapragmatic reflection showed the learner's awareness of contextual factors and formality when addressing the professor. In (4c), the learner changed in the opposite direction, from a hearer-perspective (*discúlpame* 'forgive me') to a speaker perspective (*lo siento muchísimo* 'I'm really sorry'). In the metapragmatic reflection, the learner noted that her responses reflected her identity as an intercultural speaker, showing her agency to choose the forms she feels are appropriate for her (Ishihara, 2019; Liddicoat & McConachy, 2019). She is also aware that her response in the posttest is more formal and with various forms of intensification than in the pretest. Additionally, sociopragmatic variation in the students' responses is also noted when apologizing to the friend for crashing the car. In (4d), there is a similar change in the opposite direction, using an expression of regret (*lamento mucho* 'I regret it a lot') to a speaker request (*lo siento* 'I'm sorry'). In his metapragmatic reflection, the student is aware of the contextual factors that are appropriate for an informal situation, exercising agency to choose his preference to apologize. In (4e), there is a change from a speaker request (*lo siento* 'I'm sorry' twice) to a hearer request with two different forms (*perdóname* 'forgive me [T]'). In the metapragmatic reflection, the student is aware that she used a speaker-oriented request that may not conform to the target culture, but she feels it is appropriate given the severity of the situation. Both apology forms represent an appropriate response given the severity of the situation. Finally, in (4f), the student apologized profusely in both the pre- and the posttest, using *lo siento muchísimo* 'I'm really sorry', accepting responsibility, and offering to repair the situation. In the metapragmatic reflection, the student reported that her responses followed the sociocultural norms of English, including pragmatic transfer of negative politeness (Brown & Levinson, 1987) and a high-level of formality that would not be appropriate for a friend. The student concluded that she did not know what the appropriate response was in this situation.

In sum, while most learners showed evidence of change and sociopragmatic awareness from the beginning to the end of the semester (hearer-requests, intensification, awareness of formality), they also demonstrated agency when making personal choices that did not conform to the target culture (e.g. *lo siento* 'I'm sorry'), but they thought would be appropriate in those situations to express their own intentions and personal choices (Ishihara, 2019; Liddicoat & McConachy, 2019). Overall, these learners developed metapragmatic awareness and reflection of appropriate apology forms, contextual factors, and sociopragmatic variation of levels of formality towards the end of the semester.

Refusing in the Foreign Language Classroom

Refusals belong to the category of commissives because they commit the refuser to not performing an action (Searle, 1977). According to Searle and Vanderveken (1985: 195), '[t]he negative counterparts to acceptances and consents are rejections and refusals. Just as one can accept offers and invitations, so each of these can be refused or rejected'. As a reactive speech act, a refusal functions as a response to an initiating act and is considered a speech act by which a speaker '[fails] to engage in an action proposed by the interlocutor' (Chen *et al.*, 1995: 121). In this section, I examine a refusal to a host mother's offer of food, including a two-stage speech act: an offer-response and an insistence-response. According to previous research, Spanish, like other languages with a collectivistic orientation (Shishavan, 2016; Su, 2020), shows an orientation towards ritual refusals, followed by an insistence that represents a sociocultural expectation (Félix-Brasdefer, 2008; García, 1992; Su, 2020). Following

Table 4.9 Refusing an offer of food from host mother: Stage 1 and stage 2

Refusal strategies	Study Abroad				No Study Abroad			
	Pretest		Posttest		Pretest		Posttest	
	Stage 1	Stage 2	Stage 1	Stage 2	Stage 1	Stage 2	Stage 1	Stage 2
Direct refusal (no; I can't)	63.6% (7)	27.2% (3)	36.3% (4)	9% (1)	72.7% (8)	45.4% (5)	72.7% (8)	27.2% (3)
Reason	36.3% (4)	9% (1)	63.6% (7)	9% (1)	27.2% (3)	0% (0)	27.2% (3)	9% (1)
Alternative	0% (0)	0% (0)	0% (0)	9% (1)	0% (0)	9% (1)	0% (0)	18.1% (2)
Accept	0% (0)	63.6% (7)	0% (0)	72.7% (8)	0% (0)	45.4% (5)	0% (0)	45.4% (5)
Total	100% (11)	100% (11)	100% (11)	100% (11)	100% (11)	100% (11)	100% (11)	100% (11)

Beebe et al. (1990), the linguistic expressions in a refusal sequence that were observed in both learner groups, included four strategies: a direct refusal (e.g. No; No, I can't), indirect strategies such as reasons or explanations, suggestions to make alternative plans, and acceptance of the offer. Some expressions that affirm solidarity or affiliation with the interlocutor were also evident in the data, such as expressions of gratitude, complimenting the food, or agreements used to preface a refusal (I'd love to, but…).

Table 4.9 shows the distribution of the preferred strategies used to refuse the host mother's offer of food in both groups and for each response, stage 1 (offer-response) and stage 2 (insistence-response) (11 participants for each situation). Unlike the learners without SA experience, the ones with previous SA experience reported that this situation had happened to them when living with their host families in regions of Spain and Latin America.

When refusing an offer of food from the host mother, the learners with previous SA experience were more indirect and accepted more than the students with no previous SA experience. During the pretest, stage 1, the SA abroad learners refused directly (63.6%) and indirectly with reasons (36.3%), while in Stage 2, only three refused directly, one indirectly, and seven accepted the offer (63.6%) after the insistence. During the posttest, seven refused indirectly with reasons and four directly (stage 1); while in stage 2, eight learners accepted the offer after the insistence, and three refused (one directly and two indirectly). In contrast, during the pretest, of the learners with no previous SA experience, eight learners (72.7%) refused directly and three indirectly with reasons; while in stage 2, five refused directly, one indirectly with an alternative, and five accepted the offer. During the posttest, eight refused directly and three indirectly with reasons (stage 1); while in stage 2, three refused directly, three indirectly, and five accepted the offer after the insistence. With regard to the use of mitigators to soften the refusal response or when accepting the offer after the insistence, eight learners in both groups used at least one mitigator in both the pretest and the posttest. However, most learners with previous SA experience, employed two or more mitigators (e.g. *creo que no podría comer un poquito más, pero quizás otro día como más* 'I believe I couldn't eat a little bit more, but maybe I'll eat more another day'; *vale, podría comer un poquito más* 'Alright, I could eat a little bit more').

The examples (5) and (6) show qualitative differences with regard to the pragmalinguistic strategies used and the metapragmatic reflection in both stages and in each learning group. When refusing an offer of food, all learners included an expression of gratitude and a compliment to the host mother's food, while most learners with no previous SA experience used an apology and frequent expressions of gratitude during the pretest (I'm sorry, I cannot eat more; I cannot eat more, thanks, sorry).

The metapragmatic reflections in the examples in (5) show an awareness of the notion of the insistence after an offer of food and an awareness of regional pragmatic differences in Spain and Latin America, as well as an awareness of cross-cultural differences when responding to an offer in English and Spanish. In (5a) the student used a firm refusal in Stage 1 (pretest and posttest), with compliments, reasons, and expressions of gratitude.

(5) Refusing an offer of food from host mother (SA exposure)

a. Female learner #13 (Studied in Spain [4 weeks] and Mexico [6 weeks])

Stage 1: Refusal to offer

Pretest: *Es que me encanta el guacamole, pero es que ahora yo **no puedo comer más**. No tengo suficiente espacio en mi estómago, pero la comida está muy muy muy rica hoy. ¡Muchas gracias!*
'The thing is that I love guacamole, but the thing is that right now **I cannot eat any more**. I don't have enough room in my stomach, but the food is very, very, very delicious today. Thank you!'

Posttest: *Gracias, este guacamole es riquísimo. Pero es que **no quiero comer más**. Toda la comida es riquísima gracias.*
'Thank you, this guacamole is delicious. But the thing is that **I don't want to eat any more**. All of the food is delicious, thank you.'

Reflection: In content and form, there isn't a big difference between the two responses. Both include the main speech act of a refusal with compliments as supporting movements. The first response is a bit longer with the description of being full – it represents a moment of using circumlocution (strategic competence). The second response is a little more direct with just saying 'I don't want to eat any more' (*no quiero comer más* 'I don't want to eat more').

Stage 2: Insistence-response

Pretest: *Pues puedo comer un poquito más, pero después de eso es que no tengo suficiente espacio en mi estomago – perdona.*
'**Well, I can eat a little more**, but after this the thing is that I don't have sufficient room in my stomach – I'm sorry.'

Posttest: *Okay, bueno, es que puedo comer un poco más.*
'Okay, fine, the thing is I can eat a little more.'

Reflection: In the two responses here, I accept the invitation for more food as the main head act. The first response has a reformulation of the refusal after the acceptance, but the second is just an acceptance. In the experience abroad (Spain and Mexico), everything was easier if I could eat a little more instead of simply refusing the food as is common in English.

During the metapragmatic reflection, the learner was aware of her longer response in the pretest, while in the posttest, she noted a short and direct response. In stage two, the learner accepted during the pre- and posttest, and she noted a longer response in the pretest. The student also reported that during her previous SA experience in Mexico and Spain, this situation was easier if she accepted after an insistence, unlike English where the refusal is expected. Her comments show pragmatic variation and an awareness of the cultural norm of the insistence in Mexico and Spain.

In the example in (5b), the learner refused during the pretest and the posttest (stage 1), and accepted in both responses during the posttest (insistence-response). During his metapragmatic reflections, the learner noted that while the insistence is the norm in the Hispanic culture, it is important for him to be direct and clear to end the insistence. His reflection also shows an awareness of the contextual factors as social distance with the host mother. The learner's reflection illustrates his agency to make his own decisions when speaking Spanish, such as choosing to be firm and direct to avoid further insistence.

b. Male learner #14 (Spain, 6 weeks)

Stage 1: Refusal to offer:

Pretest: *Muchas gracias, me encanta el guacamole, **pero no puedo comer más**. Gracias por ofrecerme, desearía poder comer más.*

110 The Pragmatics of Intercultural Communicative Competence

	'Thank you so much, I love guacamole, **but I can't eat any more**. Thank you for offering, I wish I were able to eat more.'
Posttest:	*Me encantó y fue lo mejor que he probado, ¡pero estoy lleno! **No podría comer** más aunque quisiera, no gracias.* 'I loved it and it was the best I have tried, but I am full! **I couldn't eat** more even if I wanted to, no thank you.'
Reflection:	In the second response, both my speech acts of praise and refusal are stronger. This is typical in Hispanic culture, especially because insistence is the most common in Spanish.

Stage 2: Insistence-response

Pretest:	*Muy bien, **una porción más**. No puedo resistirme, muchas gracias, pero después de esto no puedo comer más.* 'Very well, **one more serving**. I can't resist, thank you so much, but after this, I can't eat any more.'
Posttest:	*Está bien sólo **un poquito más**. ¡Entonces no más! ¡Estoy demasiado lleno!* 'That's fine, only **a little more**. And then no more! I am too full!'
Reflection:	My refusal is stronger at the end. While in the first I am more careful with my social distance, in the second I am more direct and clear, as a way of putting an end to the insistence.

In the example in (6), the learner with no previous SA experience refuses directly during both stages, including reasons, alternatives, and apologies.

(6) Refusing an offer of food (male learner # 6, no previous SA exposure)

(same learner as the role play interactions and metapragmatic reflections in examples 11–14)

Stage 1: Refusal to offer:

Pretest:	*Ah señora, muchas gracias por todo, es mi favorita, pero ahora mi estómago está lleno y **no puedo comer más**, pero es tan bueno.* 'Ah ma'am, thank you so much for everything, it's my favorite, but now my stomach is full and **I can't eat more**, but it's so good.'
Posttest:	*Uh, **no puedo** más discúlpame, pero la comida era muy bien. Me encanta.* 'Uh, **I can't** any more forgive me [T], but the food was very good. I love it.'
Reflection:	My refusal was more confident and more quick. I don't have to refuse in a similar situation in English.

Stage 2: Insistence-response

Pretest:	*Me gustaría, pero ahora **no puedo**, lo siento. Es posible más tarde en la noche pero no sé, **no puedo ahora**.*
	'I would like to, but **I can't** now, I'm sorry. Maybe later tonight, but I don't know, **I can't now**.'
Posttest:	***De verdad, yo no puedo** comer más, estoy lleno, pero la próxima vez puedo comer más para ti, lo siento.*
	'Truly, **I can't** eat more, I'm full, but next time I can eat more for you, I'm sorry.'
Reflection:	My refusal is more direct and stronger. Similar to what I said above.

In his metapragmatic reflections, the learner noted that his refusal was quick and confident in both pre- and posttest. He also mentioned that this situation hadn't happened to him in English. It seems that the information on the pedagogical intervention did not influence his response, but see examples (11–14), where the same learner completed the roleplay interactions for both the apology and refusal to offer food, changing his perception of the insistence during the roleplay posttest (after a visit to Europe after the class).

Metapragmatic Awareness and Reflection

After the pedagogical intervention, students were asked to reflect on their pretest and posttest responses and to comment on to what extent the posttest response reflects an improvement on their pragmatic and intercultural competence. In class, students were engaged in a discussion of the scope of these two competences and how they apply to their learning Spanish as a FL. Students were asked to reflect on the following:

- Do you think that your responses at the end of the semester reflect an improvement of your pragmatic and intercultural competence?;
- Did you observe any change in the way in which you realized the requests, apologies, and refusals according to the sociocultural norms of one of the regions of the Hispanic culture that you are familiar with? (a country you visited or a variety of Spanish with which you identify);
- How did the class help improve your pragmatic and intercultural competence and become more conscious when you interact in Spanish with others?

Following Meier (2015: 29), the learners' reflection and awareness can be explained in light of the four dimensions of intercultural communicative competence (see also McConachy & Spencer-Oatey, 2020: 409–410):

(a) Language-culture awareness of one's own and others' languages and cultures.
(b) Awareness of relevant contextual variables.
(c) Awareness of differences of others' perspectives and of varied meanings assigned to relevant contextual features.
(d) Awareness of interactional strategies.

The qualitative data were organized according to the following frequent trends observed in the data: pragmalinguistic awareness of speech act performance; sociopragmatic awareness (sociocultural and interactional norms); awareness of regional variation and agency; and awareness of improvement and lack of pragmatic competence.

In general, all learners (with and without exposure to previous study abroad) reported that the content and discussion of the pragmatic concepts helped them become aware when producing and reacting to requests, apologies, and refusals to offers at the end of the semester. Specifically, they expressed feeling more confident in expressing their own intentions, becoming conscious of sociocultural norms of the Hispanic culture (e.g. the notion of insistence after an offer; polite or impolite behavior), reflecting on their own identity, and being direct or indirect according to their own expectations, even if they do not conform to the target culture. Learner #13 stated:

> one thing that I noticed was that at the end of the semester, in general I sounded more confident in my answers. Also, I believe that my answers in the second part were much more direct and following my intentions, it makes sense that I spent my time studying abroad in Argentina.

Learners noted the effects of implicit (during the semester) and the explicit instruction during the pedagogical intervention at the end of the semester. Overall, all learners reported that the class made them more aware of pragmatic variation regarding ways of speaking in the regions of Spain and Latin America they had visited. Specifically, an awareness of producing pragmalinguistic requests such as *me da/me prestas/me pones* 'can you give/lend/put' instead of *puedo tener* 'can I have', as well as social variation of T/V forms, expressing respect and degrees of politeness in formal situations.

Pragmalinguistic awareness

Pragmalinguistic awareness refers to awareness of lexical and grammatical conventional expressions to express pragmatic intent to achieve specific illocutionary or interactional communicative functions, such as requests, apologies, or refusals (Leech, 2014; Thomas, 1983). Most learners with no previous SA experience and some with short SA experience mainly developed an awareness of and reflection for the use of pragmalinguistic forms and awareness of contextual factors. The students' reflections in (7) show the effect of classroom instruction during the semester (implicit instruction) and the pedagogical intervention at the end of the semester:

(7) Metapragmatic reflection of pragmalinguistic forms (collected in week 16)

a. Female learner #2 (no study abroad experience)

During this semester, my knowledge of pragmatics and different strategies for realizing speech acts (for example, apologies, refusals, and compliments) has increased considerably, and I think that this increase can be seen in the pragmatic competence in my responses in the communicative exercises. For example, one difference in two or three of my recordings is that when I started the semester, my requests followed the form of 'could (*podría*) or can (*puedo*) have/use/etc…' because 'Could (or can) I have/ use…' is the most common form in English. Nevertheless, we learned during the class (and at the end before the posttest) that the social norm in the majority of the Hispanic cultures is to be more direct and to orient requests toward the listener instead of the speaker. For example, my response from August (pretest) was 'Can I use a little of your shampoo, please?' (*¿Puedo usar un poco de tu champú, por favor?*), while my response on the posttest (December) was 'Can you lend me a little of your shampoo?' (*¿Me prestas un poco de tu champú?*). Because of the lessons in the class, the way in which I realize speech acts has changed.

b. Female learner #18 (three weeks in Dominican Republic)

I have improved a lot the convention that I use for a request - instead of using verbs oriented toward the speaker, I changed to using verbs oriented toward the listener, such as 'will you lend me' (*me prestas*) instead of 'can I have' (*puedo tener*). The use of 'I'm sorry' (*lo siento*) was very frequent in my first responses, but I changed to some conventions that are more typical in Hispanic culture. Before, I knew that these forms existed that show pragmalinguistic knowledge developed in class, but I didn't know the contexts in which they are used, that reflects a lack of sociopragmatic knowledge. This change in the way in which I realize speech acts made me realize that in my work with native speakers, I almost never hear the word 'I'm sorry' (*lo siento*).

As shown in the metapragmatic reflection, at the end of the semester (week 16), the learners in (7a–b) became aware of the pragmalinguistic and contextual variation regarding the forms used to perform the speech acts, making reference to the information received in class and instruction provided on the day of the pedagogical intervention. They were also aware of cross-cultural differences in use of these forms in English and Spanish, including an awareness of degrees of directness and a hearer perspective of apologies (e.g. from *lo siento* 'I'm sorry' to *discúlpame* 'forgive me') and requests (from *puedo tener* 'can I have' from to *me da/pone/prestas* 'can you give/put/lend'). The reflections of the student's pragmatic performance resulted in a successful change in the use of pragmalinguistic forms to perform speech acts in formal and informal situations at the end of the semester. The learner in (7b), who spent three weeks abroad, noted that she was not aware of these pragmalinguistic differences and the contextual differences when she studied in the Dominican Republic; her change was due to the instruction and metapragmatic awareness received at the end of the semester. Specifically, this example shows evidence of two dimensions of ICC: awareness of one's own and others' languages and cultures; and awareness of relevant contextual variables of the situation (Meier, 2015; see also, Chapter 1, Figure 1.2).

The metapragmatic reflections in (7c–d) show that students were conscious of the situation and the hearer's perspective when expressing requests and apologies in English and Spanish:

c. Female learner #1 (no study abroad experience)

    Now I am conscious to know use the words or phrases 'can I have' (*puedo tener*), or 'can I' (*puedo*), or 'I'm sorry' (*lo siento*) in specific situations, because they are not common in Hispanic culture, but they are in English.

d. Female learner #8 (no study abroad experience)

    I significantly changed the way in which I realize speech acts, especially apologies; whereas before I always used the form 'I'm sorry' (*lo siento*) after the semester, I learned to feel comfortable using new forms for apologizing that were more appropriate in a specific context.

Overall, the reflections show awareness of pragmalinguistic knowledge and variation of the contextual features of the situation, as well as feeling confident when producing apologies in formal and informal situations at the end of the semester. More importantly, these reflections illustrate the learner's agency in selecting the conventional forms that they feel most appropriate to use in specific situations.

Sociopragmatic awareness of cultural and interactional norms

Sociopragmatic awareness refers to the learner's ability to select appropriate pragmalinguistic forms or verbal cues according to the contextual factors of the situation, and how their perceptions vary according to sociocultural expectations in formal and informal situations (Culpeper, 2021; Leech, 2014). It concerns the ability to appropriately use T/V forms and vocatives, solidarity or deferential markers, and ability to use and comprehend direct and indirect styles of communication. It also includes the perception of polite or impolite behavior, awareness and negotiation of insistence to refusals of invitations or food, and an awareness of the contextual factors such as social distance, power and degree of imposition.

Learners with and without previous study abroad experience reported that they developed an awareness of sociocultural norms during the class and after the pedagogical intervention at the end of the semester. For example, in the metapragmatic reflection in (8a–b), the learner with no SA experience reported that she developed an awareness of the notion of insistence and polite behavior in both English and Spanish, and how these notions represent a sociocultural expectation across regions of Spanish.

(8) Sociopragmatic reflection of cultural norms

a. Female learner #8 (no study abroad experience)

Now I feel much more prepared to respond to insistences to a refusal and to be able to understand that in other cultures, the norm is to make an insistence, although in US culture it is generally perceived as rude.
In addition, I understand that one cannot always use a general rule of what is polite or impolite because it is totally dependent on sociocultural values and the certain context of a situation.

b. Female learner #19 (one semester in Spain)

When I was in Spain, there were some interactions that I had that I perceived as impolite, but after this class, I understand that it could be only a difference in sociocultural norms.

c. Female learner #21 (two months in Chile)

This class changed the way in which I realize speech acts according to social norms, especially because last summer I went to Chile and I heard these pragmatic concepts and conversations, but I didn't change my way.

d. Male learner #14 (6 weeks in Spain)

With this class I learned a lot about pragmatics and I really learned how to deconstruct a conversation and to analyze how it interacts and gives shape to the perceptions of the speaker. I also learned about the different cultural complexities of the various Hispanic cultures, and the behavior that is frowned upon and the behavior that is considered polite. With this I was able to improve the knowledge I had acquired when I traveled to Spain. I was definitely more direct in what I said. Also, when I needed to show respect, I changed my grammar and the structure of my speech acts to give more respect and distance, many times changing the sentence to the conditional form.

The metapragmatic reflections in (8b-d) show that even the learners with SA exposure became aware of cross-cultural differences and sociocultural norms after taking the class. Specifically, they became more aware of the interactional norms and the structure of speech act sequences. The learner in (8d) commented on his perception of impolite behavior and the expression of respect when he studied in Spain. This learner was also aware of the communicative functions of grammatical forms to express pragmatic intent, such as the conditional to convey respect and deference (Félix-Brasdefer & Cohen, 2012). Overall, these learners developed an awareness of two dimensions of ICC: awareness of cross-cultural differences with 'varied meanings assigned to relevant contextual features' and awareness of interactional features (Meier, 2015: 29).

Awareness of regional variation and agency

Awareness of pragmatic variation refers to the learners' ability to notice similarities and differences regarding the production and negotiation of speech acts across varieties of Spanish, and according to social factors such as region, age, and gender, among others (Félix-Brasdefer, 2021; Placencia, 2011). As shown in the reflections in (9), the learners with previous study abroad experience reported an awareness of regional pragmatic variation when they studied abroad in one or more regions in Spain and Latin America, reflected on the social norms, and expressed confidence in developing pragmatic competence as a result of the pragmatic instruction received in the FL classroom:

(9) Metapragmatic reflections of pragmatic regional variation

a. Female learner #12 (two months in Argentina)

I think that my responses to the second part reflect my pragmatic competence at the end of the semester and I see a lot of growth in my responses. I think pragmatic competence contributed to my confidence.
One thing I noticed was that in the second recording in general, I sounded more confident in my responses. I also think that my responses in the second part were much more direct (sometimes not similar to Spanish norms), which makes sense given my time abroad in Argentina. Really, I didn't realize how direct the Argentines were until I reflected on my conversations more in this class. I think that this class really has improved my pragmatic competence simply by making me conscious of what pragmatics is and how it influences language production.

b. Female learner #13 (six weeks in Mexico and four weeks in Spain)

I have noticed that I use various forms of communication from Mexico and Spain (I studied in Spain in the summer of 2022 and in Mexico in the summer of 2023). It is interesting how explicit instruction has increased my awareness of pragmatics and how it functions in Spanish in relation to what I know of English and what I have learned implicitly about Spanish. This pragmatics class has given me the tools to notice, process and think deeply about pragmatics and its role in my general competence in Spanish as an intercultural speaker.

The reflection in (9a) shows the learner's agency in choosing her own forms to express her intentions, not always conforming to the expectations of the Argentinean culture. She also noted that when she was in Argentina, she was not aware of the direct communication style that predominates there, and the class made her aware of that. The reflection in (9b) highlights awareness of variation in Mexico and Spain, and change in her ways of speaking as a result of both implicit (instruction during the semester) and explicit instruction at the end of the semester (pedagogical intervention).

Overall, the metapragmatic reflection helped in developing an awareness of cross-cultural differences and an awareness of sociopragmatic knowledge in both Spanish (Argentina, Mexico, Spain) and English. Both learners reported feeling confident by expressing their own intentions after the posttest, acknowledging the effects of pragmatic instruction. The learners demonstrated agency in choosing their own cultural norms to convey confidence, even if some of those norms do not conform to the target cultural expectations.

Awareness of improvement and lack of pragmatic competence

Although most learners reported a change in their speech act realization from the pre- to the posttest, others mentioned that even after the instruction, their performance still reflects influence from their L1. The learner in (10), who spent 2 weeks in Spain, mentioned that although she made an effort to use the information she learned during the posttest, her performance still reflects influence from English, specifically when apologizing and requesting with a hearer perspective.

(10) Awareness of improvement and lack of pragmatic competence

Female learner #16 (two weeks in Spain)

When it came to the questions about requests, I made a conscious effort so that my answer was oriented toward the listener instead of the speaker, because that was something we focused a lot on in class. Although I would like to think that I, as a student of Spanish, am applying what we have learned about speech acts, especially related to politeness and familiarity to my Spanish speaking, I still form sentences in the way an English speaker does. The form in which I apologize for arriving late continues to be very apologetic and uses the conditional like I would do if I were speaking English. There are select situations that we covered a lot in class and I made an effort to put those into practice while I completed this activity. In class we discussed the situation with a host mother that insists that you eat more food despite the fact that you could be full, so I tried to respond in the manner that is appropriate for native speakers of Spanish. This class changed me into a more aware student of Spanish, which will only benefit me as I continue learning Spanish.

Even after one semester and the pragmatic intervention at the end of the semester, learners with or without study abroad experience still need to practice speech acts in interaction with other learners or NSs of the target culture, as well as in different formal and informal situations. What is important in the reflection in (10) is the learner's awareness of her pragmatic competence, which reflects a change of her ability to perform and negotiate speech acts. Most importantly, while the learner in (10) acknowledged that the class made her aware of her pragmatic choices, she feels that her performance would improve with frequent practice. This learner decided to study abroad the following semester. Thus, change in the learner's ability to negotiate and comprehend speech acts is not always the result of attaining knowledge of the L2 pragmatic system; rather, change of the learner's pragmatic competence is better accounted for in the learner's understanding of the ways of speaking in the L1 and target cultures, including a reflection of the contextual variables and mindfulness of the interactional features of the situation (Liddicoat & McConachy, 2019; Meier, 2015).

Metapragmatic Reflection of Speech Acts in Interaction

In this section, I examine the negotiation of meaning in roleplay interaction with one learner at the beginning and end of the semester (apologizing to the professor for arriving late and refusing an offer of food), followed by metapragmatic reflection of the interaction. Learner #6 had no previous study abroad experience in a Spanish-speaking country. In the interaction in (11), at the beginning of semester, the learner apologizes to his professor for arriving late:

(11) Start of semester (week 1): Apologizing to the professor for arriving late

1 **Professor:** *Hola John, ¿Cómo estás?, ya son las ah.. cuatro y media, pensaba que ibas a llegar a las 4pm.*
'Hello John, how are you? [T] it's already four thirty, I thought you were going to get here at 4pm'

2 **Student:** → *Sí, hola Profe, **lo siento mucho**, ah, no tengo un buen excuso para ser tan tarde.*
'Yes, hello, Professor, **I'm really sorry**, ah, I don't have a good excuse to be late'

3 **Professor:** *Bueno, pues mira, puedo quedarme por 10 minutos, si tienes preguntas específicas.*
'Well, look, I can stay for about 10 min, if you [T] have specific questions.'

4 **Student:** *Okay, sí, yo sé que también no he estado en la clase mucho este semestre,*

5		*porque he tenido dificultades, pero espero que me pueda ayudar con las implicaturas*
6		*mucho porque no he estado en la clase.*
		'Okay, yes, I know also that I haven't attended class a lot this semester, because I've had difficulties, but I hope that you can help me with the implicatures a lot because I haven't been to class.'
7	**Professor:**	*Perfecto, ese tema es un poco complejo, vamos a repasarlo, y seguro que va a quedar*
8		*claro después de esta sesión, adelante, cuál es tu pregunta?.*
		'Perfect, that topic is a little complex, let's go over it, and I'm sure that it'll be clear after this session, go ahead, what is your question?'
9	**Student:**	*Por favor, puede explicarme la definición de la implicatura y dar ejemplos?*
		'Please, can you (V) explain the definition of implicature and give me examples?'
10	**Professor:**	((Professor explains))
11	**Student:** →	Okay, gracias, me ayuda mucho, y **lo siento otra vez**
		'OK, thanks, it helps a lot, and **I'm sorry again**'
12	**Professor:**	*No hay problema.*
		'No problem'

In line 2 the learner replies to the professor's initial response with an intensified apology (speaker perspective, *lo siento mucho* 'I'm really sorry'), and an acknowledgement of the offense. In lines 3–10 both the professor and the learner engaged in negotiation (clarification request-response), allowing the student to ask his question. The student ends the interaction with another apology (line 11, *lo siento otra vez* 'I'm sorry again'), similar to the first one in line 2, and the professor's closing of the interaction (lines 11–12).

The interaction in (12) shows a change in the student's perspective at the end of the semester, using two expressions of apology oriented towards the hearer (*perdóname* [T] 'forgive me'), an expression of forgiveness (line 3) and an apology (line 4). In both cases the learner uses the informal T form, and acknowledges responsibility for being late (line 3). After the successful negotiation (lines 5–9, clarification request-response), the learner and the professor ended the interaction successfully (lines 10–12).

(12) End of semester (week 18): Apologizing to the professor for arriving late

1	**Professor:**	*Hola John, te he estado esperando, habíamos quedado a las 4:00 p.m.*
		'Hi John, I have been waiting for you, we had agreed to meet at 4:00 p.m.'
2		*y ya son las 4:30 p.m.*
		and it's already 4:30 p.m.'

3	Student:	→	*Perdóname profesor, no podía contactar – mensajarte, lo sé, pero estoy tarde,*
			'Forgive me [T], Professor, I couldn't contact - message you, I know, but I'm late
4			*y no tengo una explicación bien. Sé que está muy ocupado, **discúlpame**.*
			and I don't have a good explanation. I know that you're very busy, forgive me [T].'
5	Professor:		*No hay ningún problema, quieres quedarte un rato? tengo media hora,*
			'It's no problem, do you [T] want to stay a while, I have half an hour,
6			*podemos hablar de las preguntas que tengas*
			we can talk about the questions that you have.'
7	Student:		*Sí, bueno, solo tengo una pregunta, pero - me gustaría mucho si me ayudas.*
			'Yes, well, I just have one question, but - I would like it very much if you [T] help me.'
8			*No entiendo la diferencia entre el significado conceptual y el procedimental.*
			'I don't understand the difference between conceptual meaning and procedural meaning'
9	Professor:		((explains)
10	Student:		*Gracias, ahora me queda claro, y mejor con los ejemplos.*
			'Thank you, now it's clear to me, and even better with the examples.'
11			*Gracias, tienes buena tarde.*
			'Thank you, have a good afternoon'
12	Professor:		*Nos vemos la próxima semana en clase.*
			'We'll see you next week in class.'

During the metapragmatic reflection, the learner commented that in the second interaction he was aware of different forms to express an apology, such as *perdón* 'sorry', *perdone/a, perdóne/ame; disculpa/e/, discúlpa/eme* 'forgive me/ I apologize'. He also noted that in the first interaction (11) he only used *lo siento* 'I'm sorry', similar to English, but now he realizes that this form is not very frequent in Spanish, and explained that he is now aware of other forms to express an apology. He used the formal address form 'professor' with the informal address form T in his apology forms (*perdóname, discúlpame* 'forgive me/ I apologize').

The same learner also improved on his ability to respond to a refusal of food and expressed his awareness of cultural norms in the Czech Republic, when he visited his girlfriend after the end of the semester. The interactions in (13) and (14) show the negotiation of a refusal of food from the host mother, at the beginning and end of the semester by learner #6.

At the beginning of the semester (Example 13), after a greeting sequence and the offer of food (lines 1–4), the student replies with a compliment and refuses directly and an explanation (line 5). After the host mother insists twice (lines 6 and 8), the student refuses with an expression of apology, and a direct refusal in both cases (lines 7 and 9).

(13) Refusing an offer of food (Pretest: beginning of semester; No study abroad experience) ((→Insistence))

1	Host mother:	*Hola John, cómo estás?*
		'Hi John, how are you [T]?'
2	Student:	*Muy bien, y tú?*
		'Fine, and you [T]?'
3	Host mother:	*Muy bien, recuerdo que me has comentado que de toda la comida que preparo,*
		'Very well, I remember that you have mentioned that of all of the food I prepare,
4		*te gusta mucho el guacamole, así que come un poco más. Lo preparé especialmente para ti.*
		you like guacamole a lot, so eat a little more. I prepared it especially for you [T].'
5	Student:	*Me encanta el guacamole, está muy rico, pero **no puedo comer más**, mi estómago está lleno.*
		'I love guacamole, it's very good, but **I can't eat more**, my stomach is full.'
6	Host mother: →	*Pero ni siquiera un poquito? ((rising intonation)), ándale, solo un poco más.*
		'But not even a little bit?, go on, only a little more.'
7	Student:	***Lo siento, no puedo,*** *yo sé que es muy delicioso, pero **no puedo** tener más espacio*
		'**I'm sorry, I can't**, I know it's very delicious, but **I can't** have more room.'
8	Host mother: →	*Bueno, qué pena, si tienes hambre y cambias de opinión, hay suficiente.*
		'Well, what a shame, if you're hungry and you change your mind, there's enough.'
9	Student:	*Okay, la próxima vez si haces lo mismo, voy a comer más, pero **hoy no, lo siento**.*
		'Okay, next time if you make the same, I'm going to eat more, but **not today, I'm sorry**.'
10	Host mother:	*De acuerdo, pues será la próxima ocasión.*
		'Okay, next time then.'

122 The Pragmatics of Intercultural Communicative Competence

The interaction in (13) shows influence from the English cultural norms, using a speaker's perspective *lo siento* 'I'm sorry' several times, and no willingness to change his response during the insistence-response phase.

The interaction in (14) was conducted five months later, after the semester ended in December. During the holiday break, the student reported that he spent the winter break with his girlfriend and her family in the Czech Republic, where he experienced this discursive practice, an offer of food, followed by one or more insistences in English from the host family. After the greeting sequence and the offer of food (lines 1–4), the student responded with an expression of gratitude, a compliment, a direct refusal, and a reason (line 5). After the insistence in line 6, the student accepted, adding affiliative expressions such as the diminutive *poquito* 'a little bit', a compliment, a reason, and an expression of gratitude (lines 7–8). The interaction ends successfully (lines 10–11).

(14) Refusing an offer of food (Posttest: week 20; four weeks the semester ended) ((→ Insistence))

1	Host mother:	*Hola John, cómo estás?*
		'Hi John, how are you?'
2	Student:	*Muy bien.*
		'Fine.'
3	Host mother:	*Qué bien, pues mira, como sabes, he preparado la comida que te gusta a ti,*
		'Great, listen, as you know, I have prepared the food that you like'
4		*sé que te encanta el guacamole, ¿por qué no comes un poco más?*
		'I know that you love guacamole, why don't you eat a little more?'
5	Student:	*Muchas gracias, es delicioso, **pero no puedo** comer ahora, estoy lleno.*
		'Thank you so much, it's delicious, but **I can't eat now**, I'm full.'
6	Host mother: →	*Solo un poco más, lo he preparado para ti, te va a encantar.*
		'Just a little more, I prepared it for you, you're gonna love it.'
7	Student:	*Bueno, puedo comer un poquitito más, porque he comido mucho,*
		'Well, I can eat a tiny bit more, because I've eaten a lot,'
8		*un poco está bien, está muy rico, gracias.* ((Acceptance))
		'a little bit is fine, it's very good, thank you.'
9	Host mother:	*Qué bien, come lo que gustes.*
		'Great, eat as much as you like.'

10	Student:	*Sí, gracias, un poco más y ya, porque lo he comido antes y me encanta.* 'Yes, thank you, a little more and that's all, because I have eaten before and I love it.'
11	Host mother:	*Aquí está, come lo que quieras.* 'Here it is, eat what you'd like.'

During the metapragmatic reflection, the student reported that this situation occurred to him in an intercultural encounter in English during his visit with his girlfriend's family in the Czech Republic: 'every time I refused an offer of food or drinks from the family or friends, they would insist two or more times'. He noted that what he learned in class about the insistence as a sociocultural expectation and a marker of affiliation, also applies to the Czech Republic. In the interaction in (14), he accepted after the insistence based on the pragmatic instruction received at the end of the semester and his experience abroad in the Czech Republic when the host mother issued or more insistence after refusing an offer of food.

Overall, change of the learner's pragmatic (apologizing and refusing offer) and intercultural competence (knowledge of one's and others' norms and expectations) changed due to the learner's metapragmatic instruction and his experience abroad, where he noted the social practice of the offer of food and insistence, which also applies to the Czech culture. His reflection of the contextual analysis of the roleplay situations demonstrates his pragmalinguistic (apology and refusal linguistic conventions) and sociopragmatic awareness (formality, social power and distance, notion of insistence). Metapragmatic reflection and analysis about the learner's own performance promotes both pragmatic and intercultural communicative learning (Liddicoat & McConachy, 2019; McConachy, 2018).

Conclusion

This chapter looked at language learning of pragmatic and intercultural knowledge among FL learners of Spanish who engaged in metapragmatic reflection of speech act production and contextual analysis during 16 weeks of classroom instruction. To examine awareness of pragmalinguistic and cultural norms, the data were triangulated using a production questionnaire, critical reflection of the learners' speech act production (requests, apologies, refusals), and open-ended roleplays, followed by a reflective analysis of the learner's negotiation of speech acts. As mentioned in Chapter 3 (and Figure 3.1), metapragmatic awareness is effective when learners are engaged in reflexivity of the language choices and cultural norms they use to communicate effectively and appropriately. Contextual analysis includes an understanding of the contextual variables (social distance, power, and degree of imposition) and cultural norms such as the notion of insistence, directness and indirectness, politeness and impoliteness, and awareness of regional pragmatic variation across varieties of Spanish. Change of the learners' production and understanding of their speech act performance and reflection was the result of pragmatic instruction and critical awareness at the end of the semester. It should be noted that the goal of pragmatic development was not to observe change in pragmatic knowledge; but rather, change over time regarding an understanding of the students' awareness of sociocultural expectations and their preference to express their own decisions about linguistic choices and identity.

Learners with and without previous experience abroad executed agency, making their own pragmalinguistic and sociopragmatic choices, which at times did not conform to the sociocultural expectations of the target culture (Ishihara, 2019; Liddicoat & McConachy, 2019; see also Chapters 5 and 6 this book). As mentioned in Liddicoat and McConachy (2019: 14), 'the development of metapragmatic awareness helps learners see language use as a form of social action and simultaneously helps them become attuned to the consequentiality of linguistic choices and the broad possibilities for the construction of their own agency' (see also McConachy, 2018). Finally, teachers should engage learners in metapragmatic reflection to develop their ethical commitment, to raise awareness of diversity and regional and social variation in intercultural interaction, and to promote critical awareness about making personal choices such as agreeing, disagreeing, or challenging sociocultural expectations.

The next chapter examines sociopragmatic knowledge through role-play interactions with reflection of speech act sequences in interaction among FL learners with previous study abroad experience.

5 Negotiating Refusals: Sociopragmatic Awareness and Insights from Study Abroad Learners

Introduction

This chapter examines the effects of study abroad contexts during the negotiation of refusal practices and the role of metapragmatic awareness on intercultural communicative competence. The study abroad context offers learners an opportunity to develop an awareness of sociocultural expectations, politeness practices, identity and social norms during intercultural interactions (McConachy & Fujino, 2022; Pérez-Vidal & Shively, 2019). The present chapter has two goals: (1) to examine how learners of Spanish as L2 (or more languages) negotiate a refusal to two eliciting acts with a native speaker (NS) of Spanish: declining a friend's invitation to attend a birthday party (-P, -D) and rejecting a professor's advice to take an additional class (+P, +D); and (2) to analyze the learners' perceptions and evaluations of (im)polite behavior, sociocultural expectations and social conventions in refusal practices. As mentioned in Chapter 4, a refusal functions as a response to an initiating act and is considered a speech act by which a speaker '[fails] to engage in an action proposed by the interlocutor' (Chen *et al.*, 1995: 121). Refusing in an L2 or Lx requires an understanding of pragmalinguistic and sociopragmatic knowledge of the target language, as well as knowledge of the sociocultural expectations. Sociopragmatic knowledge should not only include understanding of polite behavior, but also understandings of impoliteness, social distance and power between interlocutors. The degree of imposition as co-constructed in a particular situation, including an understanding of the social conventions and expected norms of interaction, is also encompassed by sociopragmatic knowledge. In particular, sociopragmatics requires 'an understanding of meanings arising from interactions between language (or other semiotic resources) and socio-cultural phenomena' (Culpeper,

2021: 27), as well as the emerging norms, reflexivity, and evaluations of (im)politeness in situated interaction.

This chapter begins with an overview of the speech act of refusal and the verbal and non-verbal strategies used during the negotiation of speech act sequences. I review three studies in L2 pragmatics in study abroad contexts. Then, I offer an overview of sociopragmatic awareness and the role of attention and reflexivity in social interaction. The next section reviews four studies that focus on different aspects of sociopragmatic knowledge as a result of intercultural interaction in study abroad contexts. The following section presents the results of an empirical study using two roleplay situations: declining a friend's invitation to a birthday party and rejecting the professor's advice. The second part includes an analysis of the learners' insights and metapragmatic awareness through the learners' verbalizations immediately after a roleplay task. The voices of the learners are analyzed in light of cognitive processes (attention to linguistic and non-verbal information), the planning and language of thought during the delivery of the refusal, and pragmatic knowledge regarding an awareness of the insistence after an invitation. Concepts from Chapter 3 (Figure 3.1) will be used to examine the negotiation of meaning in intercultural interaction (joint action), attention, emergent common ground and metapragmatic awareness.

Refusals

Refusals belong to the category of commissives because they commit the refuser to performing an action (Searle, 1977). Following Searle and Vanderveken (1985: 195), '[t]he negative counterparts to acceptances and consents are rejections and refusals. Just as one can accept offers and invitations, so each of these can be refused or rejected'. Based on previous research on refusals (Beebe *et al.*, 1990; Félix-Brasdefer, 2008), the verbal and non-verbal expressions employed in a refusal sequence may include direct and indirect strategies, and expressions to reinforce positive facework on the part of the speaker (adjuncts to refusals). For example, a direct refusal can be expressed with precision and clarity ('No'; 'No, I can't'; 'I can't'). If a refusal response is expressed indirectly, the degree of inference and the realization of politeness increases as the speaker must choose the appropriate form to soften the negative effects of a direct refusal. Indirect refusals may include the following strategies: negative ability with or without any use of internal modification ('<u>Unfortunately</u>, I don't <u>think</u> I'll be able to attend the party'), a reason or explanation ('I have plans'), an indefinite reply ('I don't know if I'll have time'), a suggestion ('Why don't we go out for dinner next week?'), a postponement ('I'd rather take this class next semester'), requests for clarification ('Did you say Saturday?') or additional information ('What time is the party?'), a promise to comply ('I'll try to be there, but I can't promise you anything'), partial repeats of previous utterance ('Monday?, I can't'), or an expression of regret or apology ('I'm really sorry; I apologize'). Finally, a refusal response is often accompanied by adjuncts to refusals which may preface or follow the main refusal response. Adjuncts to refusals include: a positive remark ('Congratulations on your promotion. I'm happy for you, but...'), an expression of willingness ('I'd love to, but...'), an expression of gratitude ('Thanks for the invitation, but...'), partial agreements used to preface a refusal ('Yes, I agree, but...'), or minimal vocalizations or discourse markers ('Oh, darn it, tomorrow I can't').

In addition to linguistic expressions, refusals can also be expressed through non-verbal forms such as gesture, eye gaze, and prosodic cues (e.g. low or final intonation, duration, slow or fast speech). The preference for these strategies depends on various factors such as the situational setting, the relationship with the interlocutor (+/– power; +/– distance), the eliciting act (an invitation, a request, a suggestion), and the gender and age of the participants, among other factors.

Beebe *et al.*'s (1990) taxonomy of refusal strategies has been mainly employed by researchers in interlanguage and cross-cultural pragmatics examining pragmalinguistic aspects of refusal strategies in situations of equal and unequal status using a non-interactive instrument, such as the Discourse Completion Test (DCT), while others focused on the negotiation of refusals across multiple turns, such as institutional discourse (Bardovi-Harlig & Hartford, 1993) or role plays (Félix-Brasdefer, 2018, 2019b). In sum, refusals are complex speech acts that require not only long sequences of negotiation and cooperative achievements, but also 'face-saving maneuvers to accommodate the noncompliant nature of the act' (Gass & Houck, 1999: 2). Direct or indirect refusals are also realized with various degrees of politeness to soften the negative impact of the rejection, such as the use of hedging, diminutives, politeness formulas (e.g. please), and indirectness to convey politeness. Negotiating refusal practices requires not only a knowledge of the pragmalinguistic expressions to express a refusal, but also additional knowledge of the following: sociopragmatic awareness of the sociocultural expectations, social conventions such as norms of politeness or impoliteness, an awareness of regional variation, and an understanding of the interactional practices of both the first and target cultures (see Chapter 3).

Refusing in study abroad contexts

I will review three studies that examined the negotiation of L2 refusals during or after study abroad using natural interactions or roleplay data between learners and NSs of the target culture.[1] Following Edmondson's (1981) and Labov and Fanshel's (1977) work on spoken discourse, Gass and Houck (1999) examined the negotiation process and the sequential organization of semantic formulas produced by three low-to-mid intermediate ESL learners across 24 roleplay interactions which included refusals to invitations, offers, requests and suggestions. Refusal interactions were analyzed in terms of episodes, which they defined as being 'bounded on one side by an eliciting act (in this case, a request) and on the other by either dialogue not directly related to the eliciting act or a recycling of the eliciting act. [It] must include some kind of response (...) directed at or relevant to the opening eliciting act' (1999: 57). A major contribution of Gass and Houck's study was the analysis of refusal strategies across episodes and how the sequencing of the strategies affected the learners' ability to negotiate a final resolution. In their study, interactions were examined as a series of episodes in which learners experimented with various responses as they learned from NS reactions and, as a result, the learners in their study revealed a sophisticated procedure for resolving their lack of pragmatic knowledge. The learners were 'actively searching for successful linguistic and attitudinal resources, and in doing so [revealed] a wide range of such resources applied in a reasonable problem-solving approach' (1999: 80). In the same US context, Bardovi-Harlig and Hartford (1993) examined the development of pragmatic competence among advanced learners of English during their study abroad at a US institution. The data included intercultural interactions between US advisors and 10 graduate students of English during the negotiation of a rejection of advice over the course of one semester. Natural interactions between the advisor and the students were taped twice, at the beginning and end of the semester. Results showed that the non-native speakers (NNSs) showed a change from a high frequency of rejections to advice and no suggestions (early in the semester) to more suggestions and fewer rejections, becoming more successful negotiators of the refusal towards the end of the semester. Also, the NNSs used fewer expressions to mitigate the rejection towards the end of the semester.

In the third study, Félix-Brasdefer (2004) used roleplay data to investigate the sequential organization of refusal strategies of 24 learners of Spanish (intermediate to mid-advanced) and to examine whether their ability to negotiate and mitigate a refusal was influenced by the length of residence (LoR) in various Latin American countries. Learners were asked to roleplay six refusal situations (three equal and three unequal statuses) with a NS of Spanish. Refusal sequences were examined throughout the interaction (head acts, pre-post refusals) and multiple conversational turns. Results showed more frequent attempts at negotiation and greater use of lexical and syntactic mitigation among learners who had spent more time in the target community while also showing a preference for solidarity and indirectness, which approximated native Spanish speaker norms. Fewer rejections to advice and more suggestions were also noted with learners who spent nine months or more studying abroad. The expressions to mitigate a refusal and the sequential patterns to appropriately refuse according to Spanish sociocultural norms improved as the duration of stay increased after nine months abroad. However, these findings need to be interpreted carefully, since previous research shows that LoR abroad is not the only factor influencing pragmatic development; proficiency level and intensity of interaction are determining factors that condition the learners' development of their pragmatic competence in study abroad contexts (Bardovi-Harlig & Bastos, 2011; Pérez-Vidal & Shively, 2019).

The aforementioned studies compared learner data with the data from NSs of English or Spanish to examine the interactional practices according to the sociocultural expectations of the target culture. These studies are representative of interlanguage pragmatics (Bardovi-Harlig, 1999; Kasper & Rose, 2002), where data from L2 learners are often contrasted with data from NSs of the target community, including evidence of negative pragmatic transfer from the native language to the L2.

While these three studies showcase how learners negotiate a refusal with a NSs of the target culture during intercultural interactions, little attention was given to the negotiation process, from beginning to end and to how both the intercultural speakers and the NSs negotiated the rejection to advice or requests/invitations. The issue of achieving intersubjectivity or mutual understanding of the refusal response to advice, request, or invitation needs to be analyzed in more detail from an intercultural pragmatics perspective (Kecskes, 2014, 2020; McConachy, 2018). Further, the concept of agency and pragmatic resistance during the negotiation of refusal was not analyzed in the aforementioned studies. **Learner agency** and **pragmatic resistance** refer to the learner's ability to choose their own way to respond, including adopting NS norms or choosing individual ways to interact which may or may not conform to the ideal NS speaker (Ishihara, 2019; McConachy, 2023). According to Ishihara and Porcellato (2022), resistance to NS norms is also agentive, as learners have multiple ways of responding to specific ways of using language in a myriad of intercultural interactions. More importantly, in addition to analyzing the negotiation of refusals, an analysis of the learners' sociopragmatic awareness and agency will shed light on the learners' intercultural understandings of refusal practices in intercultural interactions during study abroad.

Sociopragmatic Knowledge, Metapragmatic Awareness and Reflection

Sociopragmatic knowledge represents one dimension of pragmatic knowledge, which concerns the speaker's ability to use and understand communicative action according to the sociocultural expectations of the target culture. Some of these include behaviors, beliefs, social conventions and norms. Leech (1983, 2014) and Thomas (1983) offered a preliminary approach to our understanding of sociopragmatic knowledge, which Leech refers to the local conditions on language use (1983: 11) and 'the various scales of value that make a particular degree of politeness seem appropriate or normal in a given social setting' (2014: 14). Leech focused his discussion on what is considered appropriate expectations of polite behavior from a sociological perspective. Additionally, Thomas (1983: 99) elaborated on the concept of sociopragmatic failure that is the result of 'cross-culturally different perceptions of what constitutes appropriate linguistic behavior'. Further, in their framework of linguistic politeness, Brown and Levinson (1987) refer to three contextual factors that one needs to consider for the evaluation of polite behavior, specifically, during the production and perception of face-threatening acts: social power, social distance and degree of imposition. These authors take a cognitive and narrow view of assessing the interlocutor's intentions with regard to the appropriate expectations in the speaker's mind to address the interlocutor with the appropriate use of language and degrees of politeness. This perspective of sociopragmatics, which has been adopted in interlanguage pragmatics research (Kasper & Rose, 2002), takes a cognitive approach from the speaker's view with exclusive assessment of polite behavior, with little attention to the social and normative aspect of language use in interaction.

In their fresh conceptualization of sociopragmatics, Culpeper and Haugh (2021) adopted the broad approach to pragmatics (see Chapter 1, section 'Situating Pragmatics from a Social and Interactional Perspective') and included a perspective of sociopragmatics, which is conducive to metapragmatic awareness and reflection. According to these authors, a broader view of sociopragmatics should encompass three components, namely, the social, the interactional and the normative. Further, assessments of sociopragmatic knowledge should not only include understanding of polite behavior, but also understandings of impoliteness, social distance and power, and degree of imposition as co-constructed in a particular situation, including an understanding of the social conventions and expected norms of interaction. And after an incisive appraisal of previous studies, Culpeper (2021: 27) states that sociopragmatics:

> is positioned on the more social side of pragmatics, standing in contrast to the more linguistic side. It is focused on the construction and understanding of meanings arising from interactions between language (or other semiotic resources) and socio-cultural phenomena. It is centrally concerned with situated interaction, especially local, meso-level contexts (e.g. frames, activity types, genres). It often considers norms emerging in such contexts, how they are exploited by participants, and how they lead to evaluations on (in)appropriateness.

To further our understanding of sociopragmatic and metapragmatic awareness, Verschueren (2021) elaborated on the concepts of reflexivity and meta-awareness, which I adopt in my analysis (see also, Chapter 3 [Figure 3.1]). Metapragmatic awareness concerns 'whatever goes on in people's minds when language serves expressive and communicative purposes' (2021: 117). During social interaction, intercultural speakers not only pay attention to linguistic forms, but they also talk about language use, degrees of appropriate and inappropriate behavior, as well as social and linguistic variation. Following Verschueren, one way to develop metapragmatic awareness and reflexivity in language use is through the analysis of contextualization cues, that is, any linguistic or non-verbal form that speakers and listeners use to contextualize language (see Chapter 3). According to Auer (1992: 24), '*Contextualization cues* are, generally speaking, all the form-related means by which participants contextualize language. Given the general notion of a flexible and reflexive context… it is clear that any verbal and a great number of non-verbal (gestural, etc.) signantia can serve this purpose'. Following Gumperz (1982) and Auer (1992), contextualization cues encompass linguistic forms, gaze and gesture signals, prosodic cues (e.g. falling or rising intonation, slow or fast speed), or any form of code-switching with a communicative intention. Finally, Verschueren (2021: 129 [emphasis in the original]) describes the interactional role of metapragmatic awareness, and I focus on two functions: first, '*all* Indicators of metapragmatic awareness *guide listeners' or readers' interpretations.*' A second function is *commenting* through evaluations of appropriate or inappropriate behavior. For example, in this chapter (and in Chapter 6) I examine learners' evaluations of polite or impolite behavior.

Overall, this perspective of metapragmatic awareness engages the participants (speaker and hearer) in reflection and evaluation of the interaction, assessments of (in)appropriate behavior, and evaluative comments on variability of interactional and sociocultural expectations during the construction of social meaning. It also fosters an intercultural understanding of the social or normative aspects during the co-construction of meaning in social action.

In the next section, I review four studies that examine different aspects of sociopragmatic knowledge as a result of intercultural interaction. I will focus on studies that examine learners in study-abroad contexts that engage in intercultural interaction, followed by some kind of metapragmatic reflection, either during or after the study abroad experience.

Study Abroad as a Site for Social Interaction and Reflection

Study abroad programs are generally defined as pre-scheduled, educational, temporary stays where the target language is the official language (Isabelli-García *et al.*, 2018; Kinginger, 2011; Martinsen, 2008; Taguchi & Roever, 2017: Chapter 7). The issue of the context of learning has received significant attention in SLA research. Some of the topics that have been analyzed include learning context (e.g. naturalistic, foreign language, immersion, and study abroad), quality and quantity of the input, length of stay in the target culture, intensity of interaction, acculturation and socialization, the opportunities that learners have to practice in a second language (L2) inside and outside of the classroom, proficiency level, previous contact with the target culture, and the type of instruction (e.g. explicit, implicit) (Bardovi-Harlig & Bastos, 2011; Barron, 2003; Collentine, 2009; DuFon & Churchill, 2006; Freed, 1995; Kinginger, 2011, 2013; Llanes, 2021; López-Serrano, 2010; Pérez-Vidal & Shively,

2019; Taguchi, 2013). The context of learning represents '[o]ne of the most important variables that affects the nature and the extent to which learners acquire a second language' (Collentine, 2009: 218).

I review the contextual contributions of a learner's language development in study-abroad contexts with specific attention to the analysis of their progress in interactional and intercultural skills via interactions and reflection with other members of the study-abroad community. I focus on four studies that examined study-abroad as a site for situated pragmatic practice (Howard & Shively, 2022; Taguchi, 2016), including studies that examined social interaction and reflection, as a result of their study abroad experiences. The first two studies (Henery, 2015; Kinginger & Carnine, 2019) adopted sociocultural theory (Lantolf & Thorne, 2006), while the third (Shively, 2011) used language socialization to analyze the development of pragmatic learning, and the fourth examined the learners' intercultural understandings of politeness after they returned from study abroad (McConachy & Fujino, 2022). Kinginger and Carnine (2019) examined pragmatic development during mealtime interactions of two US students studying in France, and the impact that a host family had on their pragmatic development. Amelia lived for one semester with an 'empty nester' family of two, and Irene studied for a full academic year with a family of four. The data were collected during the mealtime interactions between the students and the family members, face-to-face interviews, and field notes. The results revealed instances of pragmatic and intercultural learning as a result of the two different conversational styles (high involvement for Irene [host parents and two siblings] and a less conventional style for Amelia with full attention from her two host parents. Thus, the study highlights the importance of intercultural understandings and communicative repertoires as a result of particular experiences of interaction, reflection and discussion of everyday topics with family members.

In the second study, Henery (2015) investigated the development of metapragmatic awareness of two students studying in France during one semester through pedagogical intervention: one student had access to concept-based pragmatic instruction (expert mediation), while the other followed a standard study abroad program. In their study, metapragmatic awareness is defined as 'the knowledge of the social meanings of variable second language forms, how they mark different aspects of social contexts or personal identities, and how they reference broader language ideologies' (van Compernolle & Kinginger, 2013: 284). Both participants were asked to compare and contrast language that was used in a text, and were asked to say why the speaker chose to say it. For both students, the metapragmatic data were collected at the beginning and end of the semester abroad: pre- and post-interview meetings, the language awareness interview and strategic interaction scenarios, and regular journal entries. For the participant that received instruction (the expert mediated participant), metapragmatic awareness focused on the journal discussions and the explanations that were provided to the student. The second student, who did not receive metapragmatic instruction, participated in these tasks (pre-post), but did not receive formal or project-related expert mediation, and did not meet with the expert mediator to discuss social aspects of the tasks completed. Results showed that while both participants improved various aspects of metapragmatic awareness over the semester, the student who engaged in discussion and reflection with the expert improved other aspects of metapragmatic awareness of the real everyday French, while the other participant, who did not participate in the expert mediation, relied on everyday evidence from interactions she observed during the semester abroad. This study highlights the importance of engaging students in metapragmatic discussions to raise awareness of linguistic and social aspects of language use.

In the third study, Shively (2011) used natural data from a variety of service encounters in Toledo, Spain, to examine the pragmatic development of requests for service among US learners over a semester (14 weeks). Unlike the previous studies, the learners in Shively's investigation received pedagogical intervention; specifically, explicit instruction in pragmatics with regard to requests in the context of service encounters. Results showed some changes in the opening sequences and a change from indirect (e.g. *puedo comprar…* 'can I buy…') to direct requests (e.g. elliptical requests such as *cien gramos de salchichón* '100 g of salami'), reflecting the pragmatic norm of NSs in this region of Spain. Finally, McConachy and Fujino (2022) examined the challenges and opportunities that four learners of Japanese encountered while studying in Japan for a period of 9–12 months. The authors focused on the learners' understanding of the cultural significance of politeness practices that they encountered during their study abroad experiences in Japan. The interview data were collected after the participants had been back in the United Kingdom for approximately 6–8 months. Results showed that the learners perceived differences in speech style when using informal or formal address forms (T/V) and various degrees of honorifics. The study revealed that the learners' intercultural awareness and agency to use new forms of communication improved their own preferences to engage with members of the target community.

Overall, these studies highlight the importance of engaging students in social interaction in various study abroad settings, including mealtime interactions with the host family, and as a result of intercultural interactions in everyday social practices. Henery (2015) and Shively (2011) showed that metapragmatic awareness can be improved through expert-meeting interactions to engage in discussions of the realization and negotiation of speech acts and the metapragmatic awareness of second-language variable forms through expert-mediation. McConachy and Fujino (2022) highlight the role of the learners' agency as a result of intercultural understandings of politeness practices. The notion of agency is crucial for the learners to reflect on the linguistic choices and the expected social conventions they intend to follow or not (see

Chapters 4 and 6). Thus, engaging learners in everyday interactions and guided self-reflection of linguistic and social practices fosters other dimensions of metapragmatic awareness.

This chapter has two goals: First, to examine how learners of Spanish as L2 or Lx negotiate a refusal to two eliciting acts with a NS of Spanish, declining a friend's invitation to attend a birthday party (-P, -D) and rejecting a professor's advice to take an additional class (+P, +D). Second, to analyze the learners' perceptions and evaluations of polite behavior, sociocultural expectations and social conventions in refusal practices as a result of intercultural interactions during the study abroad experience.

Negotiation of Refusal Practices and Metapragmatic Awareness

Participants

Participants included 16 learners of Spanish who studied abroad in various regions in Latin America (N = 9) and Spain (N = 7), 9 women and 7 men, during a period of 2 weeks to 6 months. All learners chose to live with a host family during the study abroad experience. Fifteen had English as L1, and one had Tamil as L1. Seven were multilingual speakers; of these, six had English as a first language, Spanish as L2, and the following languages as L3 or L4; German, Chinese, Quechua, Portuguese and Russian. One female learner had Tamil as a L1, English as L2, Spanish as a L3 and Quechua as L4. Another female learner had Urdu as L2, and Spanish as L3. Three learners had studied abroad in two different Spanish-speaking countries: Costa Rica and Mexico, Spain and Peru and Spain and the Dominican Republic. Two male learners, who studied in Chile and Spain respectively, had frequent contact with Mexican speakers at work in the US at a Mexican restaurant. All participants had Spanish as a major or minor and 14 were completing their last year of the university. Table 5.1 includes the distribution of the learner characteristics:

Overall, most learners had contact with different varieties of Spanish, other languages, and with speakers in formal and informal situations, such as host families, teachers, younger siblings within the host family, and frequent intercultural interactions in a variety of service encounters. Following the American Council of the Teaching of Foreign Languages (ACTFL) and guidelines for oral proficiency interview, all learners rated at a high-intermediate to low-advanced proficiency level. They were studying Spanish as a major or minor at a US midwestern university, and were completing their third- or fourth-year taking courses in Spanish literature or Linguistics.

Instruments

The data for the present investigation were collected using two types of elicitation instruments: (1) roleplays via Zoom; and (2) retrospective verbal reports.

Table 5.1 Learner characteristics in study abroad contexts

Participants	Gender	L1	L2	L3	L4	Countries abroad	Length of stay
1	Male	English	Spanish	Portuguese		Chile	6 weeks
2	Male	English	Spanish			Dominican Republic	6 weeks
3	Male	English	Spanish	Russian		Mexico; Costa Rica	4 weeks (Mexico); 2 weeks (Costa Rica)
4	Male	English	Spanish	Chinese		Peru	1 semester
5	Female	English	Spanish			Spain	1 semester
6	Female	English	Spanish			Panama	4 months
7	Female	Tamil	English	Spanish	Quechua	Ecuador	6 months
8	Female	English	Spanish			Costa Rica	3 months
9	Female	English	Spanish			Spain	7 weeks
10	Male	English	Spanish			Chile	7 weeks
11	Male	English	Spanish	Portuguese		Spain	7 weeks
12	Male	English	Spanish			Spain	7 weeks
13	Female	English	Spanish			Spain Dominican Republic	7 weeks (college) 1 year (elementary school)
14	Female	English	Spanish			Spain; Peru	2 months (Spain); 3 weeks (Peru)
15	Female	English	Spanish	Russian	German	Dominican Republic	3 weeks
16	Female	English	Urdu	Spanish		Spain	2 weeks

Roleplay interactions

A roleplay instrument was selected because of the following three advantages mentioned in Scarcella (1979: 1): (1) it allows the researcher to obtain complete conversational interactions, that is, data include openings and closings of conversations; (2) it allows the researcher to exert some degree of control over the conversation; and (3) it reflects a consciousness of the appropriateness of language use. Although roleplay data do not represent authentic data, the validity and reliability of this instrument has been widely acknowledged to examine different aspects of social interaction in formal and informal non-formal situations, including intercultural encounters (Félix-Brasdefer, 2018, 2019b; Kasper, 2000; Schneider, 2018; Schneider & Félix-Brasdefer, 2022). The roleplay set consisted of six

Table 5.2 Roleplay situations according to politeness systems

Politeness system	Initiating act	Power	Distance	Situation
Solidarity	Invitation to attend a birthday party	– P	– D	A friend declines his or her friend's birthday party
Hierarchical	Advice to take class	+ P	+ D	Student rejects the professor's advice to take an extra class

experimental refusal prompts and four distractor items. For the present study, two situations were selected to examine different speech styles, one formal and one informal. The description of the two refusal situations was based on two culturally-sensitive independent variables: power (P) and social distance (D). Based on these variables, the two refusal situations used in the present study were classified according to two politeness systems (Scollon & Scollon, 2001). They included a refusal to a friend's invitation (solidarity, –D, –P) and a rejection of a professor's advice to take a class (hierarchical, +D, +P). The two refusal situations classified according to the two politeness systems are shown in Table 5.2:

Interviews were conducted in Spanish between the learner and two NSs of Spanish, a student and a professor from the students' institution. For the informal situation (–P, –D), female learners interacted with a female NS of Mexican Spanish and the male learners with a male NS of Peninsular Spanish. For the formal situation (+P, +D), the learners interacted with a NS of Mexican Spanish, who was also the advisor of Spanish classes. For this roleplay situation, the advisor asked students to take a class in linguistics next semester with him, so this situation had consequences for the student's class schedule. Both situations are considered discourse practices since they are recurrent episodes in the students' L1 and L2 cultures; that is, all participants reported having experienced these situations in English (in the US) and Spanish with a NS of the target language while studying abroad. Roleplay data were recorded via Zoom and transcribed according to the transcription conventions of Jefferson (2004).

Verbal reports

Immediately after the roleplay interview, retrospective verbal reports were conducted by the researcher in order to examine the learners' metapragmatic perceptions on intercultural understanding (Cohen, 1998, 2012; Ericsson & Simon, 1993). Specifically, verbal probes requested information regarding understandings of polite and impolite behavior, the language of thought when planning and delivering the refusal, attention to linguistic and non-verbal forms during the interaction, sociocultural expectations of the insistence after declining an invitation, and cross-cultural similarities and differences regarding refusal practices at home and abroad. The aim was to elicit introspective information, engaging the students in reflection and metapragmatic awareness of intercultural understanding (McConachy, 2018; Verschueren, 2021).

Data analysis

The 32 roleplay interactions were conducted via Zoom and were examined according to a classification of refusal strategies (based on Beebe *et al.*, 1990), including direct and indirect refusals, and adjuncts to refusals. Direct refusals included a flat no or negative ability ('I can't'); indirect refusals comprised reasons, apologies, indefinite replies and suggestions. Adjuncts included expressions of positive remarks to strengthen the links of affiliation and solidarity with the interlocutor.

The interactions were transcribed following analytical tools of conversation analysis across sequences and multiple turns (Sacks *et al.*, 1974; Schegloff, 2007). These included greeting sequences, pre-sequences, invitation-refusal, insistence-refusal, suggestion-rejection and closing sequences.

The verbal report data were analyzed qualitatively following Saldaña's (2015, 2021) notation for transcribing and annotating qualitative data. By analyzing qualitative data,

> Our brains synthesize vast amounts of information into symbolic summary (codes); we make sense of the world by noticing repetition and formulating regularity through cognitive schemata and scripts (patterns); we cluster similar things together through comparison and contrast to formulate bins of stored knowledge (categories); and we imprint key learning from extended experiences by creating proverb-like narrative memories (themes).(Saldaña, 2015: 11)

The following codes were used to examine the verbal report data:

- attention to linguistic and non-verbal forms during the interaction;
- the language of thought when planning and delivering the refusal;
- intercultural understandings of impolite behavior;
- sociocultural expectations of insistence after declining an invitation.

Finally, to examine the pragmatic meaning of the main refusal response, the prosodic cues of the refusal response were analyzed regarding intonation (rising or falling tone; low-final intonation) and duration (fast or slow speech) (Brown & Prieto, 2021; Kang & Kermad, 2019).

The next section presents the results for the intercultural roleplay interactions when declining a friend's invitation to attend a birthday party (-P, -D) and when rejecting a professor's advice to take an extra class (+P, +D). Preferred actions refer to those responses that show a favorable, affiliative alignment with the previous social action, such as an acceptance to an invitation, or an agreement to a previous statement. In contrast, dispreferred responses do not align with the expected response when declining an invitation and when rejecting a professor's advice. Refusal responses are negotiated across multiple turns and, in some cultures, are generally delayed via hesitations, hedges, turn-prefaces (e.g. pre-refusals), repair initiation, insert expansions and non-verbal resources such as prosodic cues, eye gaze, head nods and body movement. The selection of and preference for the refusal responses depends on various factors such as the type of situation, the level of formality and social distance with the interlocutor, the context of learning of the learners (study abroad vs formal classroom), and the initiating act, such as an invitation or a suggestion, following the refusal, among others.

Refusing in Informal and Formal Intercultural Interactions

Situational differences were observed regarding the frequency, preference, and content of the strategies the learners used to decline a friend's invitation (-P, -D) and to reject a professor's advice to take an extra class (+P, +D). Figures 5.1 and 5.2 display the most frequent refusal responses when declining a friend's invitation in two stages: invitation-response (Figure 5.1) and insistence-response (Figure 5.2).

When declining a friend's invitation (Figure 5.1), learners frequently employed affiliative expressions (e.g. positive remarks, willingness to attend the event), apologies, reasons and explanations, and a firm refusal (e.g. 'I can't). Less frequent strategies included expressions of gratitude, indefinite replies, and suggestions to negotiate the refusal. After two or three insistences to attend the friend's party (Figure 5.2), learners introduced the refusal with an expression of positive remark, followed by either an indefinite reply, a suggestion, or a direct refusal. An insistence to an invitation represents a sociocultural expectation (Félix-Brasdefer, 2008, 2019a [chapter 7]; García 1992, 1993). Of the 16 learners, two ended up accepting the invitation in the second stage.

In contrast, when rejecting a professor's advice (+P, +D), the preference for refusing an invitation in stages 1 and 2 showed different refusal trajectories. Figures 5.3 and 5.4 display the most frequent refusal responses during the suggestion-response and insistence-response, respectively.

When refusing a professor's advice to take an extra class, students invested high levels of politeness and respect across the interaction. In the first stage (Figure 5.3), expressions of positive remarks and reasons/explanations predominated across the suggestion-refusal sequence, followed by other less frequent strategies such as expressions of gratitude, direct refusals, indefinite replies and suggestions. In this formal situation, the professor insisted only in cases where he thought the student provided a non-credible response, such as general plans (e.g. I can't take the class). In the second stage (Figure 5.4), learners politely rejected the professor's advice using positive politeness strategies (positive remarks) to introduce the refusal, followed by an indirect refusal such as indefinite replies (e.g. I'll think about it) and reasons or explanations.

Overall, in both situations, learners showed agency by choosing three strategies to successfully decline the friend's invitation to attend a birthday party and to reject the professor's advice to take an extra class: expressions

Negotiating Refusals: Sociopragmatic Awareness and Insights from Study Abroad Learners   139

gratitude   indefinitereply
apology
reason
positiveremark
suggestion
directrefusal
willingness

Figure 5.1 Refusal responses, stage 1: Invitation-response (-D, -P)

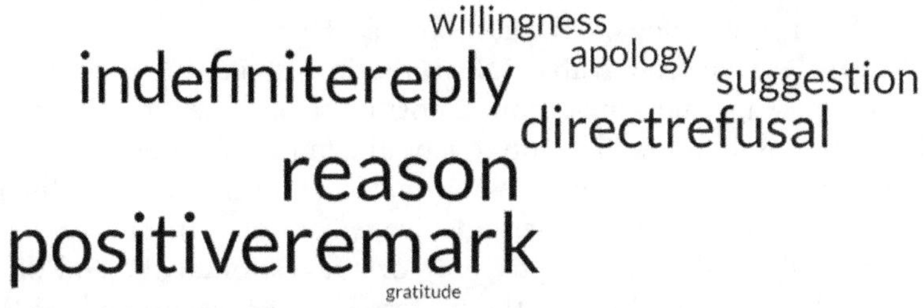

willingness
indefinitereply apology suggestion
directrefusal
reason
positiveremark
gratitude

Figure 5.2 Refusal responses, stage 2: Insistence-response (-D, -P)

willingness
gratitude
suggestion
positiveremark reason
indefinitereply
directrefusal

Figure 5.3 Refusal responses, stage 1: Suggestion-response (+D, +P)

indefinitereply
reason
positiveremark
gratitude willingness

Figure 5.4 Refusal responses, stage 2: Insistence-response (+D, +P)

of positive politeness to preface the request, a direct refusal (mainly in stage 1), and indirect strategies to achieve intersubjectivity: reasons, indefinite replies and suggestions. Choosing a suggestion to reject the professor's advice shows the learners' successful ability and agency to refuse politely and achieve intersubjectivity with the professor.

The selection and order of the expressions in the refusal response were conditioned by the situation. Table 5.3 shows the sequential distribution and order of the refusal strategies used in each situation for each learner and in each stage (N = 16; see Table 5.1). Stage 1 includes the refusal response of the 16 learners (one per learner). For stage 2, insistence-response, the NSs of Spanish issued 2–3 insistences to their friends and 1 or zero insistence from a professor. Thus, the responses when refusing a friend's invitation to a birthday party (stage 2) included 19 refusal sequences (-D, -P), and seven when refusing the professor's suggestion (+D, +P).

As can be seen from Table 5.3, in the first stage, the predominant order to refuse a friend's invitation is: positive remark, willingness, reason and direct refusal, followed by infrequent indefinite replies or suggestions. In contrast, when rejecting a professor's advice, higher levels of politeness were noted in the following order: positive remark or gratitude, reason (+ direct refusal), and an indefinite reply or suggestion at the end of the response. In the second stage, the preferred order was to end with an indefinite reply or suggestion (declining a friend's invitation) and a reason and indefinite reply (rejecting the professor's advice). Using an indefinite reply or a suggestion shows the learner's ability to negotiate a refusal response successfully. Most reasons given when rejecting a professor's advice included valid explanations such as having a full schedule, not taking an extra class to reduce anxiety, or reasons related to family or religion. Thus, the selection of an indefinite reply or a suggestion was used to express politeness, deference, and achieve intersubjectivity, as shown in previous studies where advanced learners of English chose successful suggestions to reject the advisor's advice (Bardovi-Harlig & Hartford, 1993).

In the next section, I will showcase the negotiation of the refusal across turns and across both stages, namely, refusal-response and insistence-response.

Negotiating a refusal to a friend's invitation to achieve intersubjectivity

This section presents two intercultural interactions to showcase the dynamics of refusing in informal and formal status situations: an invitation-refusal (-P, -D) and a suggestion-refusal (+P, +D). It presents an analysis of both linguistic and non-verbal resources (prosody, gesture) to better understand how the interlocutors negotiated meaning and arrived at a mutual understanding.

Table 5.3 Sequential distribution of refusal responses by situation

Situation	Learner #	Refusal response	Insistence-response
Declining Friend's Invitation	1	Positive remark, Indefinite reply	- Positive remark, Reason, Indefinite reply
	2	Positive remark, Willingness, Reason, Direct refusal	- Positive remark, Suggestion
	3	Positive remark, Willingness, Direct refusal, Reason	- Positive remark, Willingness, Reason, Direct refusal, Suggestion
	4	Positive remark, Willingness, Direct refusal, Reason	- Direct refusal, Reason, Direct refusal - Positive remark, Reason, Suggestion
	5	Apology, Reason, Apology, Suggestion	- Apology, Direct refusal, Reason, Apology, Positive remark
	6	Positive remark, Reason, Direct refusal	- Positive remark, Reason, Direct refusal
	7	Positive remark, Willingness, Reason, Direct refusal, Apology	- Positive remark, Reason, Direct refusal
	8	Apology, Positive remark, Willingness, Reason	- Positive remark, Willingness, Indefinite reply
	9	Positive remark, Willingness, Direct refusal, Reason	- Reason, Direct refusal - Indefinite reply, Reason
	10	Positive remark, Reason, Direct refusal, Gratitude	- Apology, Positive remark - Positive remark, Indefinite reply, Suggestion
	11	Positive remark, Willingness, Reason, Apology, Direct refusal	- Suggestion, Willingness, Indefinite reply
	12	Positive remark, Willingness, Reason, Direct refusal, Indefinite reply	- Positive remark, Willingness, Apology, Reason
	13	Positive remark, Direct refusal	
	14	Reason, Apology, Direct refusal, Apology	- Indefinite reply, Gratitude, Indefinite reply
	15	Positive remark, Reason, Indefinite reply	- Indefinite reply - Indefinite reply
	16	Reason	- Reason
Rejecting a Professor's Advice	1	Positive remark, Gratitude, Reason, Indefinite reply	- Positive remark, Indefinite reply - Positive remark, Willingness, Reason
	2	Positive remark, Willingness, Reason, Direct refusal	- Positive remark, Indefinite reply, Reason
	3	Gratitude, Reason, Suggestion	- Indefinite reply
	4	Gratitude, Reason	- Positive remark, Reason, Indefinite reply
	5	Gratitude, Positive remark, Reason	
	6	Positive remark, Reason, Willingness, Reason	- Indefinite reply, Reason - Positive remark, Gratitude
	7	Gratitude, Positive remark, Willingness, Reason, Direct refusal	
	8	Positive remark, Reason, Direct refusal	
	9	Reason, Direct refusal	
	10	Positive remark, Reason	
	11	Positive remark, Reason, Direct refusal, Suggestion	
	12	Positive remark, Indefinite reply, Positive remark	
	13	Positive remark, Reason	
	14	Gratitude, Indefinite reply	
	15	Positive Remark, Reason, Indefinite reply	
	16	Positive remark, Willingness, Reason	

In the first situation, the NS insisted three times, followed by responses by the learner. Example (1) shows an interaction between two friends when declining a friend's invitation, a NS from Spain and an American student (NS of English) learning Spanish as an L2. The learner spent 6 weeks in the Dominican Republic studying Spanish and was in his last year of college majoring in Spanish. (See transcription notations at the beginning of this book: ↑ shows final rising intonation; '-' short pause.)

(1) Declining a friend's invitation to a birthday party

OPENING
1 Luis: *Hombre, Paul, ¡Cuánto tiempo sin verte!*
 'Man, Paul, I haven't seen you in ages!'
2 Paul: *Sí, sí hace mucho - hace mucho, ¿qué es lo que – cómo estás?*
 'Yes, yes it's been a while–it's been a while. What is it – how are you?'
3 Luis: *Estoy bien todo:,*

INVITATION - RESPONSE
4 *uh, pero justamente este fin de semana es mi cumpleaños; cumplo 21.*
 'Everything's good; uh, but just this weekend is my birthday, I'm turning 21.'
5 Paul: *¡pues::, feliz cumple!*
 'Well–Happy Birthday!'
6 Luis: *Muchas gracias! Estoy celebrando en una fiesta, y he invitado a,*
7 *¿t'acuerdas de la, de la clase de lingüística que tomamos hace - un par de años?* ↑
8 *¿T'acuerdas de los compañeros, el grupito que teníamos?*
 'Thank you! I'm celebrating with a party, and I've invited, do you remember the linguistics class we took a few years ago?
 Do you remember the little group of friends we had?'
9 Paul: *¡Claro que sí! Que, que, que, ¡qué grupo que tenemos! sí*↑=
 'Of course! That, that, that–what a group we have! Yes↑'
10 Luis: =*sí, ¿verdad?*↑ *lo pasamos muy bien; pues, los he invitado,*
11 *para mi cumpleaños* <u>también</u>,
12 *y nada, y a ver si tú también quieres venir ir a la fiesta,*
13 *va a ser el viernes a las ocho de la noche.*   **INVITATION**
 'Yes, really? We had a really great time. Well, I've invited them for my birthday <u>as well</u>.
 And so, I wanted to see if you want to come to the party, it is going to be on Friday at 8 o'clock at night.'
14 Paul: *A las ocho, ¿de verdad?*↑   **pre-refusal**
 'At eight, that's right?'
15 Luis: *Sí*
 'Yes'
16 Paul: *Ay que no puedo*↑   **[REFUSAL 1]**
 'Oh I can't.'

INSISTENCE - RESPONSE

INSISTENCE 1
17 Luis: *¿'tás seguro?* ↑ [*¿Aunque sea un ratito* ↓ =
 'You're sure? Even if it's just for a little bit'
18 Paul: [*sí,*
19 *sí, imagino que, yo tengo que… - estoy ocupado toda la noche,*
20 *no puedo* ↓ - [*realmente.*   **[REFUSAL 2]**
 'Yes, I imagine that, I have to… I'm busy all night, I can't↓ really.'
21 Luis: [hmm

INSISTENCE 2

	22		¿Aunque sea a las- me ha- puedes venir a las ocho?
	23		'viernes de ocho, ocho y media o a las nueve,
	24		puedes venir, si quieres, con un amigo o algo,
	25		y nos tomamos una cerveza y luego ya, pero vas
	26		porque va hasta todo el grupo de lingüística juntos.

'Even if it's at – I have–can you come at eight?
On Friday at 8, 8:30 or at 9pm,
you can come, with a friend or something,
and we'll have a beer and that's all. But you're going
because the whole linguistics group will be together.'

	27	Paul:	Sí, sí, extraño a toda esa gente, toda esa – esa hombre –
	28		pero todavía tengo que mi trabajo- tengo que _trabajar_:
	29		y estoy muy ocupado esa noche,
	30		sí, imagino que no puedo ↓ [REFUSAL 3]
	31		_realmente_ yo quiero, pero – [pero no]=

'Yes, yes, I miss all of those people, all of that–but man, ahhh..
I still have to do my job, I have to work,
and I'm very busy that night.
Yes, I guess I can't
but I _really_ want to, but–but no.'

INSISTENCE 3

	32	Luis:	[y ¿ni siquiera] después de trabajar tampoco?↑

'Not even after finishing work either?'

	33	Paul:	((sound with mouth)) Sí, pues, estoy bien ocupado todos eses noches esas noches,
	34		muy.., y _realmente_ no puedo – [REFUSAL 4]

'Yes, well, I'm really busy all of these nights those nights,
really… and I _really_ can't.'

	35	Luis:	[bueno.

'Alright.'

	36	Paul:	[Discúlpame] lo siento, yo quiero

'Forgive me, I'm sorry– I want to.'

	37	Luis:→	No pasa nada, ya ves, podremos celebrar en otra ocasión la semana que viene,
	38		o dentro de un mes, o cuando sea, o después del semestre.

'It's fine, you see–we can celebrate another time next week,
or in a month, or whenever, or after this semester.'

	39	Paul:	¡Claro que sí! Claro que tenemos que reunir con todo esa gente↓

'Of course! Really, we have to meet up with all of those people↓'

	40	Luis:	¡Claro que sí, ¿verdad?↑ Uh, ya buscamos una oportunidad,
	41		pero bueno, me alegro mucho de verte, y nos vemos muy pronto.

'Yes, of course! Uh, we'll find a time soon–
but well, I'm really happy to see you, and we'll see each other very soon.'

	42	Paul:	Feliz cumpleaños
	43		[Ciao

'Happy birthday, bye!'

	44	Luis:	[Venga - gracias! ((risa))

'Bye–thanks!'

The roleplay interaction was realized across seven sequences, 21 turns, and two interventions (lines 21, 35). There were frequent instances of overlap ([ ]), expressing affiliation between the participants, non-verbal signs (eye-gaze, body movement), and prosodic cues (e.g. low and rising intonation, low and fast speech, intensity, etc.). Sequences included pre-sequences, insertions, post-expansions, repairs, and dispreferred responses. The interaction in (1) comprised seven sequences during the invitation-response sequence:

- Opening: Greeting sequence (lines 1–3)
- Invitation – response (lines 4–16) Refusal 1
- Insistence 1 – response (lines 17–21) Refusal 2
- Insistence 2 – response (lines 22–31) Refusal 3
- Insistence 3 – response (lines 32–36) Refusal 4
- Suggestion-response (lines 37–40) – Achieving intersubjectivity
- Closing sequence (lines 41–44)

The interaction was realized across sequences that comprise transactional and relational talk. The interlocutors open with transactional talk through a greeting sequence (lines 1–3). Luis begins the invitation in line 4 with a sequence across turns to preface the invitation (lines 4–11), followed by the invitation (lines 12–13). The refusal response is realized in two turns, with a pre-refusal eliciting a response and the refusal response with a nodding gesture (lines 14–16). The refusal response is direct, prefaced with an interpersonal marker to soften the dispreferred response (*Ay que no puedo* 'Oh, I can't'). This refusal is followed by three insistences as markers of affiliation, a sociocultural expectation in Hispanic cultures (Félix-Brasdefer, 2008, 2019b; García, 1992, 1999). The first insistence-response sequence is realized directly, followed by the intensifier *realmente*, 'really', accompanied by nodding and moving hands (lines 17–21). The refusal in the second insistence (Refusal 3) is more persuasive, followed by a mitigated direct refusal *imagino que no puedo* ('I guess I can't'), and an intensified direct refusal in the last line *realmente yo quiero, pero no* 'really, I want to, but no', accompanied by a nodding gesture (lines 22–31). The third insistence is brief, followed by another firm refusal, ending with an apology, *realmente no puedo, lo siento* ('really I can't, I'm sorry'), raising eyebrow and moving hand (lines 32–34). The successful apology was followed by a mutual understanding, achieving intersubjectivity (lines 37–40), followed by the closing sequence to reinforce the interpersonal relations between the interlocutors (lines 41–44).

In the last sequence, the learner negotiates meaning in the third space, a hybrid level where both speakers agree to disagree and propose mutual alternatives to end the interaction successfully, as shown below:

(2) Achieving intersubjectivity in intercultural interaction
 37 **Luis:**→ *No pasa nada - ya ves, podremos celebrar en otra ocasión la semana que viene,*
 38 *o dentro de un mes, o cuando sea, o después del semestre.*
  'It's fine - you see, we can celebrate another time next week, or in a month, or whenever, or after this semester.'
 39 **Paul:** *¡Claro que sí! Claro que tenemos que reunir con toda esa gente↓ ((left hand up))*
  'Of course! Really, we have to meet up with all of those people.'

Negotiating Refusals: Sociopragmatic Awareness and Insights from Study Abroad Learners 145

40 Luis: ¡Claro que sí, ¿verdad?↑ Uh, ya buscamos una oportunidad,
41   pero bueno, me alegro mucho de verte, y nos vemos muy pronto.
           'Yes, of course, right↑ Uh, we'll find a time soon
           anyway, I'm really happy to see you, and we'll see each other very soon.'
42 Paul: Feliz cumpleaños
43   [Ciao
           'Happy birthday, bye!'
44 Luis: [Venga - gracias! ((risa))
           'Bye–thanks!'

Prosodic analysis of the refusal response

In addition to the linguistic resources deployed to negotiate a dispreferred response and achieve mutual intersubjectivity, the learner in the interaction in (1) marked his refusal response with prosodic cues in each refusal response to express his firm and clear intentions. Prosodic resources, such as fundamental frequency (pitch), duration (slow/fast speed tempo), intensity (loudness), and vocal quality (whispery, breathy, creaky, harsh voices), represent interpersonal resources to achieve mutual understanding. Prosody in L2 discourse represents a marker of pragmatic competence, which involves the ability to perform and understand direct or indirect meaning to convey different degrees of uncertainty, affirmation, disbelief, disagreement, or annoyance.

The prosodic structure of the four refusal responses produced by the learner will be analyzed. Each refusal sequence has a different prosodic structure and conveys different aspects of the speaker's intention and attitude.

Figure 5.5 shows the spectrogram for the first refusal response *Ay que no puedo* 'Oh, I can't' (line 16, interaction 1), accompanied by a nodding gesture. The first refusal to the invitation is conveyed directly with the following internal downgraders: 'ay' to soften the direct refusal. The refusal is mitigated by means of prosodic downgraders to express hesitancy and politeness: slow speech rate and a final rising intonation which starts at 0.89 and rises to 110.3 Hertz (line 16 *Ay, que no puedo*↑ 'Oh, I can't'↑).

Figure 5.6 shows the second direct refusal introduced by *no puedo* 'I can't', followed by a brief pause and an intensifier (*realmente* 'really'), Example. The prosodic contour of the second direct refusal 'I can't' shows a rise-fall pitch contour (↗↘), which signals old information, that is, information that is known by both parties, and which is common ground, namely, the previous refusal response. Both interlocutors are aware of the refusal, with the learner conveying an impatient attitude through the rise-fall contour. (↗no puedo↘), followed by an emphatic intensifier realmente 'really'

The third refusal, in response to the second insistence, is produced in fast speech and final fall, *sí, imagino que no puedo* 'Yes, I guess I can't' (example 1, line 30). This response is accompanied by a nodding gesture, as another instance of an intensifier, as shown in Figure 5.7.

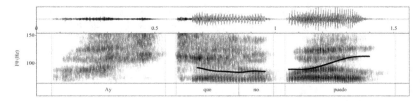

Figure 5.5 Prosodic analysis of the first refusal to invitation

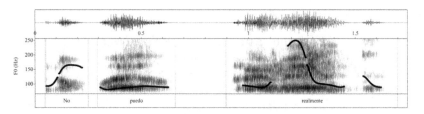

Figure 5.6 Prosodic analysis of the second refusal to insistence

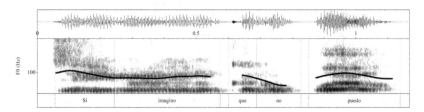

Figure 5.7 Prosodic analysis of the third refusal to insistence

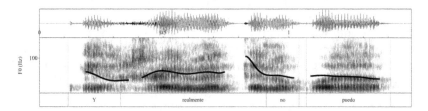

Figure 5.8 Prosodic analysis of the fourth refusal to insistence

The third refusal, in response to the second insistence, is produced in fast speech and final fall ↓, expressing the speaker's firm intention that he will not change his mind. This response is accompanied by a nodding gesture, as another instance of an intensifier.

Finally, the last refusal, in response to the third insistence, is shown in Figure 5.8 (interaction [1], line 34), *y realmente no puedo* 'and I really can't'.

In the last refusal, the speaker's flat intonation is firm and annoyed, signaling that he will not change his mind. The intensifier *realmente* 'really' receives high prominence, ending with a pause, followed by a direct refusal, ending in a low final intonation (*no puedo* 'I can't'). The refusal is mitigated with an apology (line 36), which overlaps with Luis's cue to end the insistence cycle, who suggests an alternative, expressing intersubjectivity (lines 37–40) and ending the interaction successfully (lines 41–44).

Negotiating a rejection to a professor's suggestion and achieving intersubjectivity

Unlike the refusal to a person of equal status, when refusing to a professor, the learners employed a wide range of linguistic and prosodic resources to express respect and politeness. The interactions were short and featured one insistence when it was appropriate for the professor to insist one time (10 out of 16 learners). All learners used the formal address form, *profesor* or short form (*profe*), epistemic verbs to soften the refusal (*creo que* 'I believe that'; *me parece* 'It seems to me'; *pienso* 'I think'; *siento* 'I feel') and adverbs to soften the refusal response (*quizás* 'maybe', *lamentablemente* 'regrettably', *desafortunadamente* 'unfortunately'). In (3) there are two refusal responses which show deferential resources to reject the professor's advice politely (mitigators in bold):

(3) Rejecting professor's advice to take an extra class

a. Male learner, 6 weeks studying in Chile (L1 English, L2 Spanish, L3 Portuguese)

Ah, bueno, me encantaría, Profesor, pero **creo** *que va a ser una↓ porque ya va a ser mi último año y no sé y va a ser ah un año bien ah lotado ((probably bassedin English "loaded")) ah y* **creo que no** *- no voy a poder, voy a poder hacer mi mejor, o hacer ah la clase de de de la forma que yo quiero. Entonces [***creo*** *que no...]=*
'Ah well, I would love to, Professor, but I think it's going to be a...because it's going to be my last year and I don't know and it's going to be a loaded year...and I think that I– **I'm not going to be able**–**not going** to be able to do my best, or to do the class the way that I want. So, **I don't think so**...'

b. Female learner #14, two months in Seville, Spain and three weeks in Peru

Sí, es, yo voy a **pensar** *en eso. Es - suena interesante.*
'Yes, I'm going to think about it. It's - it sounds interesting.'

In (3a) the student employed the following expressions to express a refusal politely: address form (*profesor*), the epistemic verb *creo* 'I believe' to mitigate the refusal (*creo que no puedo* 'I think that I'm not going to be able to'). The learner provided a valid reason to refuse successfully, having a full schedule in his last year of classes. In (3b), the student used an indefinite reply ('I'll think about it') to reject the professor's advice politely, achieving mutual understanding with the professor. An indefinite reply was the preferred option to reject the professor's advice by most of the learners.

The interaction in (4) takes place between learner #7 (six months in Ecuador studying Spanish and Quechua) (L1 Tamil, L2 English, L3 Spanish, L4 Quechua) and the professor, a NS of Mexican Spanish:

(4) Student rejects professor's advice to take extra class

1	Advisor:	*Hola, Mary, ¿Cómo estás?*
		'Hi, Mary. How are you doing?' [T]
2	Student:	*Hola, estoy muy bien. ¿Cómo está usted?*
		'Hello, I'm doing well. How are you?' [V]

{ Greetings }

3	Advisor:	*Muy bien,*
4		*veo que... como ya es el final del semestre ya estás planeando*
5		*tu lista de cursos para el próximo semestre y=*
		'Very good,
		I see that.. since it's already the end of the semester and you've planned
		your list of classes for next semester and =
6	Student:	*=Sí*
		'Yes'
7	Advisor:	*=y quería ese,... me imagino que ya estás casi completa,*
8		*pero como tomaste la clase de pragmática conmigo, y dado tu trabajo fenomenal,*
9		*durante todo el semestre, y además el trabajo final que completaste,*
10		*uh, ahí en esta clase nos enfocamos en temas generales de pragmática.*
11		*El curso que voy a mpartir el próximo semestre es sobre el tema de la implicatura*
12		*y el significado no convencional, y algo relacionado con el humor,*
13		*el sarcasmo y la ironía,*
14		*entonces quería sugerirte si te encantaría tomar mi curso el próximo semestre.*
		And I wanted... I guess that you're almost finished,
		but since you took the pragmatics class with me, and given your phenomenal work
		during the entire semester, and the final project you completed,
		uh, in this class we focus on general topics of pragmatics. The course I'm going to teach next semester is about implicature and
		unconventional meaning, and some of it related to humor, sarcasm, and irony,
		so I wanted to suggest to you that you'd love to take my course next semester.'
15	Student:	*Guau, pues me suena muy interesante, y me gustaría, pero es que*
16		*con todas las clases que ya tengo, voy a estar trabajando este semestre,*
17		*y me temo - que no, no podría hacerlo bien o tener tiempo para para añadir otra clase.*
		'Wow, well it sounds very interesting and I'd like it, but the thing is
		that with the classes I already have, I'm going to be working this semester,
		and I'm afraid - that I wouldn't, be able to do it well or have time to add another class.'

{ Suggestion-rejection }

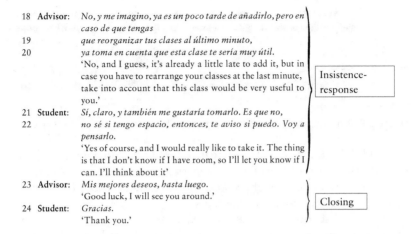

The suggestion-rejection interaction is realized across four main sequences: a greeting sequence (lines 1–3), suggestion-rejection sequence (lines 4–17), insistence-response (lines 18–22), and a closing sequence (lines 23–24). The opening sequence features an asymmetric politeness system, with the student using the deferential form (*usted*/you formal), while the professor uses the T form. The suggestion is realized in one turn, with an intervention from the student (line 6), and the rejection is accomplished in one turn (lines 15–17). The polite rejection includes a positive remark, a valid reason, and a mitigated refusal, using the conditional to express deference and respect to the professor. The insistence, in the form of an indirect suggestion, is followed by a polite and successful rejection (lines 18–22). The second rejection comprises a positive remark, a valid reason, and an indefinite reply to mitigate the negative effects of the rejection. Both the reason and the indefinite reply are effective resources to successfully end the interaction, achieve intersubjectivity, followed by the positive closing by both participants.

Prosodic analysis of the refusal response

The direct rejection was conveyed with various prosodic cues to mitigate the negative effects and to express politeness. Figure 5.9 shows the prosodic structure of the learner's rejection to the professor's advice (Example 4, line 17): *me temo: que no, no podría hacerlo bien* 'I'm afraid that I wouldn't, I wouldn't be able to do it well'.

The rejection is downgraded with the following prosodic cues: the epistemic verb is elongated, slow, and with a flat contour (*me temo::* 'I'm afraid::'), the first 'no' is longer than the second 'no' which is brief, and the rejection ends with a stressed syllable and low final intonation (*bien* 'good'). The negative ability realized with the conditional form (*no podría*

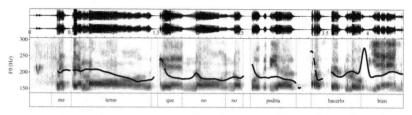

Figure 5.9 Prosodic analysis of rejection to a professor's suggestion to take class

'I wouldn't be able to') is also elongated, ending in a low final intonation. Overall, the prosodic features of elongation, slow speech, and a final low intonation are indicators of prosodic downgraders, whose function is to soften the negative impact of the refusal.

The next section examines the learner's metapragmatic awareness through the reflective verbal reports that were collected immediately after the roleplay task.

Insights on Refusal Practices and Sociopragmatic Knowledge

This section offers an analysis of the thought processes that the learners verbalized immediately after the roleplay task. As mentioned above, metapragmatic awareness concerns 'whatever goes on in people's minds when language serves expressive and communicative purposes' (Verschueren, 2021: 117). During the verbalization, the learners engaged in reflection and meta-pragmatic discussion of different aspects during the roleplay interaction, namely, cognition (attention to linguistic and non-verbal forms), politeness, and the perception of insistence, as a sociocultural expectation across varieties of Spanish. Table 5.4 includes the probes immediately after the completion of the roleplay interview.

Cognition

The retrospective verbal reports were conducted immediately after the roleplay task to obtain information that the learners attended to during the planning and execution of the refusal. An analysis of these reports indicated that learners had many things on their minds when refusing an invitation from a person of equal (declining a friend's birthday invitation) or higher status (rejecting a professor's suggestion to take an extra class). Each learner was asked the following question: What were you paying attention to when you refused in this situation? Some of the responses are included in Example (5):

(5) Attention to cognitive aspects during the negotiation of a refusal

a. Declining a friend's invitation to attend a birthday party (-D, -P)

'The truth is I was planning in Portuguese, then translating into Spanish' (Learner #1)
'I was thinking in Tamil; it's a more direct language' (Learner #7)

Negotiating Refusals: Sociopragmatic Awareness and Insights from Study Abroad Learners   151

Table 5.4 Verbal probes during the retrospective verbal interview

Cognition	What were you paying attention to when you refused in this situation?
Planning and language of thought	• When you responded to this situation, to what extent were you thinking in Spanish, English, or other languages? • Did you switch the language of thought at some point during your response?
Pragmatic knowledge	• Have you noticed any cultural differences with respect to the notion of insistence between the United States and the region you visited in Latin America or Spain? • After rejecting the suggestion from your professor, did you expect an insistence from him? If he did insist, how did it make you feel? Do you consider an insistence rude or acceptable in your culture?

'Thinking in English; planning my answer in Spanish' (Learner #9)
'Paying attention to grammar (*tú/usted*); Thinking in Spanish and Portuguese' (Learner #11)
'Focusing on grammar a lot' (Learner #6)

b. Rejecting Professor's advice to take extra class (+D, +P)

'Thinking in Chinese or Russian while I'm talking in Spanish' (Learner #2)
'I'm always learning about grammar in more formal situations' (Learner #6)
'I was paying attention to the tone of my words' (Learner #9)
'Think about it in English in my head and translating it to Spanish. Thinking particularly in my grammar, like, the conditional or the subjunctive such as "oh, I would like to go"' (Learner #13)
'Paying more attention to pronominal forms, *tú /usted*' (Learner #14)
'I wanted to show that I was thankful, but at the same time I had to say no' (Learner #13)

As shown in the verbalizations in (5), during the planning and execution of a refusal with a person of equal or higher status, most learners focused their attention on formal or informal pronominal forms (T/V), vocabulary, coming up with reasons to justify their refusals, and grammar such as the use of the conditional or the subjunctive to express politeness and respect. Regarding the selection of the language of thought, some participants were thinking in their L2, L3, or L4, while planning the refusal, such as thinking in Portuguese, Chinese, Russian, or English, then translating into Spanish. This planning predominated when rejecting the professor's advice probably because it took longer to plan, process and execute the refusal response with a formal tone. Focusing attention on pragmalinguistic aspects of the refusal predominated in the formal situation, which indicates a lack of control of the grammatical choices to express a pragmatic effect. Finally, thinking in English, or L3 or L4 to search for an appropriate excuse, was a frequent strategy reported by some learners in both situations. For instance, one learner reported that the reason came in English first, then he switched back to Spanish to continue the conversation: 'I was thinking of the excuse in English, the rest in Spanish.'

Awareness of politeness and cross-cultural differences

During the negotiation of a refusal, all learners were aware of situational differences related to politeness, respect, expressing directness and indirectness, and inter- and intra-lingual cultural differences. The verbalizations in (6a,b) show not only an awareness of situational variation and cross-cultural differences when addressing a person of equal or higher status, but also an understanding of politeness and respect that predominated in the formal situation to save face with the professor:

(6) Awareness of politeness and cross-cultural differences

a. Declining a friend's invitation to attend birthday party (-D, -P)

'I was thinking of how to maintain my relationship with my friend' (Learner #2)
'I was thinking that I didn't want to be impolite nor rude when saying no to my friend' (Learner #5)
'I used vocabulary like *tío* (dude/man) with students in Spain that I cannot use with professors in an academic setting' (Learner #11)

b. Rejecting professor's advice to take extra class (+D, +P)

'Focusing on saying something respectful' (Learner #6)
'I don't want to be impolite with my professor; I'm just more direct' (Learner #4)
'With the situation with the professor, I don't want to say, "No"; I want to say, "I think I'm unable, but I'm not sure"' (Learner #3)
'I want to maintain an amiable and professional relationship, open to the future. I don't want to offend the professor' (Learner #2)
'I tried to use *usted* (V) more, but sometimes I didn't do it' (Learner #8)
'With my professor I am paying for my education, there is distance and respect' (Learner #11)
'Based on my interactions with my Brazilian professors in my university, it's more common to use Professor [First Name], instead of "Professor [Surname]."' (Learner #1)
'There are aspects of politeness, but it seems to me that Mandarin Chinese is more direct.'
(Learner #4)
'With my Russian tutor, I only use the formal form, like *usted* ("you" formal). I imagine that if it were in Spanish, I'd use *tú* with my tutor' (Learner #3)
'In Tamil we place a lot of importance on respect, especially when talking with my grandparents and other older people. Likewise, with Quechua; it's very important to speak with respect' (Learner #7)
'I would say that there is a little more politeness in Chile than in the US' (Learner #10)
'In Costa Rica, for example, they would always say "Don" (Mister) or "el señor" (Sir)' (Learner #8)

'I was thinking about how to say 'no', but not offend the person. In Peru it is a little more formal with *usted* (V) like with older people, but in Seville, Spain they seem more direct and less tentative' (Learner #14)

As shown in the verbalizations in (6a), when learners declined the friend's invitation to attend the birthday party, they were aware of solidarity politeness, maintaining a good relationship and using the right tone with the friend so as not to sound rude. When rejecting the professor's advice (6b), all learners were aware and reflective of the impact of their response with the interlocutor. They showed a preference for deference politeness, namely, expressing indirectness, respect, and maintaining a good relationship with the professor. They were also aware of using the right address form (V) and nominal forms to show respect (e.g. professor), and elaborated excuses instead of a direct refusal. Some commented that they preferred to be uncertain by leaving the situation open by means of indirect replies (e.g. I'll think about it) or proposing suggestions. Others were aware of cross-cultural differences among their L1, L2, L3 or L4. For example, one learner who spoke four languages (L1 Tamil, L2 English, L3 Spanish, L4 Quechua) commented that Tamil is more direct, Quechua expresses more respect with elders, and English more indirect. Other learners made similar comments about Chinese and Russian, being more direct than English. Moreover, others mentioned that higher levels of indirectness represented a sociocultural expectation in varieties of Spanish such as in countries Chile, Peru and Costa Rica, than in Spain (Seville and Madrid).

These verbalizations show that learners were aware of various aspects of politeness, indirectness, respect, and regional variation when rejecting advice from a person of higher status.

Perception of insistence in the act of declining an invitation

Across regions in Latin American and Spain, and in other collectivistic cultures, an insistence after declining an invitation represents a sociocultural expectation. In various Spanish-speaking societies, after a refusal response, an insistence is considered polite and strengthens the links of affiliation between the interlocutors; conversely, not insisting is rude and gives the impression that the person issuing the invitation is insincere (Félix-Brasdefer, 2006a, 2008, 2019b; García, 1992, 1999; Placencia, 2016). In contrast, Americans generally consider an insistence as rude and imposing, and thus, they are often unexpected after a refusal. For the present analysis, immediately after the roleplay interview, learners were asked whether they were aware of cross-cultural differences in insisting after an invitation had been declined in the United States and in the target culture they had visited (Chile, Costa Rica, Ecuador, Guatemala, México, Perú, the Dominican Republic, and various regions in Spain).

With regard to the awareness of cross-cultural differences, all learners reported that after visiting a Spanish-speaking country (post-study abroad) they became aware of the differences with respect to the notion of insistence in Latin America and in Spain. The reflections in (7) show the learners' perceptions with respect to cross-cultural differences regarding the sociocultural expectation of an insistence.

(7) Perception of insistence among intercultural speakers

    a. 'Mexicans would probably not turn down a party. If they don't want to go, they'd say: "I'll go for a little bit". Americans are more direct: "Sorry, dude, I can't, I have something else to do, thanks."' (Learner #3, 4 weeks in Mexico)

    b. 'I understand that the insistence is very common in Spanish-speaking countries, so I expected it. I had a guide in Mexico because we were riding bikes, and he insisted we go to a certain restaurant to eat Yucatec food.' (Learner #3, 4 weeks in Mexico)

    c. 'A Dominican would probably arrive to the party really late, like the person knows they can't come for the whole time' (Learner #2, 6 weeks in the Dominican Republic)

    d. 'In Chile, the people don't understand when I say, "I can't" or "I don't want to;" they just think "Oh, but you'll do it, right?"' (Learner #1, 6 weeks in Chile)

    e. 'Insistence is more common in Peru than in the US when people are talking.' (Learner #14, 3 weeks in Peru)

    f. 'There were many insistences with the adults in Panama.' (Learner #6, 4 months in Panama)

    g. 'My Chilean mother just kept saying, "Oh, you'll do it" and I did end up doing it because she kept insisting.' (Learner #1, 6 weeks in Chile)

    h. 'My host mother in Peru kept insisting we try some more, but truly I was full, so I had to say, "No, I'm full, thank you so much. It's good, but I can't eat anymore."' (Learner #4, 1 semester in Peru)

    i. 'Yes, my host mother in Costa Rica would always offer me more food during breakfast and dinner. So, I would always accept it.' (Learner #8, 3 months in Costa Rica)

    j. 'With the United States, we can say "no" that is all, there isn't any insisting. Insisting is something that I have to think about, but I think that when my host family in Chile would keep saying "eat, eat, eat" after I had said no, I would say that the majority of the time I would say "yes, I'll eat more."' (Learner #10, 7 weeks in Chile)

    k. 'There was a lot of my host mom insisting that I eat more in Oviedo, Spain' (Learner #12, 7 weeks in Spain)

    l. 'Especially when I was in Oviedo (Spain), I couldn't ever refuse my host-mother.' (Learner #13, 7 weeks, Spain)

    m. 'Almost every night in Seville (Spain) would be something that they would offer me and many times I would have to refuse, but every time my host mother would ask are you sure or I can't give you anything. We were eating and the insistence was incredible. I think that one time she asked me if I wanted lucuma (Peruvian fruit) two or three times before I had to say no two or three times that I didn't want to eat anything else.' (Learner #14, 2 months in Seville and 3 weeks in Peru)

n. 'With my boss in my internship in Seville there were a few times when we were in the beginning of my practice and we were talking about my schedule and he asked to me stay after a certain time, but he had forgotten that we had discussed a different time for my schedule for that day.' (Learner #14, 2 months in Seville and 3 weeks in Peru)

o. 'If it's a situation in which I can't go, I don't want them to insist. My plans aren't going to change, so I don't want an insistence. I'm still in contact with some Dominican friends, and they always ask, "When are you coming back? When are you coming back? When are you coming back?" And I tell them I can't simply go, and they're like, "Why not? Why not?" "When are you coming back? When?"' (Learner #2, 6 weeks in Dominican Republic)

As shown in the examples in (7), all learners abroad were aware of situational variation and reported that an insistence when refusing a person of equal status was frequent across various regions in Latin America and Spain, including with friends or a person of distant relationship (7a–g). All learners were also aware that an insistence following an offer of food was a sociocultural expectation with the host family in Latin America and Spain (7h–m). In a situation of higher status, most learners abroad reported that probably one insistence (not a series of insistences) from a friend might be expected in English, but not from a boss. When asked whether they expected an insistence from a person of higher status such as a boss during the roleplay interaction (farewell), they reported that it was expected because it was a cultural expectation that they had noticed in the target culture (7n). A sociocultural awareness of cross-cultural differences between the US and the target cultures was evident among most learners (7j).

Finally, learners also showed agency when refusing in Spanish prioritizing their identity and their L1 values instead of adopting target-like sociocultural norms such as responding to the insistence according to the sociocultural expectations of the Spanish-speaking culture. One learner stated that even after one or more insistences, his plans were not going to change, and would not respond according to the expected norms he had observed in the Dominican Republic (7o). This shows an instance of the learner's agency and pragmatic resistance to the cultural norms of the target culture (Ishihara, 2019; McConachy, 2018), expressing a preference to conform to his L1 norms of the U.S. American culture.

Verbalizations as Insights for Raising Metapragmatic Awareness

All learners in the present study developed high levels of sociopragmatic awareness and reflection when refusing a person of equal or higher status as a result of their intercultural interactions during their study abroad in Latin America and Spain. Their perceptions and reflections were collected immediately after the roleplay task via Zoom, in which they interacted with two NSs of the target culture in two roleplay situations: declining a friend's invitation to attend a birthday party and rejecting a professor's advice to take an extra class. During the planning and execution of a refusal to an invitation, the learners focused their attention on various aspects of politeness, discourse, and grammar and vocabulary. Regarding their perception of politeness, during the roleplay interaction, most learners reported focusing their attention on planning a reason in order to refuse politely. Regarding discourse, some learners reported that they focused their attention on trying to compromise and offer alternatives. Alternatives and indefinite replies to rejections were often employed during the roleplay interactions to negotiate a refusal during the second stage of the conversation. The insistence–response sequence was expected by the majority of the learners, as reported in other regions in Latin America and Spain (Félix-Brasdefer, 2019a [Chapter 7]; García, 1992, 1999).

The fact that some learners focused their attention on different aspects of grammar and vocabulary caused interference in their communication. It seems that overuse of the monitor (Krashen, 1982) (i.e. being too concerned with correctness) diverted learners' attention from the message when rejecting the professor's advice where more attention was paid to politeness, respect and face management than when declining the friend's invitation. Learners were concerned with the correct uses of complex tenses and mood (e.g. past perfect, conditional, subjunctive), and even reported making grammatical corrections in their mind 'just to make sure' they were speaking correctly: 'when I speak, I consciously go through all the rules to make sure I am speaking correctly; when I make mistakes I am aware of the grammar and correct it at times' (Learner #3, 4 weeks in Mexico). Further, with respect to the use of pragmalinguistic forms when refusing an invitation, most learners in the current study tended to use a 'cover' strategy (Cohen, 2005) by using simplified constructions (e.g. the conditional instead of the subjunctive) to compensate for the inability to use more complex forms during the negotiation of a refusal.

Another conditioning factor for the planning and execution of a refusal to an invitation was the selection of the language of thought. The most common pattern was to start thinking in their L1 (i.e. planning the refusal) and then to translate it in their L2, L3 or L4. Thus, contrary to the popular belief that learners should not consult their L1 during speech-act production, the results of the current study are consistent with the ideas expressed by Cohen (1998: 5) in that consulting the native language is beneficial for the following strategic purposes: (1) to chunk material into semantic clusters; (2) to help learners keep their train of thought; (3) to create a network of associations; (4) to clarify grammatical roles; and (5) to make the input more familiar and consequently more user-friendly.

With regard to the learners' pragmatic knowledge, most learners reported that they expected an insistence from a friend, but less so from a professor. Although these learners were aware of the fact that an insistence after declining an invitation is the expected behavior in the Spanish-speaking society they visited, some exerted agency and expressed the refusal according to their L1 sociocultural expectations, being firm and not open to the negotiation of the insistence. According to Ishihara, pragmatic resistance refers to L2, L3, or Lx 'users' deliberate divergence from perceived pragmatic norms and language uses they are aware of and linguistically capable of producing' (2019: 5). For example, a successful rejection when declining a friend's invitation or when rejecting the professor's advice was often negotiated through alternatives and indefinite replies as in English, and as reported among advanced learners of English (Bardovi-Harlig & Hartford, 1993). In US English, while a direct refusal is expected ('sorry, I can't'), the predominant way to refuse indirectly and politely is with expressions that save both the speaker's face, such as *lo voy a pensar* 'I'll think about it' (rejecting professor's advice politely) or 'why don't we go out for lunch next week'.

Conclusion

This chapter examined the negotiation of refusal practices in intercultural (roleplay) interactions and the meta-cognitive processes and learner perceptions involved during the planning and execution of the speech act of refusals in formal and informal situations after they returned from studying abroad. During the negotiation of a refusal, learners used pragmalinguistic (direct and indirect refusals) and non-verbal cues (e.g. gesture, prosodic cues such as low or final intonation, low or fast speech) to negotiate a refusal across multiple turns. Retrospective verbal reports were found to be instrumental in gathering supplemental information about the learners' metapragmatic knowledge and perception of sociocultural information. It was demonstrated that by using verbal reports, one can gain insights into the strategies that learners used during the planning/execution of speech acts. In particular, verbal reports, if employed with care, can provide information with regard to cognition (linguistic and non-linguistic information attended to during the negotiation of a speech act), selection of the language of thought during the planning and execution of a speech act, and the perception of insistence after declining an invitation in a second or more languages. Finally, following previous work on agency and pragmatic resistance (Ishihara, 2019; Liddicoat & McConachy, 2019), some learners exerted agency through resistance to cultural norms of the target culture, such as refusing to conform to the several insistencies expected when refusing a friend's invitation in regions of the Spanish-speaking world.

While this chapter focused on politeness practices during the negotiation of a refusal, the next chapter looks at further instances of sociopragmatic awareness and reflexivity during the perception of impoliteness in intercultural interactions abroad.

Note

(1) Some of this information is taken from Félix-Brasdefer 2008 [Chapter 2] and adapted to intercultural contexts.

6 Intercultural Impoliteness, Reflexive Awareness, and Agency in Study Abroad Contexts

Introduction

This chapter analyzes cultural variability by examining intercultural speakers' evaluations of impolite behavior in intercultural encounters abroad. According to Culpeper (2011: 254) and Culpeper and Hardaker (2017), impoliteness is generally defined as negative evaluative attitudes towards specific social behaviors that take place in specific contexts. It is generally sustained by expectations, desires, and/or beliefs and how people's identities and behaviors are mediated in interaction. Impoliteness may occur when the speaker communicates offense *intentionally* or when the hearer perceives behavior as intentionally offensive, though it might be unintended by the speaker. In this chapter, I focus on the latter, how learners of different native languages studying abroad perceive social behaviors as offensive in a variety of intercultural encounters with host families, teachers, strangers, friends, and during the negotiation of a sales transaction. The corpus comprises 200 critical incidents which are narrations of impolite face-to-face interactions that the interlocutor experienced first-hand or that they perceived as offensive, taking into account the full communicative event: who said what, how, when, where, and to whom. Context is a key component of evaluations of impoliteness, and includes cognitive (prior knowledge), situational (setting), social (cultural expectations), co-textual (the language used in the interaction) and emerging context during the ongoing interaction (actual situational context). I focus on instrumental impoliteness (Beebe, 1995: 54), the use of impolite behavior 'to serve some instrumental goal' or Kasper's (1990) notion of 'strategic rudeness'. Two key elements of intercultural speakers are reflection and understanding of impoliteness and agency through mediation. In particular, agency 'is important in understanding the outcome of mediation, as success requires interlocutors to accept and ratify different understandings not simply receive them' (Liddicoat, 2022: 44).

This chapter contributes to our understanding of how learners of different languages studying abroad perceive offense, how they exert agency during the understanding of the perceived offense, how they mediate between cultures and conflicting interpretations and how they mediate their identity when interacting with others. I follow Chapter 3 (Figure 3.1) regarding metapragmatic awareness and variability of intercultural understanding. It begins with an overview of the theoretical considerations of (im)politeness, an assessment of agency and identity construction, and perceptions of offense in intercultural contexts. Then, I describe the method used to collect and analyze the data. An analysis of how impolite behavior is understood is presented and discussed with regard to Spencer-Oatey's model (2005, 2008a) of rapport management and Culpeper's (2011) revised model of violations of face (quality, social, identity) and sociality rights (equity and association).

Considerations of (Im)politeness in Intercultural Pragmatics

In this section, I examine theoretical considerations of impolite behavior among learners who engaged in social interactions abroad where perceived offense took place, followed by their reflection to and understanding of the perceived violations. As mentioned in Chapters 2 and 3 (Figure 3.1), metapragmatic awareness concerns the user's reflection and consciousness of what we do with language in social interaction, and the hearer's interpretation of evaluations of (im)polite behavior. This includes reflective awareness of the linguistic and non-verbal aspects during the negotiation of meaning according to the sociocultural expectations of the community of practice and the participants' previous and current context (i.e. identity, norms, previous assumptions). According to Holmes and Schnurr (2005: 122), attention to the contextual features of the situation is crucial for developing sociopragmatic awareness:

> Attention to context, to the community of practice in which people are participating..., awareness of the dynamic and negotiated nature of interaction, and of the constantly shifting assessments participants make when engaged in talk – these are all considerations which have improved the quality of the socio-pragmatic analysis of politeness.

As mentioned in Chapter 1, while pragmalinguistics refers to the conventional lexico-grammatical resources for the service of pragmatics (Leech, 1983, 2014), in this book I adopt a broad view of sociopragmatics that is situated in the social side of linguistics and that aligns with Culpeper's view of sociopragmatics and the construction and understandings of meanings (see also Chapter 5). Regarding the understanding of context, while I adopt a micro- (power, distance) and macro-perspective (ideologies, cultures, nationalities, gender, age), sociopragmatics is concerned with situated interaction, 'especially local, meso-level contexts (e.g. frames, genres, activity types, genres). It comprises norms emerging in such contexts, how they are exploited by participants, and how they lead to evaluations of (in)appropriateness' (Culpeper, 2021: 27). This broad understanding of sociopragmatics takes into account the participants' reflective awareness and attention to features of the social interaction and the target language variety, including the participants' intentions and evaluations of understandings of (im)politeness. As explained below, participants in intercultural encounters abroad pay attention to the linguistic and non-verbal aspects of the interaction of the community of practice where they interact, such as service encounters (service provider-service seeker, +P, +/-D), host family interactions (+P, +/-D), and interactions with strangers (-P, +D), friends (-P, -D) and teachers (+P, +/-D). Learners pay attention to the pragmalinguistic forms used, non-verbal cues (e.g. intonation, eye gaze, laughter), and the level of imposition, social distance and power between the participants.

An understanding of sociopragmatics determines how impolite behavior is defined. Research on politeness and impoliteness has been approached from different interdisciplinary perspectives, intercultural and cross-cultural contexts, and various methodological traditions (Culpeper, 2021; Culpeper *et al.*, 2017). According to Kádár and Haugh (2013), (im)politeness is a relational concept by which language users evaluate others' feelings and follow the social norms in situated contexts. It includes both the production of (im)polite language and the hearer's assessment of (im)polite behavior.

Research on politeness has witnessed three waves.[1] The first wave was motivated by traditional models such as speech-act theory (Austin, 1962; Searle, 1969, 1975) and Grice's (1975) cooperative principle and maxims, which mainly involve non-conventional implicature. The models of this wave generally favor a theoretical foundation on politeness, including traditional frameworks such as universals of linguistic politeness with a positive and negative politeness orientation (Brown & Levinson, 1987), rules of politeness and mitigation (Lakoff, 1973), and Leech's politeness maxims (Leech, 1983). This wave concerns issues related to second-order politeness, such as a focus on academic notions of politeness and etic considerations, including the cultural outsider and comparisons among cultures (i.e. second order politeness). These models have generally been criticized for their focus on the speaker, a limited focus on participants' understandings, a narrow view of (micro) context (power and distance), and an ethnocentric and universal approach to examine politeness practices in different languages. The main criticism of Brown and Levinson's model of politeness arises from the fact that it is individualistic and subscribes to the notion of a speaker as a rational agent 'who is, during the initial phase of generating an utterance at least, unconstrained by social considerations and thus free to choose egocentric, asocial and aggressive intentions' (Werkhofer, 2008: 156).

The second wave of politeness research emerged because of the discontent with universalistic views of polite behavior and an exclusive focus on the speaker. Research in the second wave was the result of the discursive-turn (Eelen, 2001) and researchers who consider the hearer's evaluation, rejecting a one-size-fits-all theory and seek out a more co-constructive and qualitative approach that reflects contextualized speaker/hearer interaction, and emphasizes localized communicative patterns and practices (Locher & Watts, 2005; Mills, 2003; Watts, 2003; Watts *et al.*, 1992). While this second wave pays attention to the discourse and the hearers' understandings (mainly assessments of native speakers), there is an exclusive focus on politic behavior, such as understandings of the layperson (first-order politeness), and little attention to the analyst.

The third wave of politeness emerged to encompass a more comprehensive analysis of both polite and impolite behavior in socially-situated contexts, embracing both first-order (politeness1) and second-order politeness (politeness2), and taking into account both the speaker's production and the hearer's interpretation of polite and impolite behavior in formal and informal contexts (Garcés-Conejos Blitvich, 2021; House & Kádár, 2021; Kádár & Haugh, 2013). Third-wave approaches are difficult to identify since they are broad in theoretical, methodological and analytical scope. They generally combine notions of first- and second-order politeness, combining participant understandings with observer theorizing, common-sense versus academic concepts of polite and impolite behavior, and emic and etic approaches (Culpeper & Haugh, 2021). Third-wave approaches can be seen in the work of Culpeper (2011) who examines lay perceptions of impoliteness within a theoretical framework of strategies; Kádár and Haugh's (2013) interactional model of im/politeness and participants understandings of polite and impolite behavior; and, Spencer-Oatey's (2005) model of interpersonal and relational model. The third-wave of politeness research is adopted in cross-cultural (House & Kádár, 2021: 61) and intercultural pragmatics (Kecskes, 2019, 2020), which encompass a flexible methodology to examine speech-act data in contrastive and intercultural contexts, including natural and elicited data.

In this chapter, I adopt general notions of the third wave to examine the negotiation of meaning and participants' understandings of impolite behavior. I adopt Culpeper's (2011) concepts of impoliteness and Spencer-Oatey's (2005, 2008a) model of rapport management to examine the co-construction and negotiation of understandings of impoliteness in intercultural service encounters. Culpeper (2011: 254) defines impoliteness as:

a negative attitude towards specific behaviours occurring in specific contexts. It is sustained by expectations, desires and/or beliefs about social organization, including, in particular, how one person's or group's identities are mediated by others in interaction.

Based on Kecskes (2014, 2019), a conceptualization of intercultural impoliteness should include a broad notion of context, including cognitive (prior understandings and assumptions) and the emergent (actual situational) context which develops during the co-construction of meaning with both speaker's production and the observer's evaluations of impolite behavior. In the next section, I review key concepts of the co-construction of the intercultural speakers' identity and agency, as well as their socially mediated capacity to act and negotiate meaning in study abroad contexts.

Identity, Mediation and Agency in Study Abroad Contexts

Identity is a complex and multi-layered construct that is negotiated in the course of social interaction, via face-to-face, written, non-verbal, or technology-mediated discourse. Knowledge of impoliteness is often associated with participants' sociocultural identity and agency to make their own linguistic, non-verbal, and sociocultural decisions, or lack thereof. Identity refers to our desire to be connected or affiliated with others, our language use (e.g. code choice, register, genre, accent) or ethnic identification of our L1 in relation to others, and the 'emotional ties' one experiences with the other group in relation to our L1 (Duff, 2012). Others define identity as 'how a person understands his or her relationship to the world, how that relationship is constructed across time and space, and how the person understands possibilities for the future' (Norton, 2000: 5), while Block frames the notion of identity as 'socially constructed, self-conscious, ongoing narratives that individuals perform, interpret and project in dress, bodily movements, actions and language' (2007: 27). Additionally, Pavlenko and Blackledge (2004: 35) describe identity as 'a dynamic and shifting nexus of multiple subject positions, or identity options, such as mother, accountant, heterosexual, or Latina'. In intercultural contexts with multilingual individuals, identities are co-constructed and mediated during the negotiation of meaning. These new identities are negotiated and assessed in the third space, interculturality, where intercultural speakers co-construct their identities and create new meanings (Kramsch, 2009a).

Agency refers to the intercultural speaker's capacity to negotiate, mediate, create, choose linguistic forms and non-verbal behaviors, and assume new identities. Agency has been defined from different perspectives: it refers to 'the socioculturally [or socially] mediated capacity to act [or not to act] ... action is socioculturally mediated both in its production and its interpretation' (Ahearn, 2001: 112), a 'dynamically negotiated capacity to act, assume new identities, or resist certain positionings actively or purposely' (Ishihara, 2019: 162; also Duff, 2012; Rogers & Wetzel, 2013). From a second language learning perspective, learners exert agency to select a language variety to learn (i.e. choosing their target model), including a high-status standard variety representing distance and respect or a non-standard variety, spoken by peers or parents, to express solidarity; gender and ethnicity also influence the learner's identity when socializing in an L2 (Zuengler, 1989). As agents, learners can decide which variety of English (e.g. US, Canadian, British) or Spanish (e.g. Mexican, Colombian, Argentinean, or Peninsular) they choose when selecting linguistic and non-verbal aspects of language use, embodying new sociocultural values and discursive norms, as well as adopting novel sociocultural identities and expectations associated with the target culture of their preference.

Agency has also been associated with the individual's capacity and preference to 'actively resist certain behaviors, practices, or positionings, sometimes leading to oppositional stances and behaviors leading to other identities, such as rebellious, diffident [students]' (Duff, 2012: 417). It also involves how 'an agent exercises their agency not only in conforming to perceived constraints governed by the sociocultural environment, but in performing any action (including resistance)' (Mitchell & Haugh, 2015: 211). Learners also have the right to resist choosing certain words to index a particular social function or adopt local practices that go against their L2 sociocultural values and identities. Ishihara (2019: 165) proposed the term *pragmatic resistance* to refer to the 'L2 users' *deliberate* divergence from perceived pragmatic norms and language uses they are aware of and linguistically capable of producing'. Previous research shows that learners resist using the standard local variety or a national identity, or style-shifting (selecting polite vs plain forms) against target-like conventions (Iwasaki, 2011), or learners choose to maintain an optimal distance from the L2 community rather than being in constant and complete conformity to perceived native-speaker norms (Ishihara, 2010; also 2019). From an impoliteness and pragmatic discursive perspective, Mitchell and Haugh (2015) adopt a broad view of agency and metapragmatic awareness that includes both the speaker and the recipient.

Following the aforementioned authors and Duranti's (2004) notion of agency of language as performance (i.e. any act of speaking involves some kind of agency), I adopt the view that learners of second or more languages, in a foreign and study abroad contexts, are individuals who are socioculturally aware of their own behaviors and own actions; that is, agents (i) who exert some degree of control over their own behavior and actions; (ii) whose actions in the world affect other persons (including themselves); and (iii) whose actions are the object of evaluations (by others and themselves) (Mitchell & Haugh, 2015: 211; adapted from

Duranti, 2004: 453). The view of socially-mediated agency encompasses a degree of agency and control over their actions for both the speaker and the recipient during negotiation of social action, or when their actions are being evaluated by others as polite or impolite. And following Byram's work, through mediation, intercultural speakers establish relationships, manage disfunctions, and mediate (2021: 49–50). In his appraisal of intercultural mediation, Liddicoat (2022: 42) explains two main functions of mediation in intercultural interactions: (i) mediation as problem solving when intercultural mediators resolve conflict between 'linguistically and culturally different others' and (ii) mediation as an intermediary position when the role of intercultural speakers is to use their linguistic and cultural abilities 'to mediate meanings between languages and cultures' (2022: 47).

Overall, the development of pragmatic and intercultural competence encompasses the intercultural speaker's ability to exert power and make their own decisions when choosing a particular pragmalinguistic expression or keep their own sociopragmatic norms over another, even if they contradict the target-like linguistic and sociocultural norms. Following Mitchell and Haugh (2015), I adopt the view that intercultural speakers are held accountable not only through the evaluations of impolite behavior by others, but also through their reactions or effects those evaluations have on other people. Thus, intercultural speakers exercise agency when their actions or behaviors are evaluated negatively as impolite or socioculturally inappropriate – they choose to engage in the interaction by commenting, clarifying, challenging the interlocutor, staying silent, or expressing their own stance regarding their preference for sociocultural expectations.

Evaluations of Impoliteness and Rapport Management

To examine perceptions of impoliteness, I adopted Spencer-Oatey's (2002, 2005, 2008a) relational model of interpersonal relationships. Spencer-Oatey's model was adapted with some modifications by Culpeper *et al.* (2010) to examine cross-cultural variation in the perception of impoliteness in five countries, and revised to analyze perceptions of offense. According to Spencer-Oatey, rapport management, or the management of harmony-disharmony among people, comprises three components: (i) face management, which refers to the management of face needs; (ii) the management of sociality rights and obligations, which concerns the 'management of social expectancies' [that are] fundamental social *entitlements* that a person effectively claims for him/herself in his/her interactions with others' (2008a: 13 [emphasis in the original]); and (iii), the management of interactional goals (2008a: 13). Following Culpeper *et al.* (2010), I will focus on the first two components to examine the perceptions of impoliteness and offense during intercultural interactions in study abroad contexts. The management of face includes three types: (i) quality face, related to self as an individual: '[w]e have a fundamental desire for people to evaluate us positively in terms of our personal qualities, e.g. our confidence, abilities, appearance, etc.' (Spencer-Oatey, 2002: 540); (ii) relational face, related to self in relationship with others, in particular, significant others, that is '[s]ometimes there can also be a relational application; for example, being a talented leader/and or a kind-hearted teacher entails a relational component that is intrinsic to the evaluation' (2008a: 15); and (iii) social identity face, related to the self as a group member: '[w]e have a fundamental desire for people to acknowledge and uphold our social identities or roles e.g. as a group leader, valued customer, close friend' (2002: 540); [it involves] 'any group that a person is a member of and is concerned about. This can include small groups like one's family, and larger groups like one's ethnic group, religious group, or nationality group' (2005: 106–07).

Sociality rights include two subcomponents: equity rights (i.e. personal consideration from others/autonomy-imposition) and association rights (i.e. belief of association with others). Regarding equity rights, 'people have a fundamental belief that they are entitled to personal considerations from others and to be treated fairly; in other words, that they are not unduly imposed upon, that they are not unfairly ordered about, and that they are not taken advantage of or exploited' (2005: 100). Concerning association rights, Spencer-Oatey (2005) notes:

> [...] people have a fundamental belief that they are entitled to an association with others that is in keeping with the type of relationship that we have with them. This principle [. . .] seems to have three components: *involvement* (the principle that people should have appropriate amounts and types of 'activity' involvement with others), *empathy* (the belief that people should share appropriate concerns, feelings and interests with others), and *respect* (the belief that people should show appropriate amounts of respectfulness for others) (2005: 100, my emphasis).

Unlike equity rights which involve aspects of negative politeness regarding personal consideration from others, such as the right of no imposition or being treated unfairly, association rights refer to a moral aspect which concerns the degree of involvement that we feel we have with others, the sharing of interests and concerns with others, and our right to be respected by others.

The three types of face (quality, social identity, relational) and the two types of sociality rights (equity, association) will be revised to examine understandings of impoliteness and perceptions of offense in intercultural service encounters abroad (see Method section). I follow Culpeper (2011) and Culpeper *et al.* (2010) to analyze the types of offense that learners perceived when interacting with NSs of the target culture in service encounter interactions with service providers, teachers, strangers, or members of the host family.

Research on Evaluations of Intercultural Impoliteness

In this section, I describe two studies that examine evaluations of impoliteness among intercultural speakers that exert agency and identity construction when perceiving offense in study abroad contexts. Mitchell and Haugh (2015) analyzed interactions between Australians and Americans residing in Australia, which then followed with consultations with the participants to gather additional information on evaluations of impoliteness. Results showed that some participants exercised agency when avoiding or suppressing evaluations of offense, while others took a strong negative stance when criticizing Americans. The authors highlighted the importance of focusing on the agency of recipients when examining evaluations of impoliteness, especially in instances where potentially impolite actions were not treated as offensive or intentional by the speaker. They concluded that while speakers and recipients are both held accountable when engaging in social action, recipients may choose to exercise agency based on the evaluations of impoliteness in socially-mediated situations. From a critical discourse analysis perspective, Mugford (2018) examined instances of reflexive intercultural impoliteness (e.g. aggression, insults, racial discrimination) using post facto interviews between Mexican bilingual operators (foreign language context) located in Guadalajara, México and customers calling from the US during the negotiation of service. In his study, reflexive intercultural impoliteness concerns understandings of the appropriate use of language, including language use, sociocultural expectations, and judgements of impolite behavior (p. 174). The data included interviews between the researcher and the Mexican agents. The agents were asked to recall perceived impolite situations that occurred to them during their previous interactions with the US callers. Results showed that while the callers (service seekers) have the power to request a service, the service providers exercised agency by contradicting the interlocutor, as a result of the customer's insults, criticism, and rude remarks. For example, one Mexican agent exercised power over the customer by contesting the customer's offensive remarks and insults regarding the agent's linguistic competence and attacks on the agent's Mexican identity. In this study, critical impoliteness grants the caller choices to make their own decisions when confronted with racial rejection, discrimination and racism.

Following Mitchell and Haugh (2015), I adopt the view that intercultural speakers are held accountable not only through the evaluations of impolite behavior by others but also through their reactions or the effects those evaluations have on other people. Thus, intercultural speakers exert agency or control when their actions or behaviors are evaluated negatively or are perceived as impolite or socioculturally inappropriate.

Perception of Offense Abroad through Impoliteness Events
Method
Instrument

This section presents the method used to collect and analyze the data on critical incidents or impoliteness events. Introspection or retrospection techniques are used to elicit data that trigger either a previous experience (or schema) or one aspect of participants' short-term memory after completion of a task. One type of introspection methodology is politeness events, which is a methodology grounded in psychological research and applied in politeness and impoliteness research in cross-cultural pragmatics (Spencer-Oatey, 2002; Culpeper *et al.*, 2010). Using this method, participants are asked to write about impolite events which had a positive or negative effect on them. As mentioned above, in Culpeper *et al.* (2010), the researchers asked participants from five countries to narrate a conversation that had a negative effect on them, yielding an impoliteness event (see also Culpeper, 2011: 195–219). This method produced lengthy discourse related to impoliteness events that are based on the participants' previous experience or frames. While the degree of validity of this method may be subject to the criticism that respondents may not always recall specific information (Kasper, 2000; Schneider, 2018), it has proven reliable and valid to a degree because participants activate existing mental frames based on previous experiences.

Procedures of data collection and the setting

Following the method used in Culpeper *et al.* (2010), I asked 200 learners to recall an impoliteness event that happened to them while studying abroad at a service encounter or an interaction they had at school, on the street, or with their host families. The gender distribution was predominantly female (72.5%, n = 145), followed by males (27%, n = 54), and 1 non-binary (0.5%). They were all university-level students (18–26 years). The participants represented 13 different languages as their L1, including English (83%), Spanish (4.5%), and other less frequent languages (Albanian, Arabic, Chinese, Egyptian, French, German, Hindi, Japanese, Korean, Russian, Telegu and Urdu, 12.5%). They studied abroad in 37 countries where the impoliteness event took place. The five predominant target countries included Spain (32.5%), Mexico and the US (10%), Chile (6.5%) and Peru (5.5%). The remaining countries included nine cases or below in Latin America (Argentina, Bolivia, Costa Rica, Dominican Republic, Guatemala, Panama, Venezuela), and other countries in Europe (Austria, Belgium, Czech Republic, Scotland, England, Egypt, Germany, Greece, France, Ireland, Italy, Norway, Poland), Africa (Ghana, Morocco, Senegal), and Asia (Japan, China, India, Kyrgyzstan, Malaysia, South Korea). The 200 intercultural encounters took place in the following settings shown in Table 6.1:

Table 6.1 Setting of intercultural encounters of impoliteness events abroad

Setting	N (%)
Service Encounter	130 (65%)
Host Family	34 (17%)
Friends	11 (5.5%)
Piropos 'cat calls'	9 (4.5%)
Strangers	9 (4.5%)
Classes	6 (3%)
Work	1 (0.5%)
Total	200 (100%)

Most of the service encounters took place at cafés, restaurants, hotels, with taxi drivers, supermarkets, museums and information centers. Following the method used in Culpeper *et al.* (2010), the 200 learners received an online survey in which they were asked to describe a service encounter interaction that they perceived as impolite or rude while studying abroad. In order to obtain as many details as possible, participants were asked to include what was said by all conversational participants (linguistic forms), how it was said (prosody), where the conversation took place (physical context), the relationship between conversational participants, and whether other people overheard the conversation (social context), in addition to how the learner and others reacted to the situation. Participants were instructed to construct the exchange as a written dialogue. These exchanges were the result of the learners activating a cultural cognitive frame of an impolite interaction that occurred to them.

The description of the prompt in (1) was circulated via an online survey (adapted from Culpeper *et al.*, 2010):

(1) Prompt to elicit impoliteness events in intercultural contexts abroad

Think about the time you spent studying abroad and describe a conversation that you had in person with your host family or in a service encounter place (restaurant, supermarket, store, hotel, information center, bank, customer service center, asking for directions, etc.) in which someone said something to you that made you feel bad or uncomfortable. For example, a time that you felt hurt, offended, embarrassed, humiliated, or ostracized. Please write the conversation as a dialogue (like a play) and try to include the following information:

- what was actually said and how it was said (for example, was there something different about the pronunciation, intonation?);
- where the conversation took place (for example, with host family, at the store, at the hotel, at the bar, at the restaurant, on the bus, on the street);

- your relationship to the other person in the dialogue (for example, a friend, a stranger, a host family member);
- how you reacted;
- whether other people heard the exchange;
- how they reacted.

After the participants described the critical incident, they were asked to complete four questions regarding their perception of the situation and an assessment of their intercultural experience (adapted from Culpeper *et al.* 2010). The first two questions were ranked on a 5-point Likert scale and the last two were meant to gather metapragmatic information based on their awareness of the impoliteness event:

- Emotion in the moment: On a scale from 1 (not bad) to 5 (very bad), how bad did the behavior in the conversation you described with the service provider or the host family member make you feel at the time it occurred?
- Service provider intention: On a scale from 1 (not intentional) to 5 (intentional), rate whether you think the service provider or the host family member meant to make you feel bad.
- Metapragmatic reflection: Think about the event you have described and explain how it made you feel at the time and why it made you feel this way. (Participants completed answer in a box.)
- Metalinguistic labels: How would you describe the behavior of the service provider or the host family member who made you feel bad? How would you label this kind of behavior? (Students completed the answer in a box.)

Data analysis

The data were analyzed according to a modified version of Culpeper's (2011: 28–30, 40–41) and Culpeper *et al.*'s (2010: 605–614) classification of offense types. In Culpeper's (2011) operationalization of Spencer-Oatey's (2002, 2005, 2008a) rapport management framework, the author proposed key questions that can guide the researcher in determining if a potentially impolite event violates different subcomponents of face and sociality rights. Table 6.2 shows the five components and examples: three types of face (Quality, Social Identity, Relational) and sociality rights (Equity and Association).

To understand the type of offense perceived, Culpeper and colleagues asked questions to examine understandings of impoliteness: in the context of an impolite situation, 'does the interaction evoke an understanding that something counters [filled with definitions for each of the five components]' (2010: 606–613). The examples are taken from the corpus of 200 impoliteness events in intercultural encounters abroad (Table 6.2, adapted from Félix-Brasdefer & McKinnon, 2017). Column 1 shows the offense

Intercultural Impoliteness, Reflexive Awareness, and Agency in Study Abroad Contexts   171

Table 6.2 Perception of offense in intercultural impoliteness events

Violated subcomponent of face or sociality rights	Question: In the context of an impolite situation, 'does the interaction evoke an understanding that something counters …'	Examples
Quality face	… positive values that a participant claims not only to have as a specific individual but to be assumed by other participant(s) as having?	When I was in Europe, I was speaking with our Airbnb host and she was explaining where everything was in the apartment and the rules of the stay. I had to help my grandpa with the luggage, so I told her she could explain how the laundry machine works to my brother, who also speaks French but with a worse accent than me. The following conversation was in French: Brother: Could you explain the dryer? Host: Not to you, I want to talk to the girl who actually speaks French. Me: He does. Host: Barely! We didn't know how to react because it was so rude to say he didn't speak French just because his accent isn't perfect.
Relational face	… positive values that a participant claims not only to have in common with all other members in a particular group, but to be assumed by other participant(s) as having?	I was teaching English to students in one country in South America. Conversation in class: Teacher: Hi class! Today I've got something special prepared for us. Today back home it's Thanksgiving day, and I'm missing home, and I figured it would be nice for us to see a short video of food preparation and some pictures of my favorite foods. (I show a video). Me to class: And which foods seem most appealing to you, and why? One student responds: I would like to eat the turkey. Me: You want to eat the turkey? Student Yes, turkey. I would like to eat the turkey. Another student responds: 'Fuck! This activity is stupid. The food looks bad. Well, that's my opinion..' I responded saying that you may not like all class activities, sorry (with sarcastic joke). The student rolled her eyes. I became frustrated because the student challenged my authority as the teacher and my relationship with her as student-teacher in the classroom. It offended me because she said it in front of the other students.
Social identity face	… positive values about the relations that a participant claims not only to have with a significant other(s) but to be assumed by that/those significant other(s) and/or participants as having?	I was at a dinner party for my boyfriend's sister in Europe. Her boyfriend, who was usually quiet and only watched soccer, decided that night that was going to engage in conversation with me around me being an American. We were all at the table, eating our dinner. He turns to me and says in Spanish: One of my friends spent three months in US region. You all are very reserved, no? Very distant people-- you don't share much, you don't know much. Americans don't read the news, they don't know much about politics. My reaction was to try to explain that the US is a big country, with many different people and ideologies and ways of life. I remember being a bit upset but trying not to show it.

(Continued)

Table 6.2 (Continued)

Violated subcomponent of face or sociality rights	Question: In the context of an impolite situation, 'does the interaction evoke an understanding that something counters …'	Examples
Equity rights	… a state of affairs in which a participant considers that they are not unduly exploited, disadvantaged, unfairly dealt with, controlled or imposed upon?	When I lived in (African country) I sometimes rode the 'cars rapides' minibus system. When climbing on board, a person takes your fee of 50 francs, flat rate regardless of distance. One day, I climbed on and had the following exchange with the fee collector: Her: 100 francs, please. Me: It's 50 francs, right? Her: 100 francs. Me: I ride this bus often, I know it's 50 francs. Her: I don't know who told you that. 100 francs, please. Me: Just this morning it was 50 francs! Her: 100 francs! … The exchange continued until I decided it wasn't worth fighting over such a small amount of money, so I pay her 100 francs. No one else in the bus said anything, and they looked away when I made eye contact. Later, another passenger climbs on board the bus and pays 50 francs. I angrily complain to the fee collector, and she tells me I 'should have negotiated harder' (even though the other passenger paid 50 francs immediately).
Association rights	… a state of affairs in which a participant considers that they have an appropriate level of behavioral involvement and sharing of concerns, feelings, and interests with others, and are accorded an appropriate level of respect?	Conversation took place at a café in Germany. I ordered, I received order, ate, asked for check, and received the bill. I paid in exact change. Waiter: 'Tip is not included.' (Grumpy, demanding tone) Me: 'I know, I'll leave it on the table.' I did not know this person and other people may have heard the exchange, but I did not see their reactions. I myself felt confused and bad because tipping is not required or expected in Germany (although it is nice to do when you receive particularly good service). The waiter's behavior was inappropriate and disrespectful to me as the customer. It would be considered very rude for the server to demand a tip, as he did. I felt that my rights as a customer in Germany were violated. I felt offended and disrespected by his actions and behavior; he simply didn't care about my feelings or emotions.

type; column 2 presents the question that was used to analyze the offense type identified in the impoliteness events; and column 3 displays an example for each type of offense type.

To ensure inter-coded reliability, the data were coded independently by the researcher and two additional coders, following the classification of offense type in Table 6.2. Unlike Culpeper *et al.* (2010) which analyzed primary and secondary offenses, I focused on the primary offense type. The primary offense type is the one that characterizes the impoliteness event as the major type of offense. When the results were compared, the level of agreement was 90%. The remaining 10% of the cases were discussed and the coders came to a 99% agreement.

The data were analyzed quantitatively and qualitatively. For the quantitative analysis, I used the Statistical Package for the Social Sciences (SPSS) to compare the frequencies and means for each offense type and the responses from the first two responses using the Likert-scale. Chi-squared tests were used to examine significant differences among the offense types.

Finally, the content of the offense types and the metapragmatic reflection data were analyzed following Saldaña's (2021) notation for transcribing and annotating qualitative data: content and frequent topics used regarding the type of perceived offense, the emotion felt after the impoliteness event to examine metapragmatic awareness, and the adjectives the intercultural speakers used to refer to the service provider, host family member, stranger, teacher, or friend (metalinguistic impoliteness).

Perceived Offense in Intercultural Impoliteness Abroad

This section presents the results and discussion of the perceived offense in the context of intercultural service encounters. Figure 6.1 displays the frequency for the primary types of perceived offense in the 200 impoliteness events between the intercultural speakers studying abroad and NSs of the target culture.

The most frequent type of primary offense perceived was quality face (62/200 cases; 31%), followed by social identity face (45/200 cases; 22.5%) and association rights (42/200 cases; 21%). The least frequent types of perceived offense were equity rights (30/200 cases; 15%) and relational face (21/200 cases; 10.5%). Regarding management of face, differences were found, with quality face as the most frequent type of perceived offense. With regard to the management of sociality rights (association

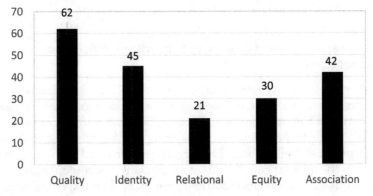

Figure 6.1 Primary types of perceived offense

and equity), differences were found, with association as the most frequent. In Culpeper et al.'s (2010) cross-cultural analysis of perceived offense in five countries among NSs (China, England, Finland, Germany, and Turkey), the three most frequent types of primary perceived offense were quality face, equity rights and association rights. The results from the present study concur with Culpeper et al. (2010), in that violations of quality face and association rights are the most frequently reported impoliteness triggers overall.

However, the data from the current study also revealed key differences from Culpeper et al. (2010), which seem to be influenced by the study-abroad context among multilingual speakers studying abroad. First, while Culpeper et al. (2010) reported that the second most frequent type of violation was either related to equity rights (Finnish, Turkish) or association rights (English, German), the present study found that violations of social identity face were the second most frequent in study abroad contexts. While issues related to social identity face (i.e. one's affiliation with a larger group) may not frequently arise in an L1 context, multilingual speakers in a study abroad context often have to navigate their L1 and host country self-identities. These two aspects of learners' identity while in the host country were seen as related to social identity face violations that involved negative comments or stereotypes about the learner's home country (e.g. 'When I was in [country], I was not let into a bar because I was American'; 'I was with my friends in [country], I was referred to as "stupid gringo" because I couldn't understand the taxi driver'). Similarly, in addition to violations of social identity face, violations to relational face were related to the study-abroad context, where host families and host-country professors were involved. Most of the impoliteness events with host families were related to differences in sociocultural norms between the L1 and the L2 cultures, while with the professors, the perceived offense was related to the learner's linguistic competence.

In the next section, I explain three common topics identified in the impoliteness events: linguistic competence, sociocultural expectations, and construction of identity, agency, and interculturality.

Quality face: Perceived offense to linguistic proficiency and personal traits

Most of the violations of quality face were related to the learners' low proficiency level in the target language and a perceived offense to personal traits. Almost half of these events were classified as an offense of the learners' low linguistic proficiency and the other half as an offense to the student's physical appearance. The negatively perceived comments were found in all four language skills (i.e. speaking, listening, reading and writing), as well as pronunciation and grammatical/lexical errors made by the learner. The example in (2) provides an exchange between a student who had recently arrived in the host country and was speaking with a NS friend in a public setting:

(2) Perceived offense to linguistic proficiency

a. Learner on a bus talking to his male friend from a Latin American country

01	NS:	((unintelligible comment))
02	Student:	what?
03	NS:	((repeats the same words))
04	Student:	I'm sorry, I don't understand, can you repeat one more time?
05	NS:	→ You are never going to learn Spanish
06	Student:	((I got very embarrassed and stopped talking))

In this exchange, after the friend used words that were unfamiliar to the learner (line 03), the student issued a clarification request (line 04). However, the NS chose to comment negatively on the student's proficiency in Spanish (line 05). This example highlights the frustration that NSs may experience while interacting with NNSs, which may result in a rude comment about their language ability. With regard to the learner's emotion at the time the interaction occurred, the learner commented 'It made me feel that I was never going to learn Spanish and that I was stupid or slow for not picking it up more quickly. I also felt hurt that my friend would say that in front of an entire bus full of people'. The learner further described the friend's behavior as 'manipulative and intentionally hurtful'. The learner described the friend's behavior as 'very bad' and very intentional.

b. At the airport in Europe

'At the airport when I first landed in Spain and was going through customs, I was speaking to the customs lady in Spanish, she replied in English: *you have a lot of work to do here to improve your Spanish.* I laughed, but already felt really embarrassed and I was not even out of the airport in the foreign country.'

The student reported that not only did he feel embarrassed, but also felt bad because the person 'answered in English when I was trying Spanish right off the bat and it hindered my confidence in the beginning of my study abroad experience.' The student described the behavior of the airport agent as 'condescending and unsupportive'. He reported that the service provider's intention was not bad (2 on a 5-point scale): 'I am sure these outcomes were very unintentional.' This shows the student's level of intercultural competence and knowledge of the sociocultural expectations of the target culture.

The second half of perceived offense to quality face included instances of offense to the speaker's personal traits such as physical appearance, as in example (3):

(3) Perceived offense to personal qualities

'It was the second day my roommate and I had been in Spain and we were staying with a 75-year-old host mom. The lady lived on the second floor of a building and had not yet shown us how to unlock/lock the door to get into the house/floor she lived on. The doors there are different, and the handle is in the middle of the door and does not require twisting to open it, and the lock is on the left side of the door where you are to insert the key, much different than doors in the US. We walk up the stairs and get to the door and attempt to unlock the door to go inside but we couldn't get it and the lady comes and opens the door and says *que torpes son* 'how clumsy you are'. We responded saying that the doors in the US are different and you didn't teach us how to open the door with the key. She didn't respond with anything and just seemed frustrated.'

The student described the behavior of the person as very intentional. The student responded that she felt 'annoyed' and 'frustrated' and described the person's behavior as rude.

Knowledge of cultural norms and metapragmatic awareness

Most examples of relational face and association rights concerned instances where the intercultural speaker perceived the interaction as offensive and rude, and the hearer's rude behavior as intentional or not (see Chapter 3, Figure 3.1). Most learners were aware that the perceived rude behavior was considered a sociocultural expectation of the target culture, which indicates a high level of intercultural competence regarding knowledge of the cultural norms and behaviors of the L1 and L2 cultures. For example, learners reported that the following actions represent a cultural expectation in Spanish-speaking countries, whereas in most English-speaking regions these values and beliefs may be perceived as offensive or inappropriate behavior: expressing unsolicited opinion, issuing direct (unmitigated) requests, interrupting and joking to express solidarity, insisting (as an affiliative marker) after refusing offers or invitations, and swearing to express affiliation (cf. Félix-Brasdefer, 2017b; Márquez Reiter & Placencia, 2005; Mugford & Félix-Brasdefer, 2021). An awareness of these sociocultural values represents a high level of intercultural competence with regard to what is considered appropriate behavior in the target culture. The example in (4) shows an instance of offense to relational face, and an awareness of sociocultural values and behavioral expectations in Spain. The student spent seven weeks with his host family, and had visited three more regions in Spain. He also spent a summer in Argentina.

(4) Perceived relational offense

'I was visiting my host mother in Spain, whom I had known for 4 years, shortly after I got engaged and she made it clear to me that she did not think it was a good idea for me to get married so young. While I was discussing my proposal and wedding plans with another friend while we were out bar-hopping as a group, my host mother said "I shouldn't get married, you are still very young". My host father and our friends heard what she said, and one of the friends tried to say something positive to downplay the comment. I reacted by ignoring the comment. It bothered me because I was very happy to be engaged and in love, but at the same time I had enough experience with the Spanish culture to know that it is considered okay to give opinions like that among a group of good friends, even about personal issues, and the fact that she was willing to express such a strong opinion showed that we have a close relationship. My host mother did not expect me to argue with her about her opinion on my engagement; she was merely expressing her own feelings, and so I believe it was perfectly appropriate for me to not respond directly to what she said.'

In this example, the host mother expressed her personal feelings and comments with regard to the student's decision to get married, which offended the student's individual wants. That is, the student perceived the host mother's unsolicited comments as an offense to their relationship. The learner was aware that expressing an unsolicited opinion represents a sociocultural expectation in this country, and he was mindful that he should not disagree or contradict his host mother. The learner realized that his host mother's comments were not meant to be offensive; instead, they represented an instance of involvement and acceptance in some regions of Spain (Hernández-Flores, 1999). What troubled the student is that his relational value as a friend or close member of the host family was threatened. In the post-event comments, the student described his emotions as follows:

> The best word I can think of to describe how I felt is probably just 'annoyed' or like I was being nagged (she is sort of my mother, so I guess that makes sense!). This situation made me feel bad, but I know her comment was not intentional or meant to be offensive.

The student commented that 'the behavior was completely culturally acceptable. The statement that she made is best described as very blunt or frank, but acceptable in this region of Spain, clearly not intentional.'

In example (5) taken from the dataset of association rights, the student shows knowledge of the behavioral expectations of tipping when she visited a restaurant in Germany:

(5) Behavioral expectations of tipping at a café in Germany

> 'I ordered, I received order, ate, asked for check and received bill. I paid in exact change.
> Waiter: Tip is not included. (Grumpy, demanding tone)
> Me: I know, I'll leave it on the table

The student reacted as follows:

> I myself felt confused and bad because tipping is not required or expected in Germany (although it is nice to do when you receive particularly good service). The waiter's behavior was inappropriate and disrespectful to me as the customer. It would be considered very rude for the server to demand a tip, as he did. I felt that my rights as a customer in Germany were violated. I felt offended and disrespected by his actions and behavior; he simply didn't care about my feelings or emotions.

In this example, the student took offense from the waiter's demanding tone and his request to leave a tip. However, the student was aware of the behavioral expectations of tipping in both the US and Germany. In the post events comments, the student noted:

> the waiter's response made me feel bad and stupid. He made me feel pressured to leave a tip and made me question my prior knowledge and experience in Germany about tipping culture.

The student perceived the waiter's behavior as 'rude and inappropriate,' and intentional.

Construction of identity, agency, and interculturality

Intercultural speakers exert agency, negotiate (im)polite behavioral expectations, and construct their identities according to the demands of the interaction. Agency allows intercultural speakers to mediate between languages and cultures and to manage interpersonal conflict and to mediate as an intermediary position by negotiating meaning as third parties (Liddicoat, 2022; Liddicoat & McConachy, 2019). Example (6) shows an intercultural encounter between an American student and the immigration officer in Mexico (adapted from Félix-Brasdefer, 2020b). The interaction took place in Spanish, and English translation is provided. The intercultural speaker perceived an offense to her association rights, expecting respect from the interlocutor: 'the belief that people should show appropriate amounts of respectfulness for others' (Culpeper *et al.*, 2010: 613). Regarding the negotiation of intercultural interaction, metapragmatic awareness, variability, and emergent common ground, see Chapter 3, Figure 3.1.

(6) Intercultural encounter at an immigration office in Mexico (US student and Mexican officer)
1   Student: Good morning, I need to renew my visa. I have these documents.
2   ((hands them over)).
3   Officer: Did you fill out form 'X'?
4   Student: ((confused face))
5   I don't know what that is. It was my understanding that I had to bring these documents.

6		((officer with an angry face, shows sign with information about the procedure de *prórroga* 'extension'))
7		
8	Officer:	Here's the information for the *prórroga*
9	Student:	*Prórroga*? What's that? I need to extend my visa.
10	Officer:	((with condescending tone))
11		well, as it says here in the sign, you need to fill out form "X".
12	Student:	But, also for the extension?
13	Officer:	Yes, for the extension
14	Student:	Ah OK, the form says it's for the *prórroga*, I need an extension,
15		not a *prórroga*.
16	Officer:	((with annoying tone, condescending, and slow tone in '*prórroga*'))
17		*Pró.rro.ga* is the same as the extension, Miss.
18	Student:	Oh, I didn't know it means the same, well, I'll fill out the form.
19	Officer:	You can give it to me when the form is ready.

The intercultural speaker, a US student visiting Mexico, opens the interaction in Spanish with the Mexican immigration officer. Both start with previous information about two different cultures, United States and Mexico (beliefs, values, ideologies and presuppositions). From line 4, it can be observed that both participants do not share common ground to begin the process of the application. The misunderstanding is the result of a lack of the meaning of *prórroga* 'extension' by the student (lines 8–9). The misunderstanding continues in the clarification-response sequence launched by the student (line 9) and followed up by the officer, with a condescending tone, who clarifies that *prórroga* is the same as extension, followed up by the student's acceptance (lines 16–18). Despite the fact that both interlocutors do not share sociocultural norms, beliefs and values (social context) or previous context, the interaction continues based on emergent context of the actual situational context (Kecskes, 2014, 2020) that is created and constructed according to the demands of the interaction in order to arrive to mutual agreement. The context of the situation is created and modified through mutual collaboration: clarification questions, repetition, reaffirmations and responses to negotiate meaning during the course of the interaction, which is created in the shared and hybrid or third space (Kramsch, 2009b, 2011) with linguistic and sociocultural input from both participants.

In this example, we can observe how the intercultural speaker exerts agency by challenging the officer through clarification requests of the meaning *prórroga*. According to previous research, agency concerns 'the negotiated capacity to act, assume new identities, or resist certain positionings actively and purposefully' (Ishihara, 2019: 162; also Duff, 2012;

Rogers & Wetzel, 2013). In the interaction in (6), the speaker mediates between two cultures and demonstrates her agency by asking clarification questions to co-construct the emergent common ground (lines 9, 12), which eventually lead to the understanding of the word *prórroga* and a mutual understanding (lines 18, 19).

During the post-event comments, the student reported that she felt angry and powerless. The student perceived the officer's response as intentional, and described the officer's behavior as inappropriate and rude. Overall, the student perceived the officer's behavior as offensive and a violation to her association rights, as result of a lack of perceived respect from the officer.

Reflexive Metapragmatic Awareness

The learners were asked two questions (ranked on a 5-point Likert scale) to reflect on their perception of impolite behavior: emotion at the moment and hearer intention. The first question asked how bad the behavior in the conversation they described with the interlocutor (service provider, host family member, teacher, friend) made them feel at the same time it occurred (Emotion at the moment). The results were ranked on a scale from 1 (not bad) to 5 (very bad). Although there was variation among the participants, the results showed an overall mean of 3.45, reporting that the majority felt bad at the moment the offense occurred. The majority of the participants rated their emotions as bad (3–4): 71% (142/200 events), and 15% (30/200 cases) ranked theirs as very bad (5). Only 14% (28/200 events) assessed their emotions as 1 and 2 (not bad/ somewhat bad). These were instances of minor offense to their relational face (a host family member) or association rights (a friend).

The second question asked whether they thought the interlocutor meant to make them feel bad (hearer intention). The results were ranked on a scale from 1 (not intentional) to 5 (very intentional). Although there was variation among the participants, the results showed that 48.5% (97/200 events) of the intercultural speakers felt that the hearer's intention to make them feel bad was not intentional (26.5% [see example 3]) or somewhat intentional (22%). The majority of the learners studying abroad reported that they perceived the hearer's offensive behavior as intentional or very intentional (51.5%; 103/200 events); most of these cases were violations of perceived offense to their quality face, identity face, or equity rights.

Metapragmatic reflection, perception of offense and emotions

After the students wrote about the impoliteness events, they were asked to reflect on the event they described and explain how and why it made them feel the way it did. Students who perceived the hearer's offense

Table 6.3 Perceived offense of hearer's intention

Offense type	Setting	Emotion felt after event
Quality	Bakery	The clerk ridiculed me for my level of Spanish, so I felt like a failure. I knew I was learning and not very good at communicating still. But, her annoyance made me feel like a burden and an idiot and that no matter how hard I tried to understand, it wasn't ever going to be good enough.
Relational face	Host family	It upset me, angered me, embarrassed me, and I felt ostracized.
Social identity face	Restaurant	I was angry. It made me feel very unwelcome because it attacked my nationality and my identity as an American. Made me feel like a dumb American.
Equity rights	Taxi	It frustrated me because even if he was just trying to get a bigger pay, he didn't have to be so rude about it and insult me. I felt unfairly treated.
Association rights	Stranger (asking for directions)	I was very annoyed. A lot of it had to do with how accepting everyone else in Japan had been with English speakers and usually went above and beyond to help us out. If this had happened in America, I definitely would not have been as annoyed as I was. I did not feel that I was treated with respect.

as intentional reported the following feelings, mainly violations to their quality face, identity face, or equity rights. Table 6.3 shows an example of each type of offense and the emotions the intercultural speakers felt during the event.

In the overall dataset, learners described their feelings with the following frequent attributes for the perceived offense: angry, hurt, frustrated, embarrassed, annoyed, upset, ridiculed, offended, uncomfortable, belittled, embarrassed, unfairly treated, disrespected, stupid, ignorant, disheartened, ostracized, horrible, and helpless. Most of these adjectives corresponded with particular types of offense, such as quality face (embarrassed, angry, stupid, ignorant, annoyed, hurt, frustrated), relational face (embarrassed, offended, uncomfortable), social identity face (embarrassed, ashamed, humiliated, ridiculed, offended, frustrated, angry, uncomfortable), equity rights (unfairly treated, upset, uncomfortable, discriminated against), and association rights (frustrated, disrespected). Most of these adjectives were modified with the following intensifiers: extremely (uncomfortable), very (upset), a little (hurt), really (bad), so (mad), and very (frustrated).

The aforementioned results are comparable, to some extent, to those found in Culpeper *et al.* (2014), which analyzed the emotions that participants from different countries (England, Turkey, Germany, Finland and China) felt after an impoliteness event. Four emotions were reported: sadness, anger, fear and surprise. Overall, sadness and anger, respectively, predominated in all groups. Cultural variation was noted in some countries: sadness was a particular emotion among the Turkish participants, while anger was strong in the Chinese groups. Similar to Goffman (1967) and Culpeper *et al.* (2014), the present study also found that violations of face are generally linked to emotions of embarrassment and anger (Quality, Social Identity, Relational), while violations of sociality rights (Equity and Association) are connected to feeling uncomfortable, frustrated and disrespected.

In addition to describing their feelings with linguistic expressions, intercultural speakers noticed non-verbal cues during the interaction. The most frequent types of body gestures and prosodic cues that learners noticed abroad are shown in Table 6.4.

The reflexive metapragmatic comments in Table 6.4 show that the learners noticed non-verbal cues (gestural and prosodic) that they perceived as offensive during the intercultural encounter. Attention to visual features of the situation (e.g. mean face, angry look, lack of eye contact, etc.) and prosodic cues (e.g. rude, sarcastic and condescending tone) represent pragmatic markers and intercultural competence during the recognition of the hearer's intention during the negotiation of the interaction. Reflexive awareness of non-verbal cues promoted high levels of pragmatic (implicit meaning, recognizing sarcastic and rude remarks) and intercultural competence (reflexive awareness of cultural norms, ways of saying, and sociocultural expectations of impolite behavior of the target culture). Finally, the reflexive awareness of non-verbal cues also promotes the intercultural speaker's agency to reflect, analyze, compare and contrast other ways of saying and cultural expectations with a second or additional culture. Based on previous work on agency and pragmatic resistance (Ishihara, 2019; Liddicoat & McConachy, 2019; McConachy, 2023), the multilingual speakers in the present study chose to follow the cultural

Table 6.4 Reflexive awareness of non-verbal cues in intercultural impoliteness

Attention to body language	Attention to prosodic cues

• Lack of eye contact
• His angry look
• Mean face
• Didn't look at me in the face
• His silence to express disagreement
• Ignoring customer's request
• The waitress and the two men exchanged glares and started speaking French like they are annoyed and shaked their heads
• Waitress just rolled her eyes and seemed annoyed that we were asking for food
• Facial expressions that we received when we were struggling with getting our information to translate
	• Tone perceived as frustrating, impatient, irritated, accusatory, annoying, upset and angry
	  – she grunted in an annoyed fashion;
	  – his intonation was rude;
	  – his slow, repetitive, and emphatic tone made me feel stupid
	• Repetition to convey condescension
	• Waiter's tone was rude and condescending
	• Service provider's way of saying was very cold and blunt without smile
	• Responses were very short brief, and in a tone that I felt was rude and careless
	• Grumpy, demanding tone
	• Patronizing and condescending
	• Sarcastic remarks
	• Loud and ironic voice

expectations of rude behavior that they noticed, opt out, disagree, maintain their own identity, and/or challenged the hearer's rude response.

Metalinguistic awareness

Intercultural speakers were asked to describe the behavior of the interlocutor with an adjective that would describe the perceived offense from the interlocutor, including a service provider, stranger, friend, teacher, or host family member. The five most frequent adjectives used to describe the interlocutor's offensive behavior (post-event comments) for the questions and the emotion felt at the moment included: rude (118 cases), mean (61 cases), impolite (12 cases), inappropriate (9) and patronizing (5 cases). There were also combinations of two adjectives to describe the offensive behavior of the interlocutor, whose behavior was perceived by the intercultural speaker as intentional:

rude and insulting	dismissive and impolite
rude and inappropriate	rude and annoying
disrespectful and rude	condescending and disrespectful

Metapragmatic reflection of how the learners described perceived offense is a way to understand first-order understandings of impolite behavior. In his study of metapragmatic impoliteness, Schneider (2012) analyzed the frequencies of *impolite* and related adjectives in two corpora, a Google search and the Corpus of Contemporary American English (oral and written), and found the following: *rude* occurs considerably more frequently than *polite*, which suggests that people in the corpora view *rude behavior* as more salient and more conscious than polite behavior. Unlike the present study, he found that *inappropriate* was used more frequently than *rude* or *impolite*. In the context of perceptions of offensive behavior with intercultural speakers studying abroad (impoliteness events), *rude* and *mean* are by far the most frequent adjectives to describe the impolite behavior of service providers, friends, teachers, strangers, and host-family members, while *inappropriate* was the least frequently used in the dataset of impoliteness events.

Conclusion

This chapter examined the perceptions of impolite behavior in a sample of 200 impoliteness events reported by intercultural speakers who studied abroad in 37 countries. I focused on impoliteness events (Culpeper, 2011; Culpeper *et al.* 2010) to elicit perceptions of offense when they interacted with NSs abroad in order to exert agency and construct their identity across the interaction in a variety of settings abroad (service encounters, host families, friends, strangers). This study adopted a novel approach to examining learners' perceptions by employing a modified version of Spencer-Oatey's (2002, 2005, 2008a) rapport management framework as applied to impoliteness (Culpeper, 2011). Rapport management offers researchers a more nuanced framework that can be applied crossculturally (Culpeper *et al.*, 2010, 2014), and as the present study demonstrated, interculturally with multilingual speakers studying abroad. Overall, the learners studying abroad described the perceived offense of the interlocutor as *rude* and *mean*, and to a lower extent *inappropriate*.

Based on Culpeper and Haugh (2021), sociopragmatic norms refer to ways of behaving (empirical norms) and thinking about conduct (moral norms). Variability of sociopragmatic norms was present across the 200 impoliteness events, including the post-event comments where intercultural speakers commented on the emotion felt during the interaction and the adjective they used to describe the behavior of the interlocutor. The sociopragmatic norms noted in the impoliteness events represent frequent sociocultural expectations and ways of behaving in intercultural interactions between a student studying abroad and NSs of the target culture. Sociopragmatic variability in the perception of offense depends on the situation where the offense took place, the interlocutor (e.g. service provider, host family member, stranger on the street), the region abroad, and the speaker's and hearer's country of origin. Individual variation was evident in 200 cases of impoliteness events because intercultural speakers represented 37 countries and 13 different languages, and because of the variation of the gender of the intercultural speaker (72.5% were women).

There were trends in the data with regard to the topics underlying the impoliteness events: the majority of events involved a violation of the learner's quality face: an offense to their low level of linguistic competence, physical appearance, skills, and insults directed to them. However, even though the learners perceived these offenses as rude, most of them were aware that the perceived offense represented a sociocultural expectation that differs from their L1 cultural norms sociocultural values (e.g. avoiding imposition, giving criticism, and offering unsolicited comments). Awareness of impolite behavior in the target culture should be part of the learner's pragmatic competence; thus, learners should be taught how to understand the comments that they perceive as impolite according to the sociocultural expectations of the target language culture (Félix-Brasdefer & Mugford, 2017).

With regard to offense to their social identity, learners perceived offense when they received stereotypes attacking their national identity (country), political affiliation and food preferences. Regarding equity rights, learners reported instances of not receiving equal rights as the NSs of the local country (e.g. being charged more than the locals). In conjunction with the types and frequencies of face and sociality rights, these findings contribute to our understanding of what may offend future multilingual speakers studying abroad.

Finally, the negotiation of perceived offense shed light on how the learners abroad exerted agency to make their own decisions, constructed their own identities, made clarifications to understand the interlocutor's intentions, chose the target language variety, challenged the interlocutor's opinions, or chose to deviate from the expected NS norms (Ishihara, 2019; Liddicoat & McConachy, 2019; McConachy, 2018, 2023). Evaluations of impolite behavior are mediated with respect to the socially-mediated agency of both the intercultural speaker and the interlocutor (Duranti, 2004; Liddicoat, 2022; Mitchell & Haugh, 2015). The analysis of impoliteness events showed that mediation should be seen as a dual process: 'a process through which learning happens and a goal to which learning leads' (Liddicoat, 2022: 56). Overall, learners exert agency when they have some control of their own behavior, an awareness of how their social actions affect the feelings or emotions of others, and when their actions are the target of evaluation as a violation of offense, or perceived as socioculturally inappropriate.

The final chapter offers concluding remarks and some directions for future research.

Note

(1) This information is taken from Mugford and Félix-Brasdefer (2021: 355–57) and adapted for intercultural impoliteness in study abroad contexts.

Conclusion

In this book, I adopted a pragmatic perspective as a way of examining Intercultural Communicative Competence (ICC) through language use and intercultural understanding in two learning contexts: study abroad and the foreign language classroom. Following the seminal work of Byram (1997, 2021) and others (McConachy, 2018; McConachy & Liddicoat, 2019; Schauer, 2024; Taguchi, 2017; Taguchi & Roever, 2017), a key objective of the approach in this volume was to broaden the concept of pragmatic competence to include the negotiation of speech acts at the discourse level; evaluations of polite and impolite behavior; sociopragmatic awareness, agency, understanding of language use, and engagement in intercultural interaction. In Chapter 1, pragmatics was defined as language use in context (cognitive, social, interactional) in social situations and how language learners produce and comprehend explicit and implicit meaning. From an intercultural learning perspective, I showed how learners negotiate their intentions according to the demands of the interaction and an understanding of the cultural norms in emergent situational contexts (Kecskes, 2014, 2020).

An issue that I addressed in this book concerns the fact that L2 pragmatics research generally adopts a bilingual view with the NS as the target model of comparison. I have emphasized, like others, a multilingual perspective on intercultural understanding, placing the language learner at the center of social interaction. Further, I have broadened the understanding of pragmatic competence to encompass a multifaceted view of social interaction (see also Barron, 2020; Schauer, 2024; Taguchi, 2017). As mentioned in Chapter 2, under the broad view of pragmatic competence, language learners perform and understand communicative action in social interaction, adjust and calibrate their intentions during the course of an interaction, pay attention to verbal and non-verbal features of the interaction, engage in reflection and collaborative dialogue, are mindful of sociopragmatic variation, and develop agency to make their own choices. And, in line with others (Jackson, 2019; Schauer, 2024), I consider that pragmatic competence represents a constituent of Intercultural Competence (IC). I agree with Deardorff (2006) and Fantini (2019) that IC is a process that develops over time according to the demands of the learning context, the situation and individual differences such as proficiency, motivation, willingness to communicate and cognitive ability, among others.

The intercultural speaker

Another goal of this book was to expand our understanding of the intercultural speaker as an individual who is responsible for making his or her own decisions. My conceptualization of the intercultural speaker is someone who engages in critical intercultural awareness; who makes decisions about what to say to whom, when, how, and where; who makes informed decisions about whether to speak or to remain silent; who agrees and disagrees; and who reflects and evaluates their own and others' perspectives. The goal of the intercultural speaker is to achieve common ground through joint interaction, reflection on intercultural understanding, and to develop metapragmatic awareness through reflection and collaboration.

My understanding of the intercultural speaker is congruent with existing work on ICC through intercultural understanding (Byram, 1997, 2021; Ishihara, 2019; McConachy, 2018; McConachy & Liddicoat, 2022; Wilkinson, 2020). Similarly, Beecroft (2022) takes a fresh look at the intercultural speaker as someone 'who can responsibly perform in communicative events by using their metapragmatic awareness to decide which linguistic structures they will use with interactants with either convergent or divergent linguacultures' (2022: 107). In Chapters 4–6, intercultural speakers are seen as learners, agents, and mediators in the foreign language classroom and in study abroad contexts. These learners engage in intercultural interaction, negotiate their identities, and reflect on issues of language use, contextual factors and pragmatic variation. In addition, agency allows intercultural speakers to communicate effectively and appropriately, making their own choices, which may or may not conform to the sociocultural expectations of the target culture.

Pragmatic competence and intercultural competence

Another aim of this book is to stimulate discussion around the relationship between pragmatic competence and IC. In Chapter 1 (Figure 1.2), I presented my understanding of ICC, which is based on an extension of Byram's model (1997, 2021). It comprises two general components: IC and communicative competence. While the former includes four dimensions for developing IC (knowledge, skills, attitudes, metapragmatic awareness), the latter comprises six competencies that allow the intercultural speaker to communicate effectively and appropriately in intercultural contexts: linguistic, pragmatic, sociolinguistic, discourse, interactional and strategic. Pragmatic competence refers to the intercultural speaker's ability to produce, comprehend, negotiate, calibrate and evaluate cultural understandings. Some of the dimensions of pragmatic competence include the negotiation and understanding of speech acts, evaluations of polite and impolite behavior, and the comprehension of implicit meanings such as irony, metaphor and sarcasm.

Previous models have proposed extensions to Byram's model of ICC. Schauer (2024), for example, examined the link between pragmatics and IC using perception data from teachers of modern languages. While the author maintains Byram's (2021) notion of IC (skills, attributes/characteristics, knowledge), she revised the notion of linguistic competence and added pragmatic competence. For Schauer, linguistic competence combines grammatical (structural elements), sociolinguistic and discourse competence; pragmatic competence includes speech acts, politeness and impoliteness. While the pragmatic component is a novel addition to her model, the linguistic component seems broad, as it includes sociolinguistic and discourse competencies. Beecroft (2022) proposed an insightful perspective to extend Byram's model adding *savoir agir*, which is placed at the interface between communicative competence and IC. According to Beecroft 2022 [Chapter 3], *savoir agir* comprises two components: (1) Perform; (2) Decide and Produce. The performative component has similar characteristics to the model I proposed in Chapter 1 (Figure 1.2) regarding interactional competence (the speaker's ability to initiate, maintain and end the interaction), pragmatic competence (the speaker's ability to produce and understand communicative action), and sociolinguistic competence (knowledge of register variation and an understanding of social factors). According to Beecroft, Decide engages the intercultural speaker through agency and metapragmatic awareness; this is reflected in my understanding of metapragmatic awareness (Figure 1.2; also Chapter 2). Finally, Beecroft's Produce aspect is responsible for the delivery of pragmalinguistic resources. This notion is reflected in the pragmatic competence component of my proposed model, for the service of pragmatics and discourse. Overall, while previous models expand our understanding and explain the link between pragmatic competence and IC, my proposed model expands on and revises the additional components of communicative competence. One of these is strategic competence, which is displayed in Figure 1.2 (Chapter 1), and is responsible for supporting the intercultural speaker with the delivery of pragmalinguistic and sociopragmatic resources.

The pragmatic-discursive approach proposed in this volume analyzes different dimensions of intercultural interaction with intercultural speakers in foreign language classroom and in study abroad contexts. The nine components illustrated in Chapter 3 (Figure 3.1) should be seen as interactive, dynamic and interdependent. Of these, metapragmatic awareness and variability highlight the intercultural speaker's agency and reflexivity. Metapragmatic awareness connects with variability to equip the intercultural speaker with reflexivity to select a linguistic form that matches the appropriate context where it is used, including an awareness of regional and social variation (Guilherme, 2022). My approach to intercultural interaction and cultural understanding engages the researcher in the analysis of data from natural and experimental sources, using qualitative and quantitative analysis. Further, it should be noted that the intercultural interaction component (Chapter 3, Figure 3.1) includes aspects of Beecroft's (2022) notion of *savoir agir*; in particular, the Perform component and Decide and Produce components, which are manifested in my model through the intercultural speaker's agency, metapragmatic awareness, and variability.

Chapters 4, 5, and 6 employed the model of ICC from a pragmatic perspective (Chapter 1, Figure 1.2) and the pragmatic-discursive approach (Chapter 3, Figure 3.1) to examine the negotiation of intercultural interaction, evaluations of politeness and impoliteness, sociocultural expectations, and understandings of contextual variables such as social distance, social power and degree of imposition.

Methodological implications

A pragmatic-discursive perspective to intercultural communication provides instructors with methodological and pedagogical resources to help learners become effective communicators in the foreign language classroom and in study abroad settings. Although natural spoken data are ideal classroom resources, the chapters in this book, and others (González Plasencia, 2019 [Chapter 4]; McConachy, 2018; Spencer & Franklin, 2009; Schneider, 2018), have shown that teachers can use the following methods to examine interaction and intercultural understanding: roleplay interactions, perception instruments (e.g. Likert scales), verbal reports, field-note data, critical incidents or impoliteness events (Culpeper, 2011; Culpeper et al., 2010; see also Félix-Brasdefer, 2018; Félix-Brasdefer & Hasler-Barker, 2017). For example, open roleplays allow teachers to examine speech acts in interactions across discourse, such as openings and closings, speech act sequences (invitation-response, complaints), markers of politeness and impoliteness, prosodic cues (low and rising intonation, duration, voice quality), as well as linguistic, situational and social variation. Verbal reports provide insights into the analysis of the learner's voice regarding reflection on and analysis of sociocultural expectations, along with instances of pragmatic resistance when learners choose to deviate from target-culture norms. Other methods used to collect evaluations of polite and impolite behavior include critical incidents or impoliteness events and Likert-scales, as in Chapter 6 (this book) and in Schauer (2024). Teachers and researchers can benefit from these methods to help students practice their oral and written skills in the foreign language classroom through intercultural dialogues, reflections on the contextual analysis of roleplay interactions, discussion of cultural and political topics, and attention to contextualization cues, such as intonation, eye gaze and body movement.

Future studies should triangulate speech-act data through gathering ethnographic data, followed by verbal reports to shed light on how learners at different stages of language development plan and execute speech acts during face-to-face interactions. This knowledge will provide a greater understanding of intercultural language-development via interdisciplinary analysis.

Pedagogical implications and intercultural citizenship

The role of the language instructor in higher education should be to prepare learners to be intercultural speakers who engage in reflection, intercultural understanding, and an awareness of global issues in the foreign language classroom and abroad contexts. Instructors should familiarize themselves with the main concepts of and frameworks on IC (knowledge, skills, attitudes metapragmatic awareness) to teach ICC through the various components of communicative competence discussed in Chapter 1 (Figure 1.2): linguistic, pragmatic, sociolinguistic, discourse, interactional and strategic. Instructors should also revise the language curriculum to include content on culture and pedagogical activities in various intercultural contexts.

Following previous research (Dimitrov & Haque 2016; Lallana & Salamanca, 2020), instructors have three main roles when teaching ICC: language mediator, trainer and social agent. As mediators they facilitate discussion and promote reflection on linguistic and global topics in the classroom; as trainers, they educate other teachers on topics related to IC and diversity; and, as social agents, they have the responsibility to promote discussion, awareness of identity, and reflection on topics that affect our world. Further, Lallana and Salamanca (2020: 5) also proposed developing IC for instructors to teach 'the ability to communicate and cooperate with multiple cultures'. For example, instructors should engage their students in the analysis of and reflection on intercultural episodes such as critical incidents through impoliteness events, complaining, and buying and selling in a variety of intercultural encounters. Instructors should also promote reflection on and analysis of contextual variables (social power and distance, degree of imposition), a discussion of stereotypes in one's own and other cultures, as well as an analysis of pragmatic variation through pluricentric languages among varieties of Arabic, Chinese, English, French, German and Spanish, among others (Schneider & Félix-Brasdefer, 2022). Overall, instructors should provide learners with an understanding of foundational concepts of IC and pragmatic competence to develop intercultural citizenship in the FL classroom and in study abroad contexts.

The ultimate goal of language learning is to prepare bilingual and multilingual learners to be intercultural citizens of the world (Barret & Golubeva, 2022; Byram & Golubeva, 2020). Intercultural citizenship, a concept proposed and developed in Byram's work (1997, 2021; Byram & Golubeva, 2020), prepares learners to become global individuals who value cultural diversity, express respect and openness to other cultures, develop linguistic, social and cognitive skills to interpret and interact, are aware of intercultural differences, agree with and challenge the opinions of others, and communicate with people from other national and transnational cultures. Future research should look at intercultural understanding of heritage language learners; that is, individuals who grow up in bilingual communities speaking the heritage language at home. With the increasing enrollment of heritage language learners in US institutions and in others around the world (Xiao-Desai, 2019), researchers should investigate how heritage language learners develop intercultural understanding in two or more languages.

The mission of higher education is to prepare students to become global citizens of the world through critical intercultural awareness. An intercultural citizen engages in interaction with people from different national varieties of pluricentric languages and communicates in contexts of *lingua franca*. These global citizens interact with individual members of minority communities, such as speakers of Nahuatl and Maya (Mexico), Quechua (Peru, Ecuador, and Bolivia), Guaraní (Paraguay), as well as engage with communities in post-colonial languages in Africa such as English (Ghana, Uganda), French (Senegal, Congo), Spanish (Equatorial Guinea), or Portuguese (Guinea-Bissau). Teachers in higher education have the responsibility to prepare students, linguistically and to become intercultural citizens of the world.

Finally, the interdependence of language and cultural understanding is part of the learner's ICC and should be included in the language curriculum. Learners should be seen as intercultural speakers who have the capacity to act as an agent and mediator: active learners who are responsible for their own pragmalinguistic and sociopragmatic choices, and someone who can make their own choices, including the ability to resist selecting the linguistic and cultural norms of the target culture. The learner represents a global citizen who is able to interact globally with peers and teachers. Overall, the chapters in this book have shown that the learning of pragmatics goes beyond the pragmalinguistic and sociopragmatic dimensions, adding an emphasis on intercultural understanding, metapragmatic awareness, agency, mediation, variation and language use in action.

References

Achiba, M. (2003) *Learning to Request in a Second Language: A Study of Child Interlanguage Pragmatics*. Multilingual Matters.
Adamson, H.D. (1988) *Variation Theory and Second Language Acquisition*. Georgetown University Press.
Ahearn, L.M. (2001) Language and agency. *Annual Review of Anthropology* 30, 109–137.
Alcón, E. and Guzmán, J. (2010) The effect of instruction on learners' pragmatic awareness: A focus on refusals. *International Journal of English Studies* 10, 65–80.
Alcón-Soler, E. (2015) Pragmatic learning and study abroad: Effects of instruction and length of stay. *System* 48, 62–74.
Arasaratnam-Smith, L.A. (2017) Intercultural competence: An Overview. In D.K. Deardorff and L.A. Arasaratnam-Smith (eds) *Intercultural Competence in International Education: International Approaches, Assessment and Application* (pp. 7–18). Routledge.
Arundale, R.B. (2009) Face as an emergent in interpersonal communication: An alternative to Goffman. In F. Bargiela-Chiappini and M. Haugh (eds) *Face, Communication and Social Interaction* (pp. 33–54). Equinox.
Auer, P. (1992) Introduction: John Gumperz' approach to contextualization. In P. Auer and A. Di Luzio (eds) *The Contextualization of Language* (pp. 1–37). John Benjamins.
Austin, J.L. (1962) *How to Do Things with Words* (2nd edn). Harvard University Press.
Bachman, L.F. (1990) *Fundamental Considerations in Language Testing*. Oxford University Press.
Bachman, L.F. and Palmer A.S. (1994) *Language Testing in Practice: Designing and Developing Useful Language Tests*. Oxford University Press.
Bardovi-Harlig, K. (1999) Exploring the interlanguage of interlanguage pragmatics: A research agenda for acquisitional pragmatics. *Language Learning* 49, 677–713.
Bardovi-Harlig, K. (2001) Evaluating the empirical evidence: Grounds for instruction in pragmatics? In K.R. Rose and G. Kasper (eds) *Pragmatics in Language Teaching* (pp. 13–32). Cambridge University Press.
Bardovi-Harlig, K. (2013) Developing L2 pragmatics. *Language Learning* 63, 68–86.
Bardovi-Harlig, K. (2014) Awareness of meaning of conventional expressions in second-language pragmatics. *Language Awareness* 23 (1–2), 1–56.
Bardovi-Harlig, K. and Hartford, B.S. (1993) Learning the rules of academic talk: A longitudinal study of pragmatic change. *Studies in Second Language Acquisition* 15, 279–304.
Bardovi-Harlig, K. and Dörnyei, Z. (1998) Do language learners recognize pragmatic violations? Pragmatic vs. grammatical awareness in instructed L2 learning. *TESOL Quarterly* 32 (2), 233–262.
Bardovi-Harlig, K. and Griffin, R. (2005) L2 pragmatic awareness: Evidence from the ESL classroom. *System* 33 (3), 401–415.
Bardovi-Harlig, K. and Bastos, M. (2011) Proficiency, length of stay, and intensity of interaction. *Intercultural Pragmatics* 8, 347–384.
Bardovi-Harlig, K., Mossman, S. and Vellenga, H.E. (2015) The effect of instruction on pragmatic routines in academic discussion. *Language Teaching Research* 19 (3), 324–50.

Barret, M. and Golubeva, I. (2022) From intercultural communicative competence to intercultural citizenship: Preparing young people for citizenship in a culturally diverse democratic world. In T. McConachy, I. Golubeva and M. Wagner (eds) *Intercultural Learning in Language Education and Beyond: Evolving Concepts, Perspectives and Practices* (pp. 60–83). Multilingual Matters.

Barron, A. (2003) *Acquisition in Interlanguage Pragmatics: Learning How to Do Things with Words in a Study Abroad Context*. John Benjamins.

Barron, A. (2019) Norms and variation in L2 pragmatics. In N. Taguchi (ed.) *The Routledge Handbook of Second Language Pragmatics* (pp. 447–61). Routledge.

Barron, A. (2020) Developing pragmatic competence in a study abroad context. In K.P. Schneider and E. Ifantidou (eds) *Developmental and Clinical Pragmatics* (pp. 429–474). De Gruyter Mouton.

Barron, A. and Schneider, K. (2009) Variational pragmatics: Studying the impact of social factors on language use in interaction. *Intercultural Pragmatics* 6 (4), 425–442.

Barron, A., Gu, Y. and Steen, G. (eds) (2017) *The Routledge Handbook of Pragmatics*. Routledge.

Beebe, L. (1995) Polite fictions: Instrumental rudeness as pragmatic competence. In J. Alatis and C. Ferguson (eds) *Languages and Linguistics* (pp. 154–168). Georgetown University Press.

Beebe, L.M., Takahashi, T. and Uliss-Weltz, R. (1990) Pragmatic transfer in ESL refusals. In R.C. Scarcella, E.S. Andersen and S.D. Krashen (eds) *Developing Communicative Competence in Second Language* (pp. 55–73). Newbury House.

Beecroft, R. (2022) *The Performativity of the Intercultural Speaker: Promoting Savoir Agir through Improvisational Tasks*. Peter Lang.

Bennett, M.J. (1993) Towards ethnorelativism: A developmental model of intercultural sensitivity. In R.M. Paige (ed.) *Education for the Intercultural Experience* (pp. 21–72). Intercultural Press.

Bennett, J.M. and Bennett, M.J. (2004) Developing intercultural sensitivity: An integrative approach to global and domestic diversity. In D. Landis, J. Bennett and M. Bennett (eds) *Handbook of Intercultural Training* (3rd edn, pp. 147–165). Sage.

Bennett, M.J. (1995) Critical incidents in an intercultural conflict-resolution exercise. In S.M. Fowler and M.G. Mumford (eds) *Intercultural Sourcebook: Cross-Cultural Training Methods*, Vol. 1 (pp. 147–56). Intercultural Press.

Bennett, M.J. (2004) Becoming interculturally competent. In J. Wurzel (ed.) *Toward Multiculturalism: A Reader in Multicultural Education* (2nd edn, pp. 62–77). Intercultural Resource Corporation.

Bialystok, E. (1993) Symbolic representation and attentional control in pragmatic competence. In G. Kasper and S. Blum-Kulka (eds) *Interlanguage Pragmatics* (pp. 43–57). Oxford University Press.

Block, D. (2007) *Second Language Identities*. Continuum.

Blum-Kulka, S., House, J. and Kasper. G. (1989) *Cross-Cultural Pragmatics: Requests and Apologies*. Ablex.

Bou-Franch, P. (2021) Pragmatics and digital discourse in Spanish research. In D.A. Koike and J.C. Félix-Brasdefer (eds) *The Routledge Handbook of Spanish Pragmatics* (pp. 533–547). Routledge.

Brown, L. and Prieto, P. (2021) Gesture and prosody in multimodal communication. In M. Haugh, D.Z. Kádár and M. Terkourafi (eds) *The Cambridge Handbook of Sociopragmatics* (pp. 430–453). Cambridge University Press.

Brown, P. and Levinson, S. (1987) *Politeness: Some Universals in Language Use*. Cambridge University Press.

Bühler, K. (1990) *Theory of Language: The Representational Function of Language* (trans. Donald F. Goodwin). John Benjamins.

Byram, M. (1997) *Teaching and Assessing Intercultural Communicative Competence* (1st edn). Multilingual Matters.

Byram, M. (2021) *Teaching and Assessing Intercultural Communicative Competence: Revisited* (2nd edn). Multilingual Matters.
Byram, M. and Zarate, G. (1994) *Definitions, Objectives, and Assessment of Sociocultural Competence*. Council of Europe.
Byram, M. and Golubeva, I. (2020) Conceptualizing intercultural (communicative) competence and intercultural citizenship. In J. Jackson (ed.) *The Routledge Handbook of Language and Intercultural Communication* (pp. 70–85). Routledge.
Callahan, L. (2009) *Spanish and English in U.S. Service Encounters*. Palgrave/Macmillan.
Canale, M. (1983) From communicative competence to communicative language pedagogy. In J.C. Richard and R.W. Schmidt (eds) *Language and Communication* (pp. 2–14). Longman.
Canale, M. and Swain, M. (1980) Theoretical bases of communicative approaches to second language teaching and testing. *Applied Linguistics* 1 (1), 1–47.
Celce-Murcia, M. (2007) Rethinking the role of communicative competence in language teaching. In E.A. Soler and M.S. Jordà (eds) *Intercultural Language Use and Language Learning* (pp. 41–57). Springer, Dordrecht.
Celce-Murcia, M., Dörnyei, Z. and Thurrell, S. (1995) A pedagogical framework for communicative competence: A pedagogically motivated model with content specifications. *Issues in Applied Linguistics* 6 (2), 5–35.
Chen, G.M. and Starosta, W.J. (2005) *Foundations of Intercultural Communication*. Allyn & Bacon.
Chen, X., Ye, L. and Zhang, Y. (1995) Refusing in Chinese. In G. Kasper (ed.) *Pragmatics of Chinese as Native and Target Language, Technical Report #5. Second Language Teaching and Curriculum Center* (pp. 119–163). University of Hawai'i at Manoa.
Chomsky, N. (1965) *Aspects of the Theory of Syntax*. M.I.T. Press.
Clark, H. (1996) *Using Language*. Cambridge University Press.
Cohen, A.D. (1998) *Strategies in Learning and Using a Second Language*. Longman.
Cohen, A.D. (2005) Strategies for learning and performing L2 speech acts. *Intercultural Pragmatics* 2 (3), 275–301.
Cohen, A.D. (2012) Research methods for describing variation in intercultural pragmatics for cultures in contact and conflict. In J.C. Félix-Brasdefer and D.A. Koike (eds) *Pragmatic Variation in First and Second Language Contexts* (pp. 271–294). John Benjamins.
Cohen, A.D. and Olshtain, E. (1981) Developing a measure of sociolinguistic competence: The case of apology. *Language Learning* 31, 112–134.
Colle, L. (2020) Pragmatic competence in autism spectrum disorders. In K.P. Schneider and E. Ifantidou (eds) *Developmental and Clinical Pragmatics* (pp. 523–544). De Gruyter Mouton.
Collentine, J. (2009) Study abroad research: Findings, implications, and future directions. In M.H. Long and C.J. Doughty (eds) *The Handbook of Language Teaching* (pp. 218–233). Blackwell.
Cordella, M. (1990) Apologizing in Chilean Spanish and Australian English: A cross-cultural perspective. *Australian Review of Applied Linguistics* 7, 66–92.
Crystal, D. (1997) *English as a Global Language*. Cambridge University Press.
Cui, G. and Awa, N. (1992) Measuring intercultural effectiveness: An integrative approach. *International Journal of Intercultural Relations* 16, 311–328.
Culpeper, J.V. (2011) *Impoliteness: Using Language to Cause Offence*. Cambridge University Press.
Culpeper, J.V. (2021) Sociopragmatics: Roots and definition. In M. Haugh, D.Z. Kádár and M. Terkourafi (eds) *The Cambridge Handbook of Sociopragmatics* (pp. 16–29). Cambridge University Press.
Culpeper, J.V. and Haugh, M. (2014) *Pragmatics and the English Language*. Palgrave Macmillan.

Culpeper, J.V. and Hardaker, C. (2017) Impoliteness. In J.V. Culpeper, M. Haugh and D.Z. Kádár (eds) *The Palgrave Handbook of Linguistic (Im)politeness* (pp. 199–225). Palgrave Macmillan.

Culpeper, J.V. and Haugh, M. (2021) (Im)politeness and sociopragmatics. In M. Haugh, D.Z. Kádár and M. Terkourafi (eds) *The Handbook of Sociopragmatics* (pp. 315–339). Cambridge University Press.

Culpeper, J.V., Marti, L., Mei, M., Nevala, M. and Schauer, G. (2010) Cross-cultural variation in the perception of impoliteness: A study of impoliteness events reported by students in England, China, Finland, Germany, and Turkey. *Intercultural Pragmatics* 7 (4), 597–624.

Culpeper, J.V., Schauer, G. and Marti, L. (2014) Impoliteness and emotions in a cross-cultural perspective. *SPELL: Swiss Papers in English Language and Literature* 30, 67–88.

Culpeper, J.V., Haugh, M. and Kádár, D.Z. (eds) (2017) *The Palgrave Handbook of Linguistic (Im)politeness*. Palgrave Macmillan.

Dávila-Romero, R. (2022) Competencia intercultural y conciencia cultural en el aula de lenguas extranjeras: Evolución del concepto de cultura en un grupo de nivel inicial. *Human Review* 22, 1–10.

Deardorff, D.K. (2004) The identification and assessment of intercultural competence as a student outcome of international education at institutions of higher education in the United States. Unpublished PhD dissertation, North Carolina State University, Raleigh.

Deardorff, D.K. (2006) Identification and assessment of intercultural competence as a student outcome of internationalization. *Journal of Studies in International Education* 10 (3), 241–266.

Deardorff, D.K. (2015) Definitions: Knowledge, skills, attitudes. In J.M. Bennett (ed.) *The SAGE Encyclopedia of Intercultural Competence, Vol. 1* (pp. 217–220). Sage.

Deardorff, D.K. and Arasaratnam-Smith, L.A. (eds) (2017) *Intercultural Competence in International Education: International Approaches, Assessment and Application*. Routledge.

Diaz, A.R. (2013) *Developing Critical Languaculture Pedagogies in Higher Education: Theory and Practice*. Multilingual matters.

DiBartolomeo, M. (2022) Moving beyond lo siento: The effect of pragmatic instruction on the production and perception of apologies in L2 Spanish. Unpublished doctoral dissertation, Indiana University, Bloomington.

Dimitrov, N. and Haque, A. (2016) Intercultural teaching competence: A multi-disciplinary model for instructor reflection. *Intercultural Education* 27 (5), 437–456.

Dings, A. (2014) Interactional competence and the development of alignment activity. *The Modern Language Journal* 98 (3), 742–756.

Dorai, S. and Webster, C. (2015) The role of nonverbal communication in service encounters. In M. Hernández-López and L. Fernández-Amaya (eds) *A Multidisciplinary Approach to Service Encounters* (pp. 211–228). Brill.

Duff, P.A. (2012) Identity, agency, and second language acquisition. In A. Mackey and S. Gass (eds) *Handbook of Second Language Acquisition* (pp. 410–426). Routledge.

DuFon, M.A. and Churchill, E.E. (2006) *Language Learners in Study Abroad Contexts*. Multilingual Matters.

Duranti, A. (2004) Agency in language. In A. Duranti (ed.) *A Companion to Linguistic Anthropology* (pp. 451–473). Blackwell.

Duranti, A. and Goodwin, C. (eds) (1992) *Rethinking Context: Language as an Interactive Phenomenon*. Cambridge University Press.

Edmondson, W. (1981) *Spoken Discourse: A Model for Analysis*. Longman.

Eelen, G. (2001) *A Critique of Politeness Theories*. St. Jerome.

Ellis, R. (1992) Learning to communicate in the classroom: A study of two language learners' requests. *Studies in Second Language Acquisition* 14, 1–23.

Ericsson, K.A. and Simon, H.A. (1993) *Protocol Analysis: Verbal Reports as Data*. MIT Press.
Escandell-Vidal, V. and Prieto, P. (2021) Pragmatics and prosody in research on Spanish. In D.A. Koike and J.C. Félix-Brasdefer (eds) *The Routledge Handbook of Spanish Pragmatics* (pp. 149–166). Routledge.
Fantini, A.E. (2006) *Exploring and Assessing Intercultural Competence*. SIT Graduate Institute.
Fantini, A.E. (2019) *Intercultural Communicative Competence in Educational Exchange: A Multinational Perspective*. Routledge.
Fantini, A.E. (2020) Language: An essential component of intercultural communicative competence. In J. Jackson (ed.) *The Routledge Handbook of Language and Intercultural Communication* (2nd edn, pp. 262–287). Routledge.
Fantini, A.E. and Tirmizi, A. (2006) Exploring and assessing intercultural competence. *World Learning Publications* 1 (1), 6–139.
Félix–Brasdefer, J.C. (2004) Interlanguage refusals: Linguistic politeness and length of residence in the target community. *Language Learning* 54 (4), 587–653.
Félix-Brasdefer, J.C. (2006a) Linguistic politeness in Mexico: Refusal strategies among male speakers of Mexican Spanish. *Journal of Pragmatics* 38 (12), 2158–2187.
Félix-Brasdefer, J.C. (2006b) Teaching the negotiation of multi-turn speech acts: Using conversation-analytic tools to teach pragmatics in the FL classroom. *Pragmatics and Language Learning* 11, 165–197.
Félix-Brasdefer, J.C. (2007) Pragmatic development in the Spanish as an FL classroom: A cross-sectional study of learner requests. *Intercultural Pragmatics* 4, 253–286.
Félix-Brasdefer, J.C. (2008) *Politeness in Mexico and the United States: A Contrastive Study of the Realization and Perception of Refusals*. John Benjamins.
Félix-Brasdefer, J.C. (2012) Pragmatic variation by gender in market service encounters in Mexico. In J.C. Félix-Brasdefer and D. Koike (eds) *Pragmatic Variation in First and Second Language Contexts: Methodological Issues* (pp. 17–48). John Benjamins.
Félix-Brasdefer, J.C. (2015) *The Language of Service Encounters: A Pragmatics-Discursive Approach*. Cambridge University Press.
Félix-Brasdefer, J.C. (2017a) Interlanguage pragmatics. In Y. Huang (ed.) *The Oxford Handbook of Pragmatics* (pp. 416–434). Oxford University Press.
Félix-Brasdefer, J.C. (2017b) The intercultural speaker abroad. In R. Giora and M. Haugh (eds) *Papers in Honor of Istvan Kecskes* (pp. 353–370). Mouton de Gruyter.
Félix-Brasdefer, J.C. (2018) Role plays. In A.H. Jucker, K.P. Schneider and W. Bublitz (eds) *Methods in Pragmatics* (pp. 305–311). De Gruyter Mouton.
Félix-Brasdefer, J.C. (2019a) *Pragmática del Español: Contexto, Uso y Variación* [Spanish Pragmatics: Context, Use, and Variation]. Routledge.
Félix-Brasdefer, J.C. (2019b) Speech acts in interaction: Negotiating joint action in a second language. In N. Taguchi (ed.) *The Routledge Handbook of Second Language Pragmatics* (pp. 17–30) Routledge.
Félix-Brasdefer, J.C. (2020a) Pragmatic transfer. In K.P. Schneider and E. Infantidou (eds) *Developmental and Clinical Pragmatics* (pp. 361–391). De Gruyter Mouton.
Félix-Brasdefer, J.C. (2020b) La comunicación intercultural [Intercultural communication]. In V. Escandell-Vidal, J. Amenós Pons and A.K. Ahern (eds) *Manual de Pragmática* (pp. 742–755). Akal.
Félix-Brasdefer, J.C. (2021a) Pragmatic variation across varieties of Spanish. In D.A. Koike and J.C. Félix-Brasdefer (eds) *The Routledge Handbook of Spanish Pragmatics* (pp. 269–287). Routledge.
Félix-Brasdefer, J.C. (ed.) (2021b) Teaching and assessing pragmatic and intercultural competence in foreign language contexts. *IU Working Papers in Linguistics* 21 (2), 1–14. Indiana University Bloomington, USAM.
Félix-Brasdefer, J.C. and Cohen, A.D. (2012) Teaching pragmatics in the foreign language classroom: Grammar as a communicative resource. *Hispania* 95 (4), 650–669.

Félix-Brasdefer, J.C. and Hasler-Barker, M. (2012) Compliments and compliment responses: From empirical evidence to pedagogical application. In L. Ruiz de Zarobe and Y. Ruiz de Zarobe (eds) *Speech Acts and Politeness across Languages and Cultures* (pp. 241–273). Peter Lang.

Félix-Brasdefer, J.C. and Koike, D.A. (2014) Perspectives on Spanish SLA from pragmatics and discourse. In M. Lacorte (ed.) *The Routledge Handbook of Hispanic Applied Linguistics* (pp. 25–43). Routledge.

Félix-Brasdefer, J.C. and Hasler-Barker, M. (2017) Elicited data. In A. Barron, Y. Gu and G. Steen (eds) *The Routledge Handbook of Pragmatics* (pp. 27–40). Routledge.

Félix-Brasdefer, J.C. and McKinnon, S. (2017) Perceptions of impolite behavior in study abroad contexts and the teaching of impoliteness in L2 Spanish. *Journal of Spanish Language Teaching* 3 (2), 99–113.

Félix-Brasdefer, J.C. and Mugford, G. (2017) (Im)politeness: Learning and teaching. In J.V. Culpeper, M. Haugh and D.Z. Kádár (eds) *The Palgrave Handbook of Linguistic (Im)Politeness* (pp. 489–516). Palgrave Macmillan.

Félix-Brasdefer, J.C. and Placencia, M.E. (eds) (2020) *Pragmatic Variation in Service Encounter Interactions across the Spanish-Speaking World*. Routledge.

Félix-Brasdefer, J.C. and Yates, A. (2020) Regional pragmatic variation in small shops in Mexico City, Buenos Aires, and Seville, Spain. In J.C. Félix-Brasdefer and M.E. Placencia (eds) *Pragmatic Variation in Service Encounter Interactions across the Spanish-Speaking World* (pp. 15–34). Routledge Press.

Fetzer, A. (2012) Contexts in interaction: Relating pragmatic wastebaskets. In R. Finkbeiner, J. Meibauer and P.B. Schumacher (eds) *What is a Context? Linguistic Approaches and Challenges* (pp. 105–127). John Benjamins.

Firth, J.R. (1935) The technique of semantics. *Transactions of the Philological Society* 34 (1), 36–73.

Firth, J.R. (1957) *Papers in Linguistics*. Oxford University Press.

Foster-Cohen, S.H. and van Bysterveldt, A.K. (2020). Pragmatic competence in down syndrome. In K.P. Schneider and E. Ifantidou (eds) *Developmental and Clinical Pragmatics* (pp. 545–580). De Gruyter Mouton.

Fraser, B. (2010) Pragmatic competence: The case of hedging. In G. Kaltenböck, W. Mihatsch and S. Schneider (eds) *New Approaches to Hedging* (pp. 15–34). Emeral.

Freed, B.F. (1995) *Second Language Acquisition in a Study Abroad Context*. John Benjamins Publishing Company.

Fried, M. (2010) Introduction: From instances of change to explanations of change. In M. Fried, J, Östman and J. Verschueren (eds) *Variation and Change* (pp. 1–16). John Benjamins.

Fuentes Rodríguez, C. (2010) *La Gramática de la Cortesía en Español/LE*. Arco Libros, S.L.

Garcés-Conejos Blitvich, P. (2021) Impoliteness and conflict in Spanish. In D.A. Koike and J.C. Félix-Brasdefer (eds) *The Routledge Handbook of Spanish Pragmatics* (pp. 371–386). Routledge

García, C. (1992) Refusing an invitation: A case study of Peruvian style. *Hispanic Linguistics* 5 (1–2), 207–243.

García, C. (1993) Making a request and responding to it: A case study of Peruvian Spanish speakers. *Journal of Pragmatics* 19, 127–152.

García, C. (1999) The three stages of Venezuelan invitations and responses. *Multilingua* 18 (4), 391–433.

Garcia, E.S. and Di Maggio, G. (2021) Teaching compliments and physical appearance in Spanish. *IULC Working Papers* 21 (2).

Gass, S.M. and Houck, N. (1999) *Interlanguage Refusals: A Cross-Cultural Study of Japanese-English*. Mouton de Gruyter.

Goffman, E. (1955) On face-work: An analysis of ritual elements in social interaction. *Psychiatry* 18 (3), 213–231.

Goffman, E. (1967) *Interaction Ritual: Essays on Face-to-Face Behavior.* Doubleday.
Goffman, E. (1981) *Forms of Talk.* University of Pennsylvania Press.
Goffman, E. (1983) The interaction order. *American Sociological Review* 48 (1), 1–17.
Golubeva, I., Wagner, M. and McConachy, T. (2022) Introduction: Michael Byram's contribution to intercultural learning in language education and beyond. In T. McConachy, I. Golubeva and M. Wagner (eds) *Intercultural Learning in Language Education and Beyond: Evolving Concepts, Perspectives and Practices* (pp. xxi–xxix). Multilingual Matters.
González Plasencia, Y. (2019) *Comunicación intercultural en la enseñanza de lenguas extranjeras.* (Intercultural Communication in the Teaching of Foreign Languages). Peter Lang.
Grice, H.P. (1975) Logic and conversation. In P. Cole and J. Morgan (eds) *Syntax and Semantics, Vol. 3: Speech Acts* (pp. 41–58). Academic Press.
Grice, H.P. (1989) *Studies in the Way of Words.* Harvard University Press.
Gudykunst, W.B. (2004) *Bridging Differences: Effective Intergroup Communication.* Sage Publications.
Guilherme, M. (2022) From critical cultural awareness to intercultural responsibility: Language, culture and citizenship. In T. McConachy, I. Golubeva and M. Wagner (eds) *Intercultural Learning in Language Education and Beyond: Evolving Concepts, Perspectives and Practices* (pp. 101–117). Multilingual Matters.
Gumperz, J.J. (1982) *Discourse Strategies.* Cambridge University Press.
Gumperz, J.J. (2015) Interactional sociolinguistics: A personal perspective. In D. Tannen, H.E. Hamilton and D. Schiffrin (eds) *The Handbook of Discourse Analysis* (pp. 309–323). John Wiley & Sons.
Guo, J. and Rodríguez, E. (2021) ¡Estás de buen ver! Teaching topic appropriateness. *IULC Working Papers* 21 (2).
Habermas, J. (1970) Towards a theory of communicative competence. *Inquiry: An Interdisciplinary Journal of Philosophy* 13, 360–375.
Habermas, J. (1987) *The Theory of Communicative Action.* Polity Press.
Hall, J.K. (2018) From L2 interactional competence to L2 interactional repertoires: Reconceptualizing the objects of L2 learning. *Classroom Discourse* 9 (1), 25–30.
Hall, J.K. and Pekarek Doehler, S. (2011) L2 interactional competence and development. In J.K. Hall, J. Hellerman and S. Pekarek Doehler (eds) *L2 Interactional Competence and Development* (pp. 1–15). Multilingual Matters.
Halliday, M.A.K. and Matthiessen, C.M.I.M. (2004) *An Introduction to Functional Grammar* (3rd edn). Arnold.
Hammer, M.R. (2012) The Intercultural development inventory: A new frontier in assessment and development of intercultural competence. In M. Vande Berg, R.M. Paige and K.H. Lou (eds) *Student Learning Abroad: What Our Students are Learning, What They are Not, and What We Can Do About It* (pp. 115–136). Stylus Publishing.
Hasler-Barker, M. (2016) Effects of metapragmatic instruction on the production of compliments and compliment responses: Learner-learner role-plays in the foreign language (FL) classroom. *Pragmatics and Language Learning* 14, 125–152.
Hassall, T. (1997) Requests by Australian learners of Indonesian. Unpublished PhD dissertation, Australian National University.
Haugh, M. (2009) Face and interaction. In F. Bargiela-Chiappini and M. Haugh (eds) *Face, Communication and Social Interaction* (pp. 1–30). Equinox.
Haugh, M. and Culpeper, J.V. (2018) Integrative pragmatics and (im) politeness theory. *Pragmatics and its Interfaces* 294, 213–239.
He, A.W. and Young, R. (1998) Language proficiency interviews: A discourse approach. In R. Young and A.W. He (eds) *Talking and Testing: Discourse Approaches to the Assessment of Oral Proficiency* (pp. 1–24). John Benjamins Publishing Company.
Henery, A. (2015) On the development of metapragmatic awareness abroad: Two case studies exploring the role of expert-mediation. *Language Awareness* 24 (4), 316–331.

Hernández-Flores, N. (1999) Politeness ideology in Spanish colloquial conversation: The case of advice. *Pragmatics* 9, 37–49.
Herring, S.C. and Androutsopoulos, J. (2015) Computer–mediated discourse 2.0. In D. Tannen, H.E. Hamilton and D. Schiffrin (eds) *The Handbook of Discourse Analysis* (2nd edn, pp. 127–151). Wiley-Blackwell.
Herring, S.C., Stein, D. and Virtanen, T. (eds) (2013) *Pragmatics of Computer-Mediated Discourse*. Mouton de Gruyter.
Holliday, R.J. (2018) *Understanding Intercultural Communication: Negotiating a Grammar of Culture* (2nd edn). Routledge.
Holmes, J. and Schnurr, S. (2005) Politeness, humor and gender in the workplace: Negotiating norms and identifying contestation. *Journal of Politeness Research* 1 (1), 121–149.
House, J. and Kádár, D.Z. (2021) *Cross-Cultural Pragmatics*. Cambridge University Press.
Howard, M. and Shively, R.L. (2022) Interculturality and the study abroad experience: Pragmatic and sociolinguistic development. In I. Kecskes (ed.) *The Cambridge Handbook of Intercultural Pragmatics* (pp. 788–814). Cambridge University Press.
Huang, Y. (2014) *Pragmatics* (2nd edn). Oxford University Press.
Huang, Y. (ed.) (2017a) Introduction: What is pragmatics. In Y. Huang (ed.) *The Oxford Handbook of Pragmatics* (pp. 1–18). Oxford University Press.
Huang, Y. (2017b) Neo-Gricean pragmatics. In Y. Huang (ed.) *The Oxford Handbook of Pragmatics* (pp. 47–78). Oxford University Press.
Hymes, D. (1962) The ethnography of speaking. In T. Gladwin and W. Sturtevant (eds) *Anthropology and Human Behavior* (pp. 13–53). Anthropological Society of Washington.
Hymes, D. (1972a) On communicative competence. In J.B. Pride and J. Holmes (eds) *Sociolinguistics: Selected Readings* (pp. 269–293). Penguin.
Hymes, D. (1972b) Models of the interaction of language and social life. In J.J. Gumperz and D. Hymes (eds) *Directions in Sociolinguistics: Ethnography of Communication* (pp. 35–71). Holt, Rinehart, and Winston.
Ifantidou, E. (2014) *Pragmatic Competence and Relevance*. John Benjamins.
Ifantidou, E. (2021) Second language pragmatics. In M. Haugh, D.Z. Kádár and M. Terkourafi (eds) *The Cambridge Handbook of Sociopragmatics* (pp. 758–79). Cambridge University Press.
Ifantidou, E. and Schneider, K.P. (2020) Pragmatic competence: Development and impairment. In K.P. Schneider and E. Ifantidou (eds) *Developmental and Clinical Pragmatics* (pp. 1–29). De Gruyter Mouton.
Isaacs, E.A. and Clark, H. (1990) Ostensible invitations. *Language in Society* 19, 493–509.
Isabelli-García, C., Bown, J., Plews, J.L. and Dewey, D.P. (2018) Language learning and study abroad. *Language Teaching* 51 (4), 439–484.
Ishihara, N. (2010) Instructional pragmatics: Bridging teaching, research, and teacher education. *Language and Linguistics Compass* 4 (10), 938–953.
Ishihara, N. (2019) Identity and agency in L2 pragmatics. In N. Taguchi (ed.) *The Routledge Handbook of Second Language Acquisition and Pragmatics* (pp. 161–175). Routledge.
Ishihara, N. and Cohen, A.D. (2010) *Teaching and Learning Pragmatics: Where Language and Culture Meet*. Routledge.
Ishihara, N. and Porcellato, A.M. (2022) Co-constructing nonessentialist pedagogy: Supporting teachers to support learners translingual agency through L2 pragmatics instruction. In T. McConachy and A.J. Liddicoat (eds) *Teaching and Learning Second Language Pragmatics for Intercultural Understanding* (pp. 151–172). Routledge.

Iwasaki, N. (2011) Learning L2 Japanese 'politeness' and 'impoliteness': Young American men's dilemmas during study abroad. *Japanese Language and Literature* 45 (1), 67–106.

Jackson, J. (2019) Intercultural competence and L2 pragmatics. In N. Taguchi (ed.) *The Routledge Handbook of Second Language Acquisition and Pragmatics* (pp. 479–494). Routledge.

Jakobson, R. (1960) Closing statement: Linguistics and poetics. In T.A. Sebeok (ed.) *Style in Language* (pp. 350–377). MIT Press.

Jefferson, G. (2004) Glossary of transcript symbols with an introduction. In G. Lerner. (ed.) *Conversation Analysis: Studies from the First Generation* (pp. 13–31). John Benjamins.

Johnstone, B. (2018) *Discourse Analysis* (3rd edn). Wiley-Blackwell.

Jones, R.H. (2017) Discourse. In A. Barron, Y. Gu and G. Steen (eds) *The Routledge Handbook of Pragmatics* (pp. 371–83). Oxford University Press.

Kádár, D.Z. and Haugh, M. (2013) *Understanding Politeness*. Cambridge University Press.

Kang, O. and Kermad, A. (2019) Prosody in L2 pragmatics research. In N. Taguchi (ed.) *The Routledge Handbook of Second Language Acquisition and Pragmatics* (pp. 78–92). Routledge.

Kasper, G. (1990) Linguistic politeness: Current research issues. *Journal of Pragmatics* 14 (2), 193–218.

Kasper, G. (ed.) (1996) The development of pragmatic competence. *Toegepaste Taalwetnschap in Artikelen* 55 (1), 103–120.

Kasper, G. (2000) Data collection in pragmatics research. In H. Spencer-Oatey (ed.) *Culturally Speaking: Managing Rapport through Talk across Cultures* (pp. 316–369). Continuum.

Kasper, G. (2006) Beyond repair: Conversation analysis as an approach to SLA. In K. Bardovi-Harlig and Z. Dörnyei (eds) *Themes in SLA Research* (pp. 83–99). John Benjamins.

Kasper, G. and Dahl, M. (1991) Research methods in interlanguage pragmatics. *Studies in Second Language Acquisition* 13 (2), 215–247.

Kasper, G. and Rose, K.R. (2002) *Pragmatic Development in a Second Language*. Blackwell.

Kasper, G. and Roever, C. (2005) Pragmatics in second language learning. In E. Hinkel (ed.) *Handbook of Research in Second Language Teaching and Learning* (pp. 317–344). Routledge.

Kecskes, I. (2014) *Intercultural Pragmatics*. Oxford University Press.

Kecskes, I. (2019) Impoliteness as a part of pragmatic competence in L2. In T. Szende and G. Alao (eds) *Pragmatic and Cross-Cultural Competences: Focus on Politeness* (pp. 51–68). P.I.E Peter Lang.

Kecskes, I. (2020) Interculturality and intercultural pragmatics. In J. Jackson (ed.) *Routledge Handbook of Language and Intercultural Communication* (pp. 67–84). Routledge.

Kecskes, I. (ed.) (2023) *Common Ground in First Language and Intercultural Interaction*. Gruyter Mouton.

Kelley, C. and Meyers, J.E. (1993) *The Cross-Cultural Adaptability Inventory*. Intercultural Press.

Kendon, A. (2010) Some topics in gesture studies. In A. Esposito, M. Bratanic, E. Keller and M. Marinaro (eds) *Fundamentals of Verbal and Nonverbal Communication and the Biometric Issue* (pp. 3–19). IOS Press.

Kinginger, C. (2011) Enhancing language learning in study abroad. Annual Review of *Applied Linguistics* 31 (1), 58–73.

Kinginger, C. (ed.) (2013) *Social and Cultural Aspects of Language Learning Context in Study Abroad*. John Benjamins.

Kinginger, C. and Carnine, J. (2019) Language learning at the dinner table: Two case studies of French homestays. *Foreign Language Annals* 52 (4), 850–872.

Klyukanov, I.E. (2021) *Principles of Intercultural Communication* (2nd edn). Routledge Press.

Koike, D.A. (2009) A grammar of L2 pragmatics: Issues in learning and teaching. In S.L. Katz and J. Watzinger-Tharp (eds) *Conceptions of L2 Grammar: Theoretical Approaches and Their Application in the L2 Classroom* (pp. 35–52). Cengage Heinle.

Koike, D. (2021) Research methods for Spanish pragmatics study. In D.A. Koike and J.C. Félix-Brasdefer (eds) *The Routledge Handbook of Spanish Pragmatics: Foundations and Interfaces* (pp. 567–582). Routledge.

Koike, D.A. and Félix-Brasdefer, J.C. (eds) (2021) *The Routledge Handbook of Spanish Pragmatics*. Routledge Press.

Kong, K. and Spenader, A. (eds) (2024) *Intercultural Citizenship in Language Education: Teaching and Learning Through Social Action*. Multilingual Matters.

Kramsch, C. (1986) From language proficiency to interactional competence. *The Modern Language Journal* 70 (4), 366–372.

Kramsch, C. (1998) The privilege of the intercultural speaker. In M. Myram and M. Fleming (eds) *Language Learning in Intercultural Perspective* (pp. 16–31). Cambridge University Press

Kramsch, C. (2009a) *The Multilingual Subject: What Foreign Language Learners Say about their Experience and Why it Matters*. Oxford University Press.

Kramsch, C. (2009b) Discourse, the symbolic dimension of intercultural competence. In A. Hu and M. Byram (eds) *Interkulturelle Kompetenz und fremdsprachliches Lernen. Modelle, Empirie, Evaluation* (pp. 107–121). Gunter Narr.

Kramsch, C. (2011) The symbolic dimensions of the intercultural. *Language Teaching* 44 (3), 354–367.

Krashen, S.D. (1982) *Principles and Practice in Second Language Acquisition*. Pergamon Press.

Labov, W. and Fanshel, D. (1977) *Therapeutic Discourse: Psychotherapy as Conversation*. Academic Press.

Lakoff, R. (1973) The logic of politeness: Or, minding your p's and q's. In C. Corum, T. Cedric Smith-Stark and A. Weiser (eds) *Papers from the 9th Regional Meeting of the Chicago Linguistic Society* (pp. 292–305). Chicago Linguistic Society.

Lallana, A. and Salamanca, P. (2020) Intercultural communicative competence in L2 Spanish: Guidelines for teaching training programs. *Journal of Spanish Language Teaching* (2), 178–192.

Lantolf, J. and Thorne, S. (2006) *Sociocultural Theory and the Genesis of Second Language Development*. Oxford University Press.

Leech, G.N. (1983) *Principles of Pragmatics*. Longman.

Leech, G.N. (2014) *The Pragmatics of Politeness*. Oxford University Press.

Levinson, S. (1983) *Pragmatics*. Cambridge University Press.

Levinson, S. (1992) Activity types and language. In P. Drew and J. Heritage (eds) *Talk at Work: Interaction in Institutional Settings* (pp. 66–100). Cambridge University Press.

Levinson, S. (1995) Three levels of meaning. In F.R. Palmer (ed.) *Grammar and Meaning: Essays in Honour of John Lyons* (pp. 90–115). Cambridge University Press.

Li, D. (2008) Pragmatic socialization. In P. Duff and N.H. Hornberger (eds) *Language Socialization: Encyclopedia of Language and Education* (pp. 71–83). Springer.

Liddicoat, A.J. (2022) Intercultural mediation in language teaching and learning. In T. McConachy, I. Golubeva and M. Wagner (eds) *Intercultural Learning in Language Education and Beyond: Evolving Concepts, Perspectives and Practices* (pp. 41–59). Multilingual Matters.

Liddicoat, A.J. and Scarino, A. (2013) *Intercultural Language Teaching and Learning*. John Wiley & Sons.

Liddicoat, A.J. and McConachy, T. (2019) Meta-pragmatic awareness and agency in language learners' constructions of politeness. In T. Szende and G. Alao (eds) *Pragmatic and Cross Cultural Competences: Focus on Politeness* (pp. 11–25). Peter Lang.

Llanes, A. (2021) The impact of study abroad on L2 Spanish pragmatics development. In D. Koike and J.C. Félix-Brasdefer (eds) *The Routledge Handbook of Spanish Pragmatics* (pp. 485–499). Routledge.

Locher, M.A. and Watts, R.J. (2005) Politeness theory and relational work. *Journal of Politeness Research* 1, 9–33.

López-Serrano, S. (2010) Learning languages in study abroad and at home contexts: A critical review of comparative studies. *Porta Linguarum* 13, 149–163.

Malinowski, B. (1923) The problem of meaning in primitive languages. In C.K. Ogden and I.A. Richards (eds) *The Meaning of Meaning* (pp. 296–336). Harcourt.

Malinowski, B. (1935) *Coral Gardens and their Magic: A Study of the Methods of Tilling the Soil and of Agricultural Rites in the Trobriand Islands, Vol. 2*. Allen & Unwin.

Marmaridou, S. (2011) Pramalinguistics and sociopragmatics. In B. Wolfram and N.R. Norrick (eds) *Foundations of Pragmatics* (pp. 77–106). Mouton de Gruyter.

Márquez Reiter, R. (2000) *Linguistic Politeness in Britain and Uruguay: A Contrastive Study of Requests and Apologies*. John Benjamins.

Márquez Reiter, R. and Placencia, M.E. (2005) *Spanish Pragmatics*. Palgrave/Macmillan.

Martínez-Flor, A. (2016) Teaching apology formulas at the discourse level: Are instructional effects maintained over time? *Estudios de Lingüística Inglesa Aplicada* 16, 13–48.

Martinsen, R.A. (2008) Short-term study abroad: Predicting changes in oral skills. *Foreign Language Annals* 43 (3), 504–530.

McConachy, T. (2018) *Developing Intercultural Perspectives on Language Use: Exploring Pragmatics and Culture in Foreign Language Learning*. Multilingual Matters.

McConachy, T. (2022) Language awareness and intercultural communicative competence: Revisiting the relationship. In T. McConachy, I. Golubeva and M. Wagner (eds) *Intercultural Learning in Language Education and Beyond: Evolving Concepts, Perspectives and Practices* (pp. 22–40). Multilingual Matters.

McConachy, T. (2023) Exploring pragmatic resistance and moral emotions in foreign language learning. In J. Shaules and T. McConachy (eds) *Transformation, Embodiment, and Wellbeing in Foreign Language Pedagogy: Enacting Deep Learning* (pp. 175–199). Bloomsbury Plc.

McConachy, T. and Spencer-Oatey, H. (2020) Developing pragmatic awareness. In K.P. Schneider and E. Ifantidou (eds) *Developmental and Clinical Pragmatics* (pp. 393–427). De Gruyter Mouton.

McConachy, T. and Fujino, H. (2022) Negotiating politeness practices and interpersonal connections in L2 Japanese: Insights from study abroad narratives. In T. McConachy and A.J. Liddicoat (eds) *Teaching and Learning Second Language Pragmatics for Intercultural Understanding* (pp. 19–39). Routledge.

McConachy, T. and Liddicoat, A.J. (eds) (2022) *Teaching and Learning Second Language Pragmatics for Intercultural Understanding*. Routledge.

McConachy, T., Golubeva, I. and Wagner, M. (eds) (2022) *Intercultural Learning in Language Education and Beyond: Evolving Concepts, Perspectives and Practices*. Multilingual Matters.

McHugh, E. and Uribe, M. (2021) ¿Se come igual en todo el mundo? Teaching intercultural competence through food. *IULC Working Papers* 21 (2).

Meier, A.J. (2015) The role of noticing in developing intercultural communicative competence. *Eurasian Journal of Applied Linguistics* 1 (1), 25–38.

Mey, J.L. (2001) *Pragmatics: An Introduction* (2nd edn). Blackwell.

Mills, S. (2003) *Gender and Politeness*. Cambridge University Press.

Mitchell, N. and Haugh, M. (2015) Agency, accountability and evaluations of impoliteness. *Journal of Politeness Research* 11 (2), 207–238.

Morris, C.W. (1938) Foundations of the theory of signs. In O. Neurath (ed.) *International Encyclopedia of Unified Science Vol. 1, no. 2* (pp. 1–59). University of Chicago Press.

Mugford, G. (2018) Critical intercultural impoliteness: "Where are you located? Can you please transfer me to someone who is American?" *Journal of Pragmatics* 134, 173–182.

Mugford, G. and Félix-Brasdefer, J.C. (2021) Politeness research in the Spanish-speaking world. In D.A. Koike and J.C. Félix-Brasdefer (eds) *The Routledge Handbook of Spanish Pragmatics* (pp. 353–369). Routledge.

Navarro, J. (2017) Intention (including speech acts). In A. Barron, Y. Gu and G. Steen (eds) *The Routledge Handbook of Pragmatics* (pp. 215–226). Routledge Press.

Norton, B. (2000) *Identity and Language Learning*. Pearson Education.

Ochs, E. (1988) *Culture and Language Development: Language Socialization and Language Acquisition in a Samoan Village*. Cambridge University Press.

Ogiermann, E. (2018) Discourse completion tasks. In A.H. Jucker, K.P. Schneider and W. Bublitz (eds) *Methods in Pragmatics* (pp. 229–255). De Gruyter Mouton.

Olshtain, E. and Cohen, A.D. (1983) Apology: A speech act set. In N. Wolfson and E. Judd (eds) *Sociolinguistics and Language Acquisition* (pp. 18–35). Newbury House.

Ohta, A.S. (2001) *Second Language Acquisition Process in the Classroom: Learning Japanese*. Lawrence Erlbaum Associates.

Oxford, R.L. (2011) *Teaching and Researching: Language Learning Strategies*. Routledge Press.

Pavlenko, A. and Blackledge, A. (eds) (2004) *Negotiation of Identities in Multilingual Contexts*. Multilingual Matters.

Pérez-Vidal, C. and Shively, R.L. (2019) L2 pragmatic development in study abroad settings. In N. Taguchi (ed.) *The Routledge Handbook of Second Language Acquisition and Pragmatics* (pp. 355–371). Routledge.

Placencia, M.E. (2011) Regional pragmatic variation. In G. Andersen and K. Aijmer (eds) *Pragmatics of Society* (pp. 79–113). Mouton de Mouton.

Placencia, M.E. (2016) Las ofertas en el regateo en MercadoLibre-Ecuador. In A.M. Bañón Hernández, M.d.M. Espejo Muriel, B. Herrero Muñoz-Cobo and J.L. López Cruces (eds) *Oralidad y Análisis del Discurso: Homenaje a Luis Cortés Rodríguez* (pp. 521–544). Editorial Universidad de Almería (Edual).

Poole, D. (1994) Language socialization in the second language classroom. *Language Learning* 42 (4), 593–616.

Riddiford, N. and Holmes, J. (2015) Assisting the development of sociopragmatic skills: Negotiating refusals at work. *System* 48, 129–140.

Risager, K. (2022) Intercultural communicative competence: Transnational and decolonial developments. In T. McConachy, I. Golubeva and M. Wagner (eds) *Intercultural Learning in Language Education and Beyond: Evolving Concepts, Perspectives and Practices* (pp. 3–21). Multilingual Matters.

Rogers, R. and Wetzel, M.M. (2013) Studying agency in literacy teacher education: A layered approach to positive discourse analysis. *Critical Inquiry in Language Studies* 10 (1), 62–92.

Rose, K.R. (2005) On the effects of instruction in second language pragmatics. *System* 33, 385–399.

Rose, K.R. and Kasper, G. (eds) (2001) *Pragmatics in Language Teaching*. Cambridge University Press.

Sacks, H., Schegloff E.A. and Jefferson, G. (1974) A simple systematics for the organization of turn-taking in conversation. *Language* 50, 696–735.

Salaberry, M.R. and Kunitz, S. (2019) *Teaching and Testing L2 Interactional Competence: Bridging Theory and Practice*. Routledge.

Salaberry, M.R., White, K. and Burch, A.R. (2019) Language learning and interactional experiences in study abroad settings: An introduction to the special issue. *Study Abroad Research in Second Language Acquisition and International Education* 4 (1), 1–18.

Saldaña, J. (2015) *Thinking Qualitatively: Methods of Mid.* Sage.
Saldaña, J. (2021) *The Coding Manual for Qualitative Researchers* (4th edn). Sage.
Savignon, S. (1972) *Communicative Competence: An Experiment in Foreign Language Teaching.* Center for Curriculum Development.
Savignon, S. (1983) *Communicative Competence: Theory and Classroom Practice: Texts and Contexts in Second Language Learning.* Addison-Wesley.
Savignon, S. (2002) Communicative language teaching: Linguistic theory and classroom practice. In S. Savignon (ed.) *Interpreting Communicative Language Teaching: Contexts and Concerns in Teacher Education* (pp. 1–27). Yale University Press.
Sbisà, M. (2002) Speech acts in context. *Language and Communication* 22 (4), 421–436.
Scarcella, R. (1979) On speaking politely in a second language. In C. Yorio, K. Perkins and J. Schachter (eds) *On TESOL '79: The Learner in Focus* (pp. 275–287). TESOL.
Scarino, A. and Kohler, M. (2022) Assessing intercultural capability: Insights from processes of eliciting and judging student learning. In T. McConachy, I. Golubeva and M. Wagner (eds) *Intercultural Learning in Language Education and Beyond: Evolving Concepts, Perspectives and Practices* (pp. 188–206). Multilingual Matters.
Schauer, G. (2004) May you speak louder maybe? Interlanguage pragmatics development in requests. In S.H. Foster-Cohen, M. Sharwood-Smith, A. Sorace and M. Ota (eds) *EUROSLA Yearbook* (pp. 253–273). John Benjamins.
Schauer, G. (2024) *Intercultural Competence and Pragmatics.* Palgrave McMillan.
Schegloff, E. (1968) Sequencing in conversational openings. *American Anthropologist* 70 (6), 1075–1090.
Schegloff, E. (2007) *Sequence Organization in Interaction: A Primer in Conversation Analysis.* Cambridge University Press.
Schiffrin, D. (2006) Discourse. In R. Fasold and J. Connor-Linton (eds) *An Introduction to Language and Linguistics* (pp. 169–203). Cambridge University Press.
Schmidt, R. (1993) Consciousness, learning, and interlanguage pragmatics. In G. Kasper and S. Blum-Kulka (eds) *Interlanguage Pragmatics* (pp. 21–42). Oxford University Press.
Schmidt, R. (1995) Consciousness and foreign language learning: A tutorial on the role of attention and awareness in learning. In R. Schmidt (ed.) *Attention and Awareness in Foreign Language Learning.* (pp. 1–63). University of Hawaii, Second Language Teaching and Curriculum Center.
Schneider, K.P. (2010) Variational pragmatics. In M. Fried (ed.) *Variation and Change: Pragmatic Perspectives* (pp. 239–267). John Benjamins.
Schneider, K.P. (2012) Appropriate behavior across varieties of English. *Journal of Pragmatics* 44, 1022–1037.
Schneider, K.P. (2017) Pragmatic competence and pragmatic variation. In R. Giora and M. Haugh (eds) *Doing Pragmatics Interculturally: Cognitive, Philosophical, and Sociopragmatic Perspectives* (pp. 315–333). Mouton de Gruyter.
Schneider, K.P. (2018) Methods and ethics of data collection. In A.H. Jucker, K.P. Schneider and W. Bublitz (eds) *Methods in Pragmatics* (pp. 37–93). Mouton de Gruyter.
Schneider, K.P. (2020) Rethinking pragmatic variation: The case of service encounters from a modified variational pragmatics perspective. In J.C. Félix-Brasdefer and M.E. Placencia (eds) *Pragmatic Variation in Service Encounter Interactions Across the Spanish-Speaking World* (pp. 251–264). Routledge.
Schneider, K.P. and Barron, A. (eds) (2008) *Variational Pragmatics: A Focus on Regional Varieties in Pluricentric Languages.* John Benjamins.
Schneider, K.P. and Placencia, M.E. (2017) (Im)politeness and regional variation. In J. Culpeper, M. Haugh and D. Kádár (eds) *The Palgrave Handbook of Linguistic (Im)politeness* (pp. 539–570). Palgrave Macmillan.
Schneider, K.P. and Félix-Brasdefer, J.C. (2022) Pragmatic variation across national varieties of pluricentric languages. In H.J. Andreas and H. Heiko (eds) *Pragmatics of Space* (pp. 637–678). Mouton De Gruyter.

Scollon, R. and Scollon, S. (2001) *Intercultural Communication* (2nd edn). Blackwell.
Searle, J.R. (1969) *Speech Acts: An Essay in the Philosophy of Language*. Cambridge University Press.
Searle, J.R. (1975) Indirect speech acts. In P. Cole and J. Morgan (eds) *Syntax and Semantics 3: Speech Acts* (pp. 59–82). Academic Press.
Searle, J.R. (1976) A classification of illocutionary acts. *Language in Society* 5 (1), 1–23.
Searle, J.R. (1977) A classification of illocutionary acts. In A. Rogers, B. Wall and J. Murphy (eds) *Proceedings of the Texas Conference on Performatives, Presupposition, and Implicatures* (pp. 27–45). Center for Applied Linguistics.
Searle, J.R. and Vanderveken, D. (1985) *Foundations of Illocutionary Logic*. Cambridge University Press.
Shishavan, H. (2016) Refusals of invitations and offers in Persian: Genuine or ostensible? *Journal of Politeness Research* 12 (1), 55–93.
Shively, R.L. (2011) L2 pragmatic development in study abroad: A longitudinal study of Spanish service encounters. *Journal of Pragmatics* 43 (6), 1818–1835.
Shively, R.L. (2015) Developing interactional competence during study abroad: Listener responses in L2 Spanish. *System* 48, 86–98.
Sidnell, J. (2010) *Conversation Analysis: An Introduction*. Wiley-Blackwell.
Solon, M. (2013) Cross-cultural negotiation: Touristic service encounters in Yucatán, Mexico. In C. Howe, S.E. Blackwell and M.L. Quesada (eds) *Selected Proceedings of the 15th Hispanic Linguistics Symposium* (pp. 252–268). Cascadilla Proceedings Project.
Spencer-Oatey, H. (2000) A problematic Chinese business visit to Britain: Issues of face. In H. Spencer-Oatey (ed.) *Culturally Speaking: Managing Rapport through Talk across Cultures* (pp. 272–288). Continuum.
Spencer-Oatey, H. (2002) Managing rapport in talk: Using rapport sensitive incidents to explore the motivational concerns underlying the management of relations. *Journal of Pragmatics* 34, 529–545.
Spencer-Oatey, H. (2005) (Im)politeness, face and perceptions of rapport: Unpackaging their bases and interrelationships. *Journal of Politeness Research* 1, 95–119.
Spencer-Oatey, H. (2008a) Face, (im)politeness and rapport. In H. Spencer-Oatey (ed.) *Culturally Speaking: Culture, Communication, and Politeness Theory* (2nd edn, pp. 11–47). Continuum.
Spencer-Oatey, H. (2008b) Introduction. In H. Spencer-Oatey (ed.) *Culturally Speaking: Culture, Communication, and Politeness Theory* (2nd edn, pp. 1–8). Continuum.
Spencer-Oatey, H. and Franklin, P. (2009) *Intercultural Interaction: A Multidisciplinary Approach to Intercultural Communication*. Palgrave Macmillan.
Sperber, D. and Wilson, D. (1986) *Relevance: Communication and Cognition*. Blackwell.
Sperber, D. and Wilson, D. (1995) *Relevance: Communication and Cognition* (2nd edn). Blackwell.
Spitzberg, B.H. and Changnon, G. (2009) Conceptualising intercultural competence. In D. Deardorff (ed.) *The Sage Handbook of Intercultural Competence* (pp. 2–52). Sage.
Stalnaker, R. (2002) Common ground. *Linguistics and Philosophy* 25 (5–6), 701–721.
Sternberg, R.J. (2000) Images of mindfulness. *Journal of Social Issues* 56 (1), 11–26.
Streeck, J. (1980) Speech acts in interaction: A critique of Searle. *Discourse Processes* 3 (2), 133–153.
Su, Y. (2020) Yes or no: Ostensible versus genuine refusals in Mandarin invitational and offering discourse. *Journal of Pragmatics* 162, 1–16.
Taguchi, N. (2013) Production of routines in L2 English: Effect of proficiency and study-abroad experience. *System* 41 (1), 109–121.
Taguchi, N. (2015) Instructed pragmatics at a glance: Where instructional studies were, are, and should be going. *Language Teaching* 48, 1–50.
Taguchi, N. (2016) Contexts and pragmatics learning: Problems and opportunities of the study abroad research. *Language Teaching*, 1–14.

Taguchi, N. (2017) Interlanguage pragmatics: A historical sketch and future directions. In A. Barron (ed.) *The Routledge Handbook of Pragmatics* (pp. 153–167). Mouton de Gruyter
Taguchi, N. and Roever, C. (2017) *Second Language Pragmatics*. Oxford University Press.
Takahashi, S. (2013) Pragmatic awareness in second language learning. In C.A. Chapelle (ed.) *The Encyclopedia of Applied Linguistics* (pp. 4505–4509). Wiley-Blackwell.
Tecedor, M. (2023) Negotiated interactions in cross-cultural video-mediated virtual exchanges. *Computer Assisted Language Learning*, 1–24.
Terkourafi, M. (2012) Between pragmatics and sociolinguistics: Where does pragmatic variation fit in? In J.C. Félix-Brasdefer and D.A. Koike (eds) *Pragmatic Variation in First and Second Language Context: Methodological Issues* (pp. 295–318). John Benjamins.
Thomas, J. (1983) Cross-cultural pragmatic failure. *Applied Linguistics* 4 (2), 91–112.
Tiffany, C. (2021) Teaching openings and requests in French café encounters. *IULC Working Papers* 21 (2).
Timpe-Laughlin, V., Wain, J. and Schmidgall, J. (2015) Defining and operationalizing the construct of pragmatic competence: Review and recommendations. *ETS Research Report Series* 2015 (1), 1–43.
Ting-Toomey, S. (1999) *Communicating Across Cultures*. Guilford Press.
Torrás, M.C. and Gafaranga, J. (2002) Social identities and language alternatives in non-formal institutional bilingual talk: Trilingual service encounters in Barcelona. *Language in Society* 31 (4), 527–548.
Usó-Juan, E. and Martínez-Flor, A. (2006) Approaches to language learning and teaching: Towards acquiring communicative competence through the four skills. In E. Usó-Juan and A. Martínez-Flor (eds) *Current Trends in the Development and Teaching of the Four Language Skills* (pp. 3–25). Mouton de Gruyer.
van Compernolle, R.A. (2014) *Sociocultural Theory and L2 Instructional Pragmatics*. Multilingual Matters.
van Compernolle, R.A. and Kinginger, C. (2013) Promoting metapragmatic development through assessment in the zone of proximal development. *Language Teaching Research* 17 (3), 282–302.
van Dijk, T.A. (1979) Pragmatic connectives. *Journal of Pragmatics* 3 (5), 447–456.
van Ek, J.A. (1986) *Objectives for Foreign Language Learning*. Council of Europe.
Verschueren, J. (1999) *Understanding pragmatics*. Edward Arnold.
Verschueren, J. (2021) Reflexivity and meta-awareness. In M. Haugh, D. Kádár and M. Terkourafi (eds) *The Cambridge Handbook of Sociopragmatics* (pp. 117–139). Cambridge University Press.
Vygotsky, L.S. (1978) *Mind in Society: The Development of Higher Psychological Processes*. Harvard University Press.
Vygotsky, L.S. (1997) *Educational Psychology*. St. Lucie Press.
Wagner, M., Perugini, D.C. and Byram, M. (2018) *Teaching Intercultural Competence Across the Age Range: From Theory to Practice*. Multilingual Matters.
Watts, R.J. (2003) *Politeness*. Cambridge University Press.
Watts, R.J., Ide, S. and Ehlich, K. (eds) (1992) *Politeness in Language: Studies in its History, Theory, and Practice*. Mouton de Gruyter.
Weinreich, U., Labov, W. and Herzog, M. (1968) Empirical foundations for a theory of language change. In W. Lehmann and Y. Malkiel (eds) *Directions for Historical Linguistics* (pp. 97–195). University of Texas Press.
Werkhofer, K.T. (2008) Traditional and modern views: The social constitution and the power of politeness. In R.J. Watts, S. Ide and K. Ehlich (eds) *Politeness in Language: Studies in Its History, Theory, and Practice* (pp. 155–199). Mouton de Gruyter.
Wilkinson, J. (2020) From native speaker to intercultural speaker and beyond: Intercultural (communicative) competence in foreign language education. In J. Jackson (ed.) *The Routledge Handbook of Language and Intercultural Communication* (pp. 283–298). Routledge.

Wilson, D. (2017) Relevance theory. In Y. Huang (ed.) *The Oxford Handbook of Pragmatics* (pp. 79–100). Oxford University Press.
Wilson, D. and Sperber, D. (2004) Relevance theory. In L. Horn and G. Ward (eds) *The Handbook of Pragmatics* (pp. 607–632). Blackwell.
Wittgenstein, L. (1958) *Philosophical Investigations* (trans. G.E.M. Anscombe). Blackwell.
Xiao-Desai, Y. (2019) Heritage learner pragmatics. In N. Taguchi (ed.) *The Routledge Handbook of Second Language Acquisition and Pragmatics* (pp. 462–478). Routledge.
Young, R.F. (2011) Interactional competence in language learning, teaching, and testing. In E. Hinkel (ed.) *Handbook of Research in Second Language Teaching and Learning, Vol. 2* (pp. 233–268). Routledge.
Young, R.F. (2019) Interactional competence and L2 pragmatics. In N. Taguchi (ed.) *The Routledge Handbook of Second Language Acquisition and Pragmatics* (pp. 93–110). Routledge.
Yule, G. (1996) *Pragmatics*. Oxford University Press.
Žegarac, V., Spencer-Oatey, H. and Ushioda, E. (2014) Conceptualizing mindfulness-mindlessness in intercultural interaction. *International Journal of Language and Culture* 1 (1), 75–97.
Zuengler, J. (1989) Identity and IL development and use. *Applied Linguistics* 10 (1), 80–96.

Index

agency 3, 9, 54, 72, 81, 105, 116–117, 124, 129, 133, 155, 163–165, 167, 178–180
Alcón-Soler, E. 78
attention 57–60, 62–63
Austin, J.L. 6, 27, 57–59

Bardovi-Harlig, K. 41, 44–45, 77–78
Barron, A. 34, 40–41, 57, 69–70
Beecroft, R. 1, 11, 187
Bennett, M.J. 18–20
Byram, M. 1, 11, 16–189, 22–25, 35, 83, 182

Celce-Murcia, M. 27–32
Clark, H. 6, 59, 65,
Cohen, A.D. 29, 35, 54, 67, 87, 98
context 6–7, 20, 27, 30, 40, 47, 58, 63–65
contextualization cue 62, 71
critical intercultural awareness, 19, 68, 187, 191
Culpeper, J. 12–13, 57, 67, 114, 130, 160–162, 165–166, 168–170

Deardorff, D.K. 16–19, 21, 24, 35, 186
DiBartolomeo, M. 45
directness, 44, 70, 74, 76, 89, 91, 97, 113, 152
discourse competence 22, 27, 29, 34
discourse completion test (DCT) 82, 86, 188

emergent common ground 58, 65–66

Fantini, A.E. 16, 18–19, 23–24, 35
felicity conditions 7, 14, 59, 61
Félix-Brasdefer, J. C. 3–4, 13, 31, 44–46, 53, 57, 66, 69–71, 76–77–79, 86–87, 89, 97, 116, 126–128, 138, 144, 153, 156, 176, 184, 189

García, C. 87, 106, 138, 144
Goffman, E. 7, 30, 182
Golubeva, I. 17, 21, 191
González Plasencia, Y. 189
Grice, H.P. 14–15, 41–42, 57, 60–63, 161
Gudykunst, W.B. 16
Guilherme, M. 19, 68, 73, 189
Gumperz, J. J. 57, 62, 71

Hasler-Barker, M. 66, 71, 78, 86, 198
Huang, Y. 13, 61

incidental learning 44, 76–77
identity 8, 160, 163–164, 166
impoliteness 51, 53, 67, 74, 89, 159, 161, 163, 165–170
indirectness, 44, 59, 70, 74, 76, 89, 91, 93, 96–97, 127, 152–153
insistence 87, 89, 112, 115, 121–123, 137–138–40
intention 14–15, 27, 29, 42, 47, 57–58, 60, 61
interactional competence 23, 30–31, 35, 51, 188
intercultural communicative competence 3, 11, 17–19, 21–22, 33, 63, 67, 75
intercultural competence 3–4, 15–19, 21–22, 2–25, 32–33, 35–36, 78, 80, 97
intercultural speaker 2–3, 7, 17, 19, 21, 25, 28, 36, 52–53, 71–72, 163, 165, 167, 178, 183–184
intercultural understanding 1–3, 6, 38, 56, 58, 74, 132
Ishihara, N. 2, 46, 52, 54, 56, 77–78, 105–106, 124, 129, 155, 164, 182

Kasper, G. 2–3, 31, 40–41, 44–45, 53, 66–67, 76, 78, 85–86
Kecskes, I. 2–6, 12, 15–17, 32, 40, 42, 50–52, 57, 63, 65–66, 72, 129, 16–63, 179, 186
Kinginger, C. 32, 49, 90
Koike, D.A. 13, 40, 42, 45, 66
Kramsch, C. 17, 30–31, 35, 163, 179

Leech, G.N. 34, 41, 44, 76, 112, 114, 129, 160
Liddicoat, A. J. 1–3, 11, 36, 50, 52, 54, 56, 58, 68, 74, 76, 80–81, 84, 106, 118, 123, 157, 165, 178, 182
Likert-scale 67, 173

Martínez-Flor, A. 29, 31–32
McConachy, T. 1–4, 7–8, 11, 17, 36–37, 50, 52, 54, 56, 58, 68, 74, 78–79, 81–82, 8, 90, 105–106, 123–125, 129, 132, 155, 157, 178, 182
Mediation 51–52, 56, 68, 133, 159, 163, 165
Meier, A.J. 16, 18, 67, 68, 111
metapragmatic awareness 4, 6–7, 33, 36, 38, 40, 48–49, 52, 58, 67–69, 84, 100, 111, 130, 133–134
mindfulness 68
Mugford, G. 167, 176, 184

politeness 161–162
pragmalinguistic 76, 160

pragmatic competence 3, 29, 34, 38–39, 40, 42–44, 47–48, 51–52
pragmatic resistance 164

relevance theory 47, 62–63
roleplays 66–67, 86, 134

Schauer, G. 1, 3, 11, 32, 38, 54, 67, 186
Schneider, K.P. 34, 57, 70
Searle, J.R. 7, 27, 41, 57, 59
Shively, R.L. 32, 125, 132–133
sociocultural expectations 4, 34, 41, 46, 49, 51, 54, 58, 67
sociocultural theory 48
sociolinguistic competence 22, 26, 28, 34,
sociopragmatics 76, 161
sociopragmatic awareness 9, 33, 82, 84, 112
Spencer-Oatey, 8, 18, 36, 52, 71, 74, 79
strategic competence 26, 35–36

Taguchi, N. 1, 4, 41–42, 44, 54, 76, 78, 131–132, 186
Timpe-Laughlin, V. 35, 40–41

utterance-type meaning, 14–15

variability 58, 69, 72
variational pragmatics 69–71
verbal reports 67, 82, 136, 150, 189
Verschueren, J. 8, 13–14, 38, 57, 68–69, 130–131

Žegarac, V. 68

For Product Safety Concerns and Information please contact our EU Authorised Representative:

Easy Access System Europe

Mustamäe tee 50

10621 Tallinn

Estonia

gpsr.requests@easproject.com